MASTERS OF CHANGE:

Why Today's Most Successful Individuals Learn
to Harness Life's Most Challenging Moments
to Become Who They Want to Be

MASTERS OF CHANGE:

Why today's most successful individuals learn to harness life's most challenging moments to become who they want to be

JULIE BROWNE, MPH, LCSW

NEW DEGREE PRESS

MASTERS OF CHANGE:
Why today's most successful individuals learn to harness life's most challenging moments to become who they want to be

ISBN   979-8-88926-847-5 *Paperback*
          979-8-88926-848-2 *Ebook*

Dedicated to Dwayne.

After all is said and done, this is for you.

*We are all artists. Sometimes we are sculptors
needing to remove the unnecessary. Sometimes we
are painters deciding if we are going to use adversity
as the primary color or only an accent color for
contrast. But we are always building a mosaic.
The question is, are we doing it consciously?*

*Every event in our life is a stone in that mosaic.
The excitement is found in approaching it
with curiosity to see how all the pieces will fit
in place. My late wife is a beautiful shining
gemstone in my mosaic and I am truly blessed
for having spent time with her on this earth.*

*Take the tool of your choice in hand and start to create
the most beautiful life art you can, consciously and
intentionally. You are unique and your masterpiece
will be a stone others can use in their mosaic.*

—ROBERT PARDI

Table of Contents

Praise for Masters of Change

"I've experienced severe loss of identity on a few occasions and had no idea what was going on or how to overcome it. Browne's book explains this difficult phenomenon. There's a great balance between research on identity, stories of people who've lost their identity, and practical tools and exercises to help create a new, bolder identity."
—Dr. Leonaura Rhodes, MB (Surgeon), Speaker, Executive Coach, Corporate Wellness Trainer, Leadership Trainer, DISC Analyst

"With honesty, vulnerability, wisdom, and strength, riveting stories and practical tools and concepts explain this invisible phenomenon—forced identity transition—and provide a roadmap on how to move forward. *Masters of Change* will help someone who doesn't even realize what's happening to her and needs detailed guidance and direction."
—Nurzhan Sterbenz, Foreign-born mama with childhood trauma, Podcast Host of *Foreign-Born Mama*

"I wish I had Julie's book when I was in forced identity transition myself. She's articulated the emotional landscape of each stage of the process, along with what's going on in the psyche, for someone processing grief alongside an identity transition. Her writing is clear, direct, empathetic, and loving. She gave me relief and hope."

—Nadhira Razack, Life Coach and Strategist

"For anyone seeking the light but struggling with carrying the crushing burden of past psychological and emotional hurts and injustices, this tome is a must-read. Browne offers hope and a possible way of going on the offensive for families with family members with mental illness. Should be required reading in relevant university curricula."

—David Prestage, Retired Sr. Psychiatric Technician, Founder and Former Director of Camp Country Jamboree -a national award-winning camp for kids with cancer

"All I can say is wow! This is exactly what I need right now! I feel seen and not alone...dare I say, 'normal.' I enjoy the clarity and structure of Julie's success strategies for overcoming loss and adapting to forced change. Many will walk away resourced with her thoughtful research and analysis."

—Becca Rae Eagle, Former Teacher, Author of *Embodying Joy: A Heart Journal*, Writing Doula, Host of *The Joyful Journaling Podcast*

"As I read *Masters of Change* I felt a sense of peace inside my soul, resonating throughout my body. I witnessed my bare-naked worthiness creating a new plot in my story line. This book gives meaning to loss of identity and inspires hope for moving forward with tools to navigate an unknown path as we learn to go beyond, think beyond, and find peace."

—Maria McKeon, Health and Wellness Coach, Yoga and Pilates Teacher

"*Masters of Change* should be a staple in everyone's personal library. Whether you are going through a difficult transition, know someone who is, or you're fascinated with the human story, this book holds so much wisdom. It also offers a support group through the stories of others, accessible 24/7, shining beacons of light into very dark places."

—Jean Olney, Mother, Forever caregiver to disabled child

"The shame of addiction kept me stuck in a self-imposed emotional prison for more than a decade. *Masters of Change* gave me the tools and courage I needed to face the shame and learn to trust, accept, and love myself again, emerging stronger and happier than I've ever been. I got more out of it than five years of therapy."

—Andrew Prestage, District Director, Information Systems State Center Community College District, Fresno, California

"I am so excited for Julie's words and work to be put out in the world! Reading *Masters of Change* I felt hopeful that a new path is emerging, whereby pain can be alchemized into allowing us to become a more pure and joy filled version of ourselves, offering hope where it may feel hopeless."

—Laura Thomas, Certified Wayfinder Life Coach, Healthy Living with Juice Plus

"*Masters of Change* gives us permission to acknowledge and truly feel identity loss. It provides the tools to navigate back to a new sense of empowerment. I keep it next to my bed and read relevant sections every day. It fills me with hope after layers and layers of identity loss. Julie was the missing link to moving out of pain, loss, grief and stuckness."

—Niki Thomson, Reiki Master, Learner and transformer of identity loss

"A soul-tickling delight to read, *Masters of Change* is for anyone looking for the formula to get unstuck and intentionally create the next version of themselves. This eye-opening book shows how your identity defines all that you believe you are (and are capable of) and how to use those insights when life throws you curveballs. An empowering, insightful, and actionable read, reminding us that we are in control of our personal identity and showing us how to take ownership of our journey and change the course of our lives to create ones that light us up."

—Stephanie Brentin Rose, Intrailluminologist, Enthusiast for self-knowledge

"Reading *Masters of Change*, I couldn't resonate more with it. I'm in the middle of a forced identity transition after becoming a mom four months ago and discovering my daughter has a very rare genetic disorder. It's changed our entire life. I'm navigating all these emotions and find so much value in Julie's approach to face these unexpected life events. Thank you, Julie, for sharing your life with the world."

—Liseth Kingery

"Wow! So much to chew on here! Browne has clearly explored this topic fully and there's enough here for three books! This is the real work. Rarely have I seen such an actionable, thoughtful, insightful and thorough treatise on the subject of transformation. As a growth focused person, this might just be my new favorite book."

—Josh Routh, Showman and Proprietor of Circus Kaput

"I love this book! Julie's beautifully woven in cutting-edge science of identity formation and identity loss into the fabric of everyday life events. Even better, she's maintained an empathetic, compassionate, and supportive tone raising ambition and calling on courage in the service of an individual's next evolution."

—Mark Matthews, PhD Candidate - Psychology Graduate Fellow at The Ohio State University, Certified High-Performance Coach™

"If you're struggling with a pandemonium life change then *Masters of Change* is a must-have. Not only will it help you survive but it will elevate your journey, and you'll not miss the hidden gifts that are uniquely for you. Julie helps you create a more fulfilling life than what you ever dreamt was possible. Your future self will thank you."

—KR Miller, MSW

"I got tired of dimming my light and am reinventing myself as we speak, this time with more clarity, courage, and conviction than ever before! Julie's book will serve as a lifeline to those whose heads are just above water, the souls where the walls are closing in, and for that tiny spark left that's seeking a flame of hope to reignite the way out of darkness."

—Cara Lynn, Trauma Alchemist

"Julie's book helps one know that identity loss is a common feature in life and no-one needs to feel bad about it. It helps assure them that one is on track, it is a slow process, and to have empathy for oneself. As I read, some pages repeatedly, I keep a deck of cards with me, picking out sentences. I write them as reminders for myself and paste them on my wall."

—Dr. Molamma Panicker, PhD

"*Master's of Change* is a modern day handbook for the human condition. It provides practical tools and guidance for the many ways life can upend our plans yet emerge better for it. It calls forth our capacity to empower ourselves and take charge of our destinies as we master how to meet life's unexpected challenges."

—Joan Advent, MSW and Author of *The Radiance Equation: Catalyzing Emerging Visionary Leaders Here to Change the World*

"Sometimes I have to convince SPED parents that their child will not outgrow the disability. Your book will help so many to better cope with having a family member with struggles. Thank you for your candor in making this book available."

—Maryjane Gertz, MSE, Educational Specialist

"Browne offers a clear pathway for more easily navigating the perilous journey of having your identity pulled out from under you or simply shift away from what you expected it was going to be. Through research and storytelling, Browne's book will guide you to gracefully accept and adapt to the identity changes that are inevitable in life."

—Dayna Del Val, Co-Founder/Producer at *Daily Dose of Dr Marry & DD—alcoholism, recovery and marriage insights,* President and CEO at The Arts Partnership, Motivational Speaker

"Julie Browne's expertise with the transformation process highlights the ease of change but the troubling distrust of the process to bring us to safety and growth in the end. Her ability to highlight the process of change through forced identity transition provides a new take on navigating fear, change, hardship, agony, and coping."

—Michelle Greenwell, PhD, Wellness Industry - speaker, author, podcaster, lecturer, researcher, multi-modality practitioner

Introduction

"Hold on!" Kevin yelled. When the car spun out of control, that corner became the turning point in Brendon's life.

A kid in his first year of college, all Brendon Burchard wanted was to get away. He was "miserable, terrified, upset with the world, and didn't know what to do." His high school sweetheart had just cheated on him. Deeply in love, every part of his life had been tied up in that relationship, and when it fell apart, so did he.

"I was wrecked." He wasn't getting out of bed. He couldn't go to class because *she'd* be there. He stopped caring about the world, refusing to do anything other than read. Severely depressed, he created a detailed suicide plan, notes and all.

One day he saw an ad in the school newspaper that read, "ESCAPE!" Reading that saved his life. It was for summer student jobs in the Dominican Republic. Brendon didn't know where that was. All that mattered was *she* wouldn't be there. Without tools to deal with his emotional struggle, he escaped to the Caribbean with his friend Kevin to become "glorified tour guides."

On the night of the accident, they had just dropped off a client in a newly developed part of the country. Enjoying life and speeding at eighty-five miles per hour, they came upon a hairpin turn with no warning sign. The car careened off the road and crashed, and they both miraculously survived.

Standing on the car's hood, Brendon stared down at blood pooling at his feet. Then, looking up at the moon and connecting with God, he had the mortality moment that fueled the rest of his life. In those few moments, wondering if he'd survive, he evaluated what kind of person he had been.

Watching his life pass before him in slow motion, he asked three questions:

- Did I live?
- Did I love?
- Did I even matter?

Unhappy with his answers and realizing he wasn't going to die and had been given a second chance, Brendon made made a pact with God. He'd make sure to change those answers.

The gift of intention is a tool that helped solve his psychoemotional struggle with identity loss.

Every day, for the past two decades, Brendon's made good on his promise. He designs his life so at the end, he'll be happy with his answers to those questions. He teaches others to use those questions as tenets for daily living.

Brendon is an ordinary guy who became a master of change. He wasn't set up better than anybody else. In his own words, he's not "special or extra smart." His ambition in high school was to start a landscaping business. He was really good at pushing a lawnmower.

Because of a demarcation line, a no-going-back moment, a decision branded into his heart while standing in a pool of his own blood, Brendon changed.

He stopped being a person wanting to end his life. He became a global force, teaching people that life's short, to treat it like a gift, and to live with intention. Brendon helps people live more fully, love more openly, and make a difference *today*. He created a new, unifying self-image. He set new standards and chooses, every day, to live into them (Burchard 2017).

...

You're about to learn that mastering change doesn't have to be as difficult, painful, and scary as you might be experiencing it.

A challenge we all face is the pace of change. Most of us will have more life transitions than previous generations, and we must adapt at ever-faster rates to more and more changes.

The world is different now. Life's more dynamic. It used to be like an escalator; we grow up, join the workforce, maybe raise a family, and grow old and die. Now it's flooded with nonstop choices, like a bank of elevators in a skyscraper. With more options, change happens faster and is inevitable (and you'll need to be ready for it).

In a Clarendon lecture on self-identity and career transition, organizational change expert Herminia Ibarra spoke of career changes: "In many ways you are on your own. There used to be paths, sequences, clear trajectories. We don't do that anymore. There are more transitions to navigate, and you navigate them yourself" (Ibarra 2017).

I have a fascination with how individuals adjust to uninvited major role shifts because it's happened to me many times. I want to understand why it's often so difficult and painful, and why it takes so darn long to adapt. I want to know how we change and become who we become, how to become happy in our own skin, how to smile at ourselves more, and how to, as my friend Robert Pardi puts it, "bounce beyond" crisis.

We face loss and major role shifts when the rug's pulled out from under us and life as we knew it irrevocably changes. We can feel as if our core is eviscerated. Catapulted into "forced identity transition" (Ibarra 2017), we lose touch with a coherent sense of self as our identity crumbles. Many people land in a vacuum, finding life void of meaning and purpose.

It can be from an abrupt, catalytic event that changes your world from one day to the next:

- Divorce.
- Health and career losses.
- Loss of a loved one, including a pregnancy.
- Loss of our sovereignty to caregiving roles (e.g., motherhood, becoming responsible for a person with a disability).
- A violent assault.
- An empty nest.
- Retirement.

Or it can be from gradual catalysts:

- Addiction.

- Aging parents.

- Loss of your identity in a relationship.

- Ongoing physical or sexual abuse (e.g., domestic violence, incest, commercial sexual exploitation).

- Awakening to a different sexual orientation or gender identity.

- Losing connection with your faith.

While you may have never heard of the term forced identity transition (FIT), catalysts causing it are common. The following are US stats.

- The 2022 divorce rate was 40 to 50 percent (Vuleta 2022).

- In 2021, about one in four adults and 54 percent of people in their forties were part of the sandwich generation (Horowitz 2022).

- In 2022, about ten thousand people retired every day (Lazic 2022).

- In 2019, about 5.8 million people were unemployed (Edwards 2020).

- In 2019, almost 3 million deaths occurred (Kochanek 2020).

- In 2018, a disability impacting major life activities affected about one in four adults (Okoro 2018).

- In 2020, nearly 20 percent (one in five) adults lived with a mental illness, and 5.6 percent (about three in fifty) lived with severe mental illness (schizophrenia, bipolar, depression) (NIMH 2020).

- In 2019, almost one in four adults struggled with addiction (Kacha-Ochana 2022).

- In 2018, at least one in nine girls and one in fifty-three boys under the age of eighteen experienced sexual abuse (RAINN 2018).

- In 2017, around one in three women and one in four men experienced severe physical violence by an intimate partner (NCADV 2022).

Life is full of crushing personal events causing untold grief, pain, and uncertainty. These can cause significant psychological changes and challenges. How is it that some individuals come out the other end with more strength, confidence, courage, grit, purpose, freedom, and joy than they ever imagined possible?

> Many people think change is complicated.
> I believe it becomes much less complicated
> when we stop resisting and become comfortable
> being uncomfortable.

What if surrendering to discomfort led to harnessing freedom? What if you only find the treasures you're meant to find when you're uncomfortable?

While change can be messy, painful, and scary, this is where we become fully alive. Being comfortable isn't where feeling energized, engaged, excited, and fulfilled resides. Boredom, frustration, and restlessness are roommates with comfort.

What we strive for and what we're capable of are passion and being fully present—firing on all cylinders, doing our best work, having our best relationships, being filled with joy, peace, and a sense of freedom as we tackle life's challenges.

FIT gives us the opportunity to level up if we embrace the process and if we refuse to settle before we've created transformation.

This book is about how to navigate FIT more effectively. Tools and practices exist to soothe emotional distress and help you move forward and find happiness to move from being lost to loving your life.

I discovered how to turn transitions into transformation. I harnessed opportunities to become a master of change. Now, I offer lessons learned from my own pain, struggle, and growth to help *you* transform and prevent you from spiraling down.

I learned the foundation of successful change is developing a sense of empathy for myself and others, and what keeps us from making our best choices are self-betrayal and lack of self-compassion.

With a handful of my own unexpected identity losses, my license in clinical social work including more than ten years as a social worker, the diversity of influences on my life, and my current work as a certified high-performance coach, personal growth and transformation trainer, speaker, and host of the *Bold Becoming* podcast, I have the skills, perspective, and tools needed to guide others through what my friend Cecilie Holter calls "The Hairy Passage."

I'm bringing the pain of identity change out of the closet. I'm naming, normalizing, and giving a container for what is often an invisible and lonely journey. We tend to downplay and overlook the value of this transition.

FIT is replete with grief and loss. My mission is to expand the traditional concept of grief and loss and to turn forced identity transition into an acknowledged and cherished rite of passage, a process capable of producing immense, positive transformation.

But transformation only happens when you stay the course, refuse to settle, and don't let discomfort and fear win.

In this book I lay out a framework of eight principles of change. Masters of change, whom I call bold becomers, use these for navigating life's most difficult challenges. They're the needle movers. This is where leverage lies. The principles are:

1. Courage
2. Purpose
3. Grief
4. Clarity

5. Self-care
6. Mindset
7. Productivity
8. Support

PART ONE

This is the big picture. I explain FIT and place your experience in a container with a landscape and a roadmap. I detail the roles creativity, intuition, and expectations management play. I discuss how to turn transition into transformation—accessing your essence to become all of who you are, despite and sometimes *because* of what you lost.

PART TWO

This section provides a concrete discussion of the eight principles. It gives you tactical information and workshopping. Be sure to keep a notebook on hand. Through personal stories you'll see how others harnessed these principles to become someone they had never imagined. The stories are from people I interviewed, a few are from secondary research, and at the end of each chapter in part two is a story about me.

PART THREE

Here, I group story catalysts under three umbrellas: career, health, and relationships. I provide a short analysis with each story, giving tangible connections to our principles.

I incorporate more workshopping, where you start applying the principles in your own life.

This journey doesn't have shortcuts. Transformation takes time. Getting stuck is expected, but staying stuck is a choice. With understanding and guidance, change doesn't have to take as long or be as complicated and painful as you might expect.

As much as I'm hopeful my book will help a lot of people through difficult life transitions, I'm aware some people may have trauma history that makes going through this process on their own too overwhelming. This book should not be used as a substitute for qualified care or treatment by professionals.

Change and struggle are part of life. They're gifts we can learn and grow from.

Focusing on choice over circumstances creates options that open a path to wholeness.

The key to transformation is respecting your inner knowing. That's connected to self-love. It always knows how to guide you. Its job is not to let you settle. Since it won't force itself on you, it's your choice whether to act on its whispers. If that's what you want, I'm here to help.

You'll love this book if you:

- Are in transition;
- Want to find treasure in your tragedy, or other radical life changes;
- Are rediscovering what brings you joy, meaning, and purpose;
- Want tips on how to get unstuck or manage this journey with less angst;

- Find yourself saying, *I don't know who I am anymore*;

- Seek ways to access, strengthen, and use self-agency to accept change and move forward;

- Wish to choose courage every single day; and

- Yearn to honestly say, *I love my life.*

This book also helps allies of people in identity crisis, those who want to learn what's normal and how to be more supportive. People in forced identity transition go underground with this process. They need you *not* as advisor, but as their confidant, witnessing their journey.

Whatever context you're coming from, this book offers models for navigating life's most difficult changes. Find out what happened after a pencil took me out and I lost my social work career to a hand disability. Learn how Lena, who was sold into sexual slavery, survived and is living a fulfilling life, and how Arletha can be filled with joy after losing her husband and children in a car accident.

Gain the tools and practices needed to leverage your challenge for all it's worth. Learn to create a better experience for yourself as you let go of outdated ideas and beliefs. Intentionally apply new principles so you see things from a fresh perspective.

Open your heart and release
what no longer serves you.

I invite you to discover how to harness this reset opportunity and to become aware of your innate radiance. As your new identity emerges, congruent with your deepest values and updated beliefs, you'll boldly become the person who has always been who you really are. Then you can enjoy your sparkle and share it with others.

In the words of my macrobiotic teacher David Briscoe, "The world needs this you."

FORCED IDENTITY TRANSITION BASICS

*Peace is the result of retraining your mind
to process life as it is, rather than as you think it should be.*

—WAYNE W. DYER

CHAPTER 1

From Forced Identity Transition to Transformation

May you remember your ability to choose
what is deeply nourishing. May you ignite your power
to make choices that align with your soul.
May you take action in the name of your authentic fire.
May you find the courage to heal, be free, and grow.

—TANYA MARKUL

...

You're here because you are or someone you care about is struggling. A catalytic event (or series of events) inserted chaos into your life, changing who you are. You're being exposed to new worlds and relationships and taking on new roles. Identity transition expert Herminia Ibarra describes this as "lingering between identities" (2003, 14). You are neither who you used to be nor who you will become.

You're experiencing FIT or *forced identity transition* (Ibarra 2017), and I've written this book to help you navigate it. You've lost your rudder and need to regain your sense of direction and purpose. The rug's been pulled out from under you, and you're having an identity crisis. It could have been pulled out slowly, over time, or suddenly. It could have happened recently or as far back as childhood.

You likely feel broken. You need to feel whole again. You're ready to heal and make purposeful change happen, to find the life you seek and lose the fear to live it. To push your personal limits to rediscover all parts of yourself so the new version can be consciously connected with and driven by your essence.

There is light at the end of the tunnel. Bold becomers find that light and, in the process, transform. Once they reach it, they're stronger than they could imagine and have a new drive and zest for life they might never have had before. They've embraced a radical new self. They're living life on their own terms now. They feel at peace. Their life makes sense, and they have the audacity to articulate and get what they want.

All the details add up to something beautiful and powerful despite, and partly because of, the pain and suffering it took to get there.

Many of those I've interviewed build legacy out of their loss. The change catalyst is integrated as a vital, an enriching, and even, as strange as it might seem, a welcome component of their life journey. They learned to harness the unfamiliar, unusual, and uncomfortable.

WHY THE STRUGGLE?

People struggle with FIT for many reasons:

- The catalytic event is uninvited and often unexpected, so we're caught off guard and forced into a personal growth journey we didn't sign up for.

- We must contend with grief and loss.

- We, and those around us, get tired of seeing us continue to struggle.

- Those around us want us to return to who we were, and that's not going to happen.

- What we need most—clarity—is what we tend to have least of (at least in the beginning, crisis stage). So it's hard to trust our decisions.

- It is an iterative process where one thing leads to the next. Ideas and decisions are fluid. They morph or make sudden, dramatic changes, or are abandoned. Goal posts keep shifting as we refine what we're really after (Ibarra 2017).

- Transition "always takes much longer than we expect because to make room for the new, we have to get rid of some of the old selves we are still dragging around and, unconsciously, still invested in becoming" because of "taken-for-granted priorities and assumptions about how the world works" (Ibarra 2003, 13–14).

The image below represents what FIT is like: living in a jumbled-up mess of thoughts, emotions, actions, inactions, and aspirations. While lingering between identities, also referred to as being in *liminality* (Ibarra 2017), you're experiencing *divergence*, and it's uncomfortable. This is what the middle phase of identity transition (discussed later in this chapter) looks like—messy.

Divergence in Liminality

© 2023 - Current Courage-Ignite Breakthrough Institute, LLC

I've struggled with my fair share of *unexpected identity losses*. At ten or eleven, when I gave up fighting gender inequality, I lost my identity as a person who acted congruently with her beliefs. In my twenties, when I got saddled with chronic pain and fatigue, I lost my identity as a healthy person who could choose to do anything. My physical strength and capabilities, especially as a star athlete, had been the psychoemotional backbone of who I was, my greatest source of joy, and where I felt my sense of freedom. At forty-one, I lost my financial independence, and sense of purpose in being a valuable member of society when I lost my social work career due to disability.

I didn't have a name for what was happening.
I certainly didn't know the term
forced identity transition.

I didn't even know the underlying theme of my struggle was identity loss. All I could see was the cause of my losses—the catalysts—and their situational fallout.

What I did know was that I had to reset. I had to find my center again. I knew I wasn't going to just drift or settle. I knew the grief and loss I felt was legitimate. It was the same as grieving the death of a loved one, only it was grieving the death of a part of myself that became forever inaccessible.

Because I was still knee deep in a forced identity transition, I had an existential crisis one day in 2019. That was when, in an exercise class, the words "identity loss" dropped in my lap.

Those two, simple words encapsulated the heart of my struggle after losing my social work career. In fact, it was a central thread in my life—handling the grief, fear, and the moving forward process after multiple identity losses. I could happily help others with this topic. Crisis intervention had always been my favorite part of social work. It's where I could make the biggest bang for the buck. The difference I made was palpable. I felt whole, with full access to all my potential, wisdom, and skills emanating from every cell in my body, rising to the occasion because of high stake situations.

I began developing an *overcoming identity loss* workshop. Then I started hearing from others that they'd like my help. Within an hour of posting my vision of the workshop in a business development class, a classmate gave just the validation I needed:

"I just read your workshop plan. I have recently gone through unexpected identity loss. What you are proposing is incredibly useful and valuable. For a year I swam in the muck. Had an offer like yours existed, I would have signed up in a minute. Please use me as a sounding board."

The reason I'm here today, writing on this topic, is largely because of that message. Connection with others around my topic has propelled me forward. It moved me over the threshold and out of what I'll explain below: liminality (a.k.a. limbo). It led me to establish the Courage-Ignite Breakthrough Institute and start coaching, launch the *Bold Becoming* podcast, become a speaker and trainer, and write this book.

Finding a topic and connecting with others was what I needed. I'd been searching for a way back to using my therapeutic voice. Finding a topic was key to overcoming my identity loss after losing my social work career. It was one of many steps in how I overcame that identity loss. It opened the door to my next life chapter as a thought leader.

THIS BOOK'S GOALS

This book plans to help you:

- Gain perspective, courage, self-clarity, and confidence;

- Decrease the angst inherent in FIT;

- Harness the power of this uninvited opportunity for transformation; and

- Heal, level up, and thrive.

My mission is to bring FIT into the limelight and honor it as a valuable rite of passage. This book shows how to navigate FIT more effectively.

(Note: Part 1 is theory heavy, setting you up for the rest of the book. Parts 2 and 3 are chock full of stories that add context by giving concrete examples. For an overview of story topics, see appendix A. Stories in part 3 give detailed analyses on how individuals used the eight principles of change.)

WHAT IS IDENTITY?

Identity is how we define ourselves. It informs our sense of belonging and is driven by where and how we fit in. It's how we think about ourselves, built around activities and relationships central to who we are. We normally see and understand ourselves in the context of and in relation to others (Ibarra 2017). Dr. Ibarra teaches the building blocks of identity, which are the following (Ibarra 2017):

1. What we do;

2. The company we keep; and

3. The story we tell about ourselves.

"It is very difficult to be something if no one else thinks that is what you are... Whatever you identify as, if it is not confirmed and endorsed by those around you, it is very hard to hang on to that identity" (Ibarra 2017).

Herminia Ibarra, author of *Working Identity: Unconventional Strategies for Reinventing Your Career (2003)* and formerly a professor at the Harvard Business School, currently teaches at the London Business School and is a recipient of the 2022 Thinkers50 Award, a global recognition honoring leaders. I draw heavily upon her identity transition frameworks to help people overcome unexpected identity loss.

WHAT IS FORCED IDENTITY TRANSITION?

In passing, Ibarra mentioned the term "forced identity transition." During the 2017 Clarendon lecture on career transition, she noted differences between chosen and forced identity transition (Ibarra 2017).

I am indebted to Dr. Ibarra for giving me the language, theory, and mechanics of identity transition. She gives us practical applications for successfully navigating a challenging process. Much of this chapter's material is adapted from her work on career transition, a chosen process. Extrapolating from that, her work elucidated, normalized, and validated my experiences with FIT.

Forced identity transition is a process. It results from a catalytic event or series of events causing a loss. Ibarra describes *identity transition* as a disruption of "the continuity of identity and sense of a persistent self" (Ibarra 2017).

In FIT, the catalytic event causes what I refer to as unexpected identity loss.

We lose a part of who we are because of the loss from the catalytic event. This then forces a person into an identity transition process. Internalized skills, competencies, and preferences are disrupted because we are no longer doing and being like before (Ibarra 2017).

FIT commences a deep psychological shifting and translation process as we reformulate who we are. Parts of who we were get translated into the new person. Everything fits differently now. This rearranging process takes time and is difficult. Our old self is catapulted into translating its relevant and existing parts to belong in a new configuration. We shift away from other parts that no longer fit our emerging identity. For parts we choose to keep, we often see a shift in their meaning and use. In systems theory, since everything is interrelated, when one part changes the whole also changes. The fundamental shift that occurs is our perspective, which then influences everything about our choices.

Ibarra describes the beginning of an identity transition as leaving a person feeling the following (Ibarra 2017):

- In midair;
- Neither here nor there;
- At loose ends;
- Unmoored;
- Broken;
- Lost; or
- Asking, *Who am I?*

An exhaustive list of FIT loss catalysts does not exist. Also, determining the catalyst can sometimes be like the chicken or the egg, and/or are overlapping. Throughout parts 2 and 3 of this book, you'll read stories about how these kinds of catalysts impacted individuals. Common ones include:

- A major relationship ends, leaving you feeling unhinged.

- You lose your job or career due to a health condition, a layoff, or you get fired and are left feeling high and dry with no idea what to do next.

- You lose your health:
  - You receive a life-threatening diagnosis.
  - Physical and/or cognitive functioning is dramatically altered.
  - You develop a permanent disability such as loss of a limb, and/or certain functioning is limited.

- You lose your identity to mental illness or addiction:
  - You're no longer fully in control of your life.
  - The addictive urge overpowers your will, and you've lost sovereignty over your life.

- Mental illness may have taken your ability to live independently.
- You lose an identity tied to a future dream such as having:
  - A baby.
  - A healthy baby.
  - Your child grow up to become independent.
  - A career which is now out of reach.
  - The retirement you envisioned.
- You lose your identity in an abusive relationship.
- You lose your identity after rape or another kind of violent assault.
- Your identity is aborted, stunted, or unable to develop on its normal trajectory due to:
  - Child sexual, physical, or emotional abuse or neglect. (Identity formation is nipped in the bud early in life, limiting your ability to find an identity outside of the harm you experienced.)
  - Racism, sexism, ableism, nationalism, and other forms of systemic discrimination.
- You lose your identity from the demands of motherhood or another caretaking role.
- You lose custody of your children, you are estranged from family members, or you or a family member is incarcerated.
- You lose your faith.
- You awaken to a different sexual orientation or gender identity than you'd thought you were.
- You're adopted and have no connection to and/or knowledge of your birth family.
- You lose your identity after retirement or from an empty nest.

The common denominator in these scenarios is a major loss. It results in role changes and status shifts.

One's sense of stability, integrity, wholeness, and belonging shifts dramatically. A sense of *disorientation* and *ambiguity* is the hallmark of identity transition (Ibarra 2017). You experience divergence while in a state of liminality (defined below). What you counted on doing, or what you did, is no longer possible. This catapults you into an identity crisis.

You're forced to redefine who you are based on a different set of variables. A cascade of reprioritizations must begin immediately. Ibarra explains this is different from a chosen identity transition (e.g., career change), where one has time to slowly awaken to new desires (Ibarra 2017). It's the difference between taking a leap and being pushed over a cliff.

THE THREE PHASES OF IDENTITY TRANSITION

The following three phases are from Ibarra's career transition framework: a form of *chosen identity transition*. I've added to it to address forced identity transition. The image below represents the major steps in chosen *or* forced identity transition and personal transformation.

It's important to trust the process, commit to the process, and avoid premature commitment to outcomes. By cycling through enough times, you transform. If you stop early, you settle (Ibarra 2017).

Steps for Transition & Transformation

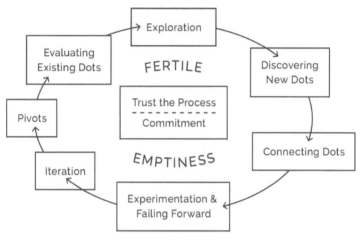

The goal of any identity transition is to reach a sense of coherence with who you are, what you do, and feeling whole (Ibarra 2017). You're working to:

- Have clarity and stability;

- Feel comfortable in your own skin;

- Have all parts of you represented and supported (at least by you); and

- Experience a sense of ease and fulfillment.

Transition, whether chosen or forced, provides possibility and challenge. Unlike chosen identity transition, those in FIT have an additional challenge. They're grieving a major loss.

Ibarra's framework for a career transition process consists of three phases: beginning, middle, and end. A person in FIT skips the beginning phase and starts in the middle. Much of what happens in the beginning phase carries over into the middle phase. Therefore, it's important to understand the complete model (Ibarra 2017).

THE BEGINNING PHASE

Before we begin, to dissuade you of any notion that it's because of circumstances you're stuck and not making the change you seek happen, this is what Ibarra found regarding desired career change. A person's circumstances—be they financial, skillset, social, etc.—did not have a predictable impact on those who wanted change and got it versus those who didn't. And no checklist of attributes separates those who make successful career transitions and those who stay stuck in frustration and discontent (Ibarra 2017). Both she and I offer principles of how to successfully change, independent of circumstances.

These principles are the foundation supporting the quest for self-determination and personal freedom. They're key to exiting status quo.

The beginning phase starts when a person feels restless or dissatisfied and entertains thoughts of change. You experience a push away from your current status. At the same time, you lack a sufficient pull toward attractive ideas and possibilities. Without this, you lack necessary motivation to take action (Ibarra 2017).

When you discuss change, your core network favors the status quo. This can lead to, as Ibarra puts it, "ties that bind and blind" (Ibarra 2017). In order not to rock the boat, you're apt to wait for change to happen instead of making it happen. She warns this strategy can lead to choosing the wrong thing (Ibarra 2017).

Waiting in the comfort zone restricts interfacing with the full range of opportunities life has to offer. You aren't doing the necessary exploration, discovery, and experimentation that change requires. This sets you up to settle unnecessarily (Ibarra 2017).

Without a strong enough set of ideas pulling you away from the status quo, you stay put. Life events causing self-reflection don't lend enough sway for you to take action (Ibarra 2017).

Once the pull is strong enough, this is the key to getting you out of your head and into action (Ibarra 2017). You start experimenting and learning about "possible new selves." You try on new identities to see how they fit (Ibarra 2003, 35). This begins the transition process.

> "You're moving away from something," Ibarra describes, "with not yet having left it, while moving toward something without knowing what it is" (Ibarra 2017).

The whole transition process is what Stanford professor Dr. Hazel Markus (whose work informs Ibarra's) calls a "working identity, working draft, or a work in progress" (Ibarra 2003, 37).

Dr. Markus describes (Ibarra 2003, 38) this as exploring and enacting, among other selves, the:

- Desired self;
- Ought to self;
- Ideal self; and
- The feared self.

The process can be both exciting and uncomfortable. Ibarra emphasizes those already successful are the most uncomfortable with chosen change because of what they have to lose (Ibarra 2017).

THE MIDDLE PHASE

This is where you take action while relinquishing your old self (Ibarra 2017). For the person in FIT, an uninvited push landed them directly in the middle phase. They haven't experienced the pull part of the equation (from the beginning phase).

Like people in chosen identity transition, people in FIT explore and experiment with new options. But they do it with a powerful brake on because of grief over their loss and losing the plot to their life's narrative. They're forced to take action with the brakes on while grief and fear make it like walking through quicksand. But this is where they level up. It's where masters of change harness opportunity like no one's business.

The middle phase is the difficult, in-between period between the old and new you, and it's harder and takes longer than expected (Ibarra 2017).

In layman's terms, we call it being in limbo. In anthropology they call it *liminality*—the middle stage—in reference to rites of passage. Ibarra shares these three definitions by other experts (Ibarra 2017):

- "The middle stage of archaic rites of passage: the actual passing through the threshold marking the boundary between past and future social positions" (Arnold van Gennep).

- "A psychological state in which the individual lacks or loses a self-defining connection to an important social domain such as work" (Blake Ashforth).

- "An inter-structural situation, between and betwixt well-defined positions in the social structure… Suspended in social space, lacking a firm identity, they have shed their old identities and have not been given new ones, so they are neither one thing nor another… A state of being neither one thing or another, or maybe both; or neither here nor there; or maybe nowhere" (Victor Turner).

The middle phase is the critical stage where change takes place. It's where a person in FIT lands (Ibarra 2017) without preparation or having a vote.

The middle phase is where both those in chosen and forced identity transition experience ambiguity and disorientation (Ibarra 2017). Clarity is elusive.

It's the place where the potential for "fertile emptiness" resides… and the best way to leverage it is by "avoiding foreclosure on the experience" (Ibarra 2017).

It's important to keep temptation for premature commitments squarely on your radar. You can do this by understanding, by not resisting that it is what it is, and by honoring that the process takes longer than you expect and is harder than you can imagine.

The middle phase for those in FIT is where your identity gets stripped down to the core. You discover who you really are, unsupported by status or skills—just your bare-naked worthiness, the parts of you that nobody and nothing can take away from you.

This is where you oscillate. It's a difficult period for you and others because you pivot a lot. People worry you'll make foolish decisions while being unmoored. What you feel, seek, and want are fluid (Ibarra 2017). It drives you and others nuts!

And it's where Ibarra says to explore opportunities without following the normal rules of engagement (Ibarra 2017). Allow yourself to open a Pandora's box of opportunity. Risk hoping for and chasing seemingly unattainable dreams. If not, you risk spiraling downward, losing out on the gifts this challenge has in store for you, or living in a holding pattern.

> Achieving outcomes is not how success is measured while in liminality (Ibarra 1017).

You measure success by the amount of action you take and how many things you try and reject. Especially by how much action you take outside of your comfort zone (Ibarra 2017).

Delayed commitment is the rule, and divergent exploration is the game plan. You generate alternatives. You invite serendipity into the mix and enter through the doors it opens for you (Ibarra 2017).

All of the pivots can make you feel unstable, and it's hard to evaluate progress or to even feel you're making progress at all.

It's much easier to know what you don't want than what you do. This information is no less valuable. Indeed, it should be the crux of your focus. It clears your path forward by providing you with the tool of compare and contrast (Ibarra 2017).

FIT requires a divergent trajectory, which makes clarity elusive. This contributes to making the process longer, messier, and harder than anticipated. And while much of the time you may doubt progress is being made, this is unlikely true.

The change and growth phenomena of taking two steps forward and one step back still results in net gain. Incremental progress is often hard to detect. That doesn't mean it's not happening.

> As you gain clarity and proximity to your
> destination, the goal posts move (Ibarra 2017).

Each new move and experience are part of an iterative process as you grow and change. Therefore, you're constantly redefining your target (Ibarra 2017). You can either rejoice or recoil. Regardless, you're eliminating what doesn't work.

Each identity loss catalyst creates a unique situation. Each person enters transition with a different set of variables. A generic, straight path forward doesn't exist, nor can anyone effectively guide you. Rebuilding your new identity is virgin territory. It's up to you to figure it out as you test new versions of yourself, without certainty or clarity.

Since identity is about how we see ourselves, we must act our way into a new identity; we cannot think our way there (Ibarra 2003, xi–xii).

> "No amount of self-reflection can substitute for the
> direct experience we need to evaluate alternatives
> according to criteria that change as we do…
> We start this process by taking action" (Ibarra 2003, 2).

Simultaneously in FIT, you're deciding what other parts of your identity to let go of, in addition to what was lost, while force-fed a comprehensive and soul-baring examination of the essence of who you are and daring to peek at who you aspire to become.

As you compare and contrast new options for resetting your identity, you begin to see patterns in the emerging new you. Eventually, a whole, cohesive picture is revealed (Ibarra 2017). But you only get there one step at a time, and only a few next steps are revealed at a time.

You're at the precipice of rewriting the plot of your life's story. It's a matter of persistence, self-love, faith in the process, and taking consistent action that gets you to the threshold where you will exit liminality.

Moreover, you're going through a parallel process. You're called to process grief over your losses—the primary loss the catalytic event caused and all the secondary losses caused by the primary loss.

THE END PHASE

Reaching the end phase doesn't mean you've reached your destination. You haven't yet stepped out of transition and into your new identity. It's where you've gained enough clarity that you can plan and implement steps toward it (Ibarra 2017).

A story about who you are becoming crystalizes. You start telling a story, to yourself and others, that you believe and makes sense. When this happens, it indicates you're close to the end of the process. You're close to stepping over the threshold and out of liminality (Ibarra 2017).

You've become the author of your own life again and have a focus on something more rewarding than where you've been. You've restructured a new plot to your life's storyline.

Identity forms by taking action over time, by being and doing. While you identify with this new person you've chosen to become, it takes time to embody that person. You may still need to learn new skills and to embrace new mindsets (Ibarra 2017).

The important thing is who you're becoming
is congruent with who you need to be.
You have clarity and certainty.
This is what feeling whole is.

Feeling whole doesn't mean everything is taken care of. It means you feel comfortable in your own skin. You agree with who you are. You don't have internal civil wars happening with sides vying for control. Your vision and intentions and actions are all going in the same direction. You're living in congruence with who you need to be.

You'll continue to iterate, and for the time being no more huge pivots are happening (Ibarra 2017). Your activities complement each other, and momentum is easier to gain and maintain. Feelings of being overwhelmed diminish, and focus takes less effort because your path becomes more linear.

People around you are relieved, happy, and hopeful you've finally pulled yourself together. They see there was method to the madness. They stop meddling with your business because of your newly minted clarity, confidence, and resolve.

Life now has deep meaning and purpose and your emotions are available in full tilt. By this time, you might even see a silver lining in your misfortune, or you may never. Some things don't have silver linings.

Bold becomers tend to have exponential growth resulting from hardship and suffering. They recognize and harness the power of opportunity in FIT. They come to view it as a rite of passage and honor the struggle. By understanding the identity transition process and applying the principles of mastering change covered in part 2, you can embrace the challenge with pride and anticipation despite the pain, knowing transformation awaits you on the other side.

STABILITY SNAPSHOT

The following visual is what it looks like once you're in the end phase. It shows the interrelatedness and interdependence of the major factors that come into play in FIT. Consistent and conscious attention to these elements is necessary for a successful and quicker transition. These elements, along with the graphic showing the steps in transition, are what this book discusses. I introduce them here and discuss them in different contexts throughout the book.

The pyramid's bottom tier is about being. These attributes and conditions impact levels above. The second tier is actions and mindsets. The third tier can only be activated fully and well-managed when the lower two tiers are well-managed. It's important to keep a good check on any temptation to settle. Your vision and clarity help do this. The goal of transition and transformation is to have psychoemotional access to joy, passion, and contentment. All elements below drive you toward these states of self-actualization—realizing your dreams, being true to yourself, and achieving inner peace. This is how you achieve joy, passion, and contentment.

The Stable Snapshot of a Person in Identity Transition

Joy · Passion · Contentment

Vision · Clarity · Settling Temptations

Letting Go · Allowing Opportunity · Choice · Decisions · Expectations

Fear · Courage · Sovereignty · Health (Physical, Mental, Spiritual) · Grief (Pain, Loss) · Personal Agency · Self-Compassion

© 2023 · Current Courage-Ignite Breakthrough Institute, LLC

IMPORTANT CONSIDERATIONS FOR AN EASIER FIT

Ibarra gives several specifics to keep in mind during an identity transition, whether chosen or forced.

TESTING NEW POSSIBLE SELVES

It's important not to worry about being authentic or an impostor and to "flirt with possibility" (Ibarra 2017). You're perfectly positioned to test drive new thoughts, beliefs, values, and activities. Adopt new ones that make sense and release old ones that no longer fit. Ibarra stresses the need to actually act in ways that feel inauthentic. This creates scenarios of compare and contrast. It's easier to know what you don't want than what you do (Ibarra 2017).

Since you're already stripped of something essential to who you were, your job is to try on new identities to fill the void of your loss. This happens by practicing new identities through *doing* rather than *thinking* (Ibarra 2017).

By leaving your familiar zone and doing things that *do* make you feel inauthentic, you create a compare and contrast filter to better discover what you desire.

The best way to try on new identities is by adding new activities, engaging with new people and interests, and reconnecting with old passions. New networks give you new perspectives and broaden your potential to find new opportunities and interests. Spending time searching for answers inside yourself only gives static information based on the past. This self-knowledge can even be a defense against change (Ibarra 2017).

Your intuition is different than self-knowledge and invites you to act on hunches and serendipity. Take action, accumulate new information, and create new personal assets. Transformation takes time, and FIT asks you to allow yourself to evolve over time while giving equal weight to your head and your heart. During FIT, bold becomers recalibrate their decision-making instrument.

CHOOSING THE BEST CHANGE MODEL FOR IDENTITY TRANSITION

Ibarra describes two separate change models (2003, 29-34):

- Plan-and-Implement.
- Test-and-Learn.

She advises not to depend on the common Plan-and-Implement model for identity transition because it's answer driven. It's dependent on a logical series of linear steps while identity transition is anything but linear and logical (Ibarra 2017).

The Plan-and-Implement model relies on static self-assessment and self-knowledge as well as on reflection and introspection. It doesn't factor in that we learn in iterative, circular, multilayered ways, nor does it consider the reality of serendipity and value of welcoming it (Ibarra 2017).

A fulfilling identity transition makes room for serendipity, which results in a plethora of pivots and restarts.

In contrast, the Test-and-Learn model is iterative and process driven. This is where you *seek answers through doing*. Then evaluate and iterate on next steps. You learn through gaining new information. You generate new options as you allow this information to influence how you seek and absorb information.

You continually change as you grow, so naturally, goal posts are moving targets. It invites you to pivot as necessary, since growth implies you are never the same person (Ibarra 2017).

It's natural to try to escape the void in FIT. We all want to hurry up the process and settle because of discomfort, fear, doubt, or exhaustion. But if we do this, if we commit prematurely, we squander the latent potential in this fertile emptiness. Stay the course until you fully understand yourself and what's driving you (Ibarra 2017).

Use this book to educate your loved ones about the process. Believe in yourself. The world, your community, your team, your family, and *you* need the transformed version of you FIT can deliver. Allow yourself to set high expectations. It's your time. This is a now-or-never opportunity.

KEY IDENTITY TRANSITION TAKEAWAYS

DOS AND DON'TS

- Don't worry about changing your mind often.
- Create an environment for continual growth. Allow options, for opinions to be fluid, and for choice to rule the day. Change your beliefs, desires, values, actions, and aspirations as you lean into transformation. Don't adjust. Transform.

- Don't try to plan your way out of this.
- Doing is the fastest way out. Planning requires adequate knowledge of major variables and how they interact. All variables are interacting differently now that some are missing. You're no longer functioning on the same cylinders. You have yet to discover new variables, which will become part of the equation. Build the plane while you're flying it.

- Don't worry about being an impostor.
- This is the perfect time to shed others' expectations. Follow desire. Make decisions as if you were already that self you seek to become.

- Don't rely on static information.
- Break up your routines. Help dormant parts of you emerge and expand your horizons. Follow your hunches. Act on serendipity.

- Don't be a people pleaser. Beware of spending too much time with people uncomfortable with you changing, who can't tolerate your "wild ideas" and frequent pivots.
- Be willing to pay the price for change. Find the change that's worth the price. Decide what to do with your life and develop the courage and skills to do it. Find what excites and fulfills you and chase those dreams. Give yourself permission to flirt with endless possibilities. Open the Pandora's box of desire.

- Don't delay taking action while waiting for clarity and a logical strategy.
- Take action with minimal clarity, certainty, and direction. Allow for massive and continual trial and error. Adopt a "fail forward" mindset.

- Don't allow self-betrayal to make you settle, to get the better of you, or to even rear its ugly head.
- Do intervene with self-compassion every time it shows up. Tame your self-betrayal villain that lives inside you with a will as strong as steel. Show it who's boss. Show it where it belongs. Then give it grace because it's a legitimate part of you, doing its job. It belongs in you, and you can't make it an orphan.

RESILIENCE

When you feel like throwing in the towel and settling, when things are falling apart, first check where you rate on the self-betrayal/self-compassion spectrum. How well are you managing that villain?

Now figure out which of the eight principles in this book you can focus on leveraging. It could be where you need the most growth. It could be where your greatest strength lies. It could be a combination of any of these. You can be sure the solution lies somewhere in adjusting that equation.

THREE MISTAKES KEEPING THE CHANGE YOU SEEK OUT OF REACH (AND WHAT TO DO ABOUT IT)

REWAC is a framework to help you avoid three common mistakes, harness your challenges, and make the change you seek to make. It incorporates needle movers from material outlined above and later in the book. It's an effective, simple tool for mastering change.

Three common mistakes keeping people stuck:

1. Thinking you know what you want (false clarity).

2. Planning too much.

3. Succumbing to fear.

The Three Mistakes

False Clarity Impedes:
- Curiosity
- Exploration
- Discovery

Causes Opportunity Loss

Too Much Planning Impedes:
- Interactive process
- Information only accessible through doing

Succumbing to Fear:
- Trapped in indecision and planning.
- False expectation — believing you must make "The Right" decision.
- Wanting retrospect to be available in the moment.

© 2022 - Current Courage-Ignite Breakthrough Institute, LLC

HOW TO AVOID THE THREE MISTAKES:

1. THINKING YOU KNOW WHAT YOU WANT

When it comes to identity transition, it's easier to know exactly what you don't want than to clearly articulate what you do want (Ibarra 2017).

Thinking you know what you want keeps you from fully engaging in the discovery process. It thwarts needed curiosity. Since discovery can be uncomfortable, it causes people to stay put.

Allow time for discovery. Courageously engage in discovery. You don't know what you don't know. This is where clarity gestates and is born.

Wallow in the void and chaos of divergence and liminality. Flirt with possibility. Allow yourself to be uncomfortable. Do new things. Talk to new people. Test drive new identities (Ibarra 2017).

2. PLANNING TOO MUCH

Planning is something we're taught and expected to do. To be sure, it's an important tool. But it happens in your head. Change requires a transition, and that requires doing.

Planning too much puts you at risk of falling into a vortex of ever-expanding options and obstacles. These then beg for more planning to decrease risk and improve the odds of success.

All the while planning stalls action, insights, and breakthroughs. Transition and transformation require iteration, and iterating on a plan is wasting time. A plan needs to be tested and evaluated before iteration is of value.

Experiment instead of plan. Embrace trial and error. Learn to fail forward.

3. SUCCUMBING TO FEAR

As you allow enough time to experiment and discover, to wallow in liminality and flirt with possibility, resist premature commitment (Ibarra 2017). Over time, you'll get used to the goal posts moving, and pivoting will become easier.

But to do all of this, you must contend with fear. The antidote to fear is, of course, courage.

This requires willingness to express yourself—your real thoughts, feelings, needs, and ambitions—to others and, most importantly, to yourself.

The winning formula is to consistently take bold action *while* wallowing in liminality and, as my teacher Seth Godin says, "dancing with fear."

(Note: More on fear in the Courage and Grit chapter.)

HARNESS YOUR CHALLENGES USING REWAC

- Resist premature commitment. Don't settle.
- Experiment versus plan.
- Wallow in liminality.
- Allow enough time to discover what you really want.
- Courageously dance with fear.

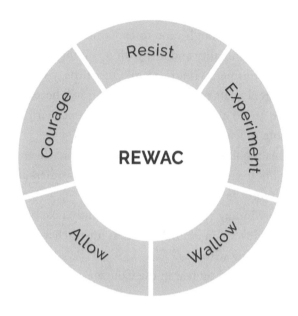

YOU'VE GOT THIS

The fact that you're reading this book proves you have what it takes to be a master of change. It shows you have a growth mindset, meaning you believe things can change. You believe a better way forward exists and are taking steps to discover it by reading this book.

I honor and applaud your courage and willingness to rebuild your identity on your own terms. Personal development is available to all, and you've raised your hand to learn. Because you're reading this book, I'm confident you're willing and able to implement the suggestions this book has to offer. You're ready to join other bold becomers to harness your challenge, grow, and transform.

CHAPTER 2

Creativity, Intuition, and Expectations Management

I have no special talents. I am only passionately curious.

—ALBERT EINSTEIN

...

While in forced identity transition, you're required to make decisions about things you're likely unprepared to face. Clouded judgment from emotional turmoil overlays this demand. You might want to crawl up and hide in a hole, but you can't. You have to get out of this pickle. Liminality isn't a destination.

You need creativity in full force right now. You're dealing with things you've likely never dealt with. You are in a disoriented and ambiguous state of divergence. You've parted from your habitual ways of being, doing, and thinking and don't yet have a new foothold. You are living in liminality.

Creativity and experimentation, as discussed in chapter 1, go hand in hand. They're your primary tools for extricating yourself from wherever your catalyst landed you.

If you're reading this book, you are intentionally creating the next version of yourself. You're not satisfied with just letting life happen to you.

What built you into who you are today, a gradual evolution, isn't going to get you over that threshold and out of the liminal space any time soon. To not stay stuck or spiral downward, you need creativity to generate new options for who you wish to become and how to carry that out.

Intuition is tied to creativity so learning to hear, trust, and act on it is essential. Chapter 1 explains why logical planning can only get you so far in this type of situation. Intuition fills in where strategy and past experience falls short. It tames logic's overbearing, overrated confidence, and attempts at omnipotence.

Logic gives great excuses to avoid change:

- It doesn't make sense.
- It would be too hard.
- It is (theoretically) impossible.
- It's not necessary.
- I don't want to change anything else and lose more than I've already lost.

But during FIT, logic needs to play second fiddle in managing the chaos of divergence and living in liminality. And expectations need to be played in a different key.

> Managing expectations and logic differently
> than you're used to is essential.

This allows the process to ebb and flow while what you want are straightforward, quick outcomes. The creative process is not to be rushed. Pivoting is its love language.

Many things make change during FIT difficult:

- It's something so big it impacts basically every aspect of your life.

- It upsets the applecart, disrupting almost everything.

- Your mind is always searching for answers while your heart and soul just want to stop the world, escape reality, and lick your wounds.

- Others get tired of hearing about your struggle.

Perhaps the most challenging part is much of the help from others isn't all that helpful. When it comes down to it, this is an inside job. That's where intuition comes in.

I know a bit about logic's desire for omnipotence and its promise of predictability and comfort. I have two master's degrees in planning (public health and social welfare).

But I learned a lot about logic's shortfalls when I lost my social work career (full story in chapter 7). At that time, logic was impotent. It failed me big time. Sometimes, no amount of brainstorming can give you the solution you need. Forced identity transitions are this kind of situation.

My skill and dependence on strategic planning and reverse engineering solutions went out the window. Life threw me a curveball. I couldn't connect the dots because many of them didn't yet exist in my universe.

Against all schemes and logical arguments, my journey demanded I allow for serendipity and heed intuition.

This was where I learned, kicking and screaming, to stop trying to push the river, to allow for what was showing up, to make courageous choices without any reasonable expectation of success, and to trust my intuition.

I learned to measure success differently by taking action one day at a time. And that was enough.

I learned what accepting moving goal posts meant. How I measured success at the start of my journey changed over time. I replaced it with other measurements. I counted actions taken, not outcomes achieved. Truthfully, it took some painful years before I changed what I measured and even more years to accept how long this process was taking.

I learned FIT is different from a chosen identity transition. I treat it differently now, and I hope you will too. I'm able to be kind to myself about the time it takes. I've released the guilt of not being productive in the ways I used to measure productivity.

Learning the concepts in this chapter will make decision-making easier. My hope is for you to embrace these early on and then apply them while using the eight principles of change outlined in part 2.

You now have a guide for reducing the angst inherent in FIT. You likely only have an idea of where you're headed. These are some tools and practices needed to get you there.

Let's talk about how you can do it faster, feel stronger and more competent, and do this better than you would have alone. You'll avoid some of the pitfalls and be more likely to harness the benefits that are always part of this journey.

THE POWER OF CREATIVITY

Each individual life is a creative process. Some people are highly ambitious, seeking accolades and compensation for their accomplishments and making that happen. Others scrape by doing the bare minimum to survive. Then there's everyone in between.

Everyone is making something of their lives—some by design and some by default. Some venture into many distant pastures, always seeking greener grass. Others stay close to what's familiar. Some deeply contemplate the meaning of life. Others are content with daily living. Each of our lives is as individual as our fingerprints, even when we share similar circumstances.

FIT invites us to become proactive designers of our lives.

It's where we get to examine and decide on a litany of details, many of which we've never thought much about before, if at all. We've grown up and become who we are based on many other people's and our own ideas and aspirations for us.

Now is the time to differentiate and to decide consciously what parts are truly ours and how to bolster them. Clues to who this self is are likely found in the seven-year-old version of yourself or some version who got buried long ago.

Now is the time to not only become the designer of your life but to be like a couturier—a designer *and* maker of fashionable, high-quality custom clothing made to the customer's every specification.

In couture, cost is not a determining factor. You choose the highest quality fabrics, use the most labor-intensive construction techniques, and create the most refined garments. You make as many changes as needed along the way. You give yourself the gift of time with the goal of enhancing and highlighting the customer's essence. Everything is there for a reason. Nothing is superfluous. The result is one-of-a-kind luxury garments.

FIT can be this kind of creative process. You have the opportunity to design a couture-quality life, with no compromises on quality, filled with high impact and high rewards. But it takes time. It's messy. It's not linear, and it takes investment.

THE CREATIVE PROCESS

Creativity isn't just for artists. We use it in our daily lives, especially when we're trying to create change or when change is thrust upon us. It involves making choices, and this can be messy and risky. By definition, creativity disrupts the status quo.

It requires courage to explore the unknown, to risk not finding what you're after, and to be disappointed in what you find.

Creativity involves curiosity. Sometimes we hold back from asking questions because we don't want to know the answers. They might reveal things that compel us to make decisions we don't want to make.

If you're in FIT, you have no choice *but* to be curious and creative. You're in a state of divergence and need to get things straightened out. Tough questions need answers. Curiosity helps you ask better questions. It helps the divergence process move toward convergence faster, where things will fit together again and make sense. To piece your life back together, you're called to explore courageously and harness the creative process for all it's worth.

Here's the one rule: The creative process
cannot have predetermined outcomes.

While navigating in liminality and experiencing divergence, you will have some sort of vision of where you're
headed. But be on the alert for premature commitments.
This is an iterative process through which ideas get refined.
It takes time for options to emerge. You will experience discomfort and doubt in the uncertainty, and it takes courage
and resolve not to abandon ship.

FIT lays your cards out on the table. It's a time when
you review everything for meaning and purpose. Then, you
get to pick and choose. You build upon what could be a very
different, even stronger foundation than you had before your
catalytic event.

As you evaluate your life, you assess what worked and
what didn't, what you want for yourself now, and what you
will no longer allow.

The process feeds you information from doing and from
your subconscious, brought to you by intuition—knowledge,
flashes of insight, etc. Creative divergence is about collecting
dots of information and finding patterns. Eventually, it gives
you enough dots to start reconnecting pieces of yourself back
together. With this, you'll eventually see patterns, which forge
openings for all parts of you to show up, parts that belong in
the new version of you.

A critical element of healing and moving forward
involves grief and loss. Processing grief allows you to transform the meaning of things you've lost and channel this
through new avenues. In FIT, meaning is in a state of divergence on steroids. It may seem impossible to re-establish
order, but you will.

You will experience a metamorphosis of meaning from your loss. Through the process of convergence, you will transform important aspects of your loss and find ways to carry this with you into the future. All that seems lost is not lost.

Each idea, each new angle of the vision
of the life you're working your way into,
is waiting to be discovered.

Your starting point is just a point in time. You've crossed over a threshold into unknowing. Your job is to build a new threshold to cross over into a new version of yourself—your best self.

The creative process is experimental and experiential. It's *feeling* guiding intellect, logic, and planning.

It requires time as you go through many either/or and back-and-forth moments. It's not possible to envision exactly what you want and where you're headed. You can have an idea. The details of life's choices and taking action invite serendipity and reveal your path forward.

In taking bold action and then evaluating, we discover what the new version of ourselves is becoming.

In this iterative process, we only know we've finished and stepped over the new threshold when it feels right, when we feel complete (Ibarra 2017), and when we no longer doubt our choices.

Until then, it's normal and okay to doubt, even *as* you trust the process. The FIT creative process takes on a life of its own, if you allow it. You are the artist. An artist lets design elements speak to and lead her.

EMPOWERING YOUR INTUITION

Intuition is direction we receive from our higher self. It is our soul's tool—our soul's voice—designed to help us survive and achieve its goals.

Intuition supports and promotes self-actualization. Your higher self is compassionate and caring but soft with its directives. It always allows for free will. It treats fear with empathy. It understands, respects, and tries to assuage fear.

Another voice comes from the lesser self. Your intuition does not emanate from here. This voice pushes you toward self-betrayal and self-sabotage. It's critical and can be downright abusive. Guilt, shame, and fear are common feelings associated with this voice.

The lesser self wants to keep you put by whatever means necessary. It believes self-actualization to be too risky, too big of a cost, too much expended energy for an unguaranteed outcome. Its job is to preserve status quo.

We recognize intuition when we say things like:

- "I can't really explain it, but…"
- "It just felt right."
- "It just felt wrong."

It's when you have a gut feeling or a hunch or hear an inner whisper and know your higher self has your back.

Within each of us lives a gentle, persistent, and positive inner voice—our soul's voice. This voice is unmeasurable by reliable scientific and social science instruments, and it is the driving force behind our will and conscience.

Our soul's presence has many names:

- Higher self
- Best self
- Ideal self
- Inner knowing
- Truest self

Intuition becomes more apparent and accessible during FIT. We're questioning so much of what we thought to be true as so many new opportunities appear before us. This loosens our grip on logic to allow for intuition.

Intuition can conflict with logic, our personality, and what we believe. These are driven, in part, by needs to fit into social settings. Our personality and belief system often collude with things against our best interest.

But our higher self and the messages it sends us through intuition never steer us wrong. From here we may draw upon our self-compassion.

Self-compassion is always available.
It is our internal mediator, defending us against
unworthy external and internal demands.

In a *Psychology Today* article titled "The Science of Intuition," the authors urge us not to bypass our intuition. "It may be easier to passively absorb the views of others without consulting ourselves. But quieting the noise from the outside world and turning inward long enough to listen to the signals from our own minds, bodies and brains make us better equipped to make sound decisions" (Cozolino, Drulis, Samuelson 2021).

Intuition is often discounted or overlooked. For many, it's not something we can call upon at will. We learned to seek answers from authority and that unless we can justify something backed with proof, our ideas don't count.

What makes it hard for people to take action on intuition is they can't prove they're right. So they doubt what they feel, hear, or know and push intuition aside. And we may avoid it because it often rubs up against logic.

Cozolino et al. explain traditional decision-making theories. These are based on "logical and rational application of conscious cost-benefit analyses... lists of pros and cons... Yet it seems that there are other processes going on inside us which influence our choices... These sometimes override what we think is most logical... There's a sixth sense they may not even be able to articulate" (Cozolino, Drulis, Samuelson 2021).

Intuition is more than our past experiences and learnings feeding us information in the present.

Cozolino et al. point to neuroscience. Our body evolved to give us cues that help us make quick survival decisions. These "somatic markers" translate unconscious emotions and sensations into felt instinct. These appear in different forms— unidentified or vaguely recognized feelings, unpleasant body sensations, etc. In the modern world, somatic markers interweave with rational thinking, improving decision-making (Cozolino, Drulis, Samuelson 2021).

Many books teach about intuition in depth. For the purposes here, it's enough to know it's real. It's a necessary part of making the most of the human experience. And it's one of the main tools bold becomers harness to become the next version of themselves.

When you acknowledge intuition's value and take action based on it, you will benefit from what can support and change you in positive ways. To reap these benefits, we need to become more familiar with our intuition and its value. When we become masters at interpreting our lives and act on our inner wisdom, we make better decisions. The more we trust and act on intuition, the faster our intentions, actions, and outcomes align. We replace lesser quality or no longer best choice beliefs, behaviors, and routines with elevated ones.

Intuition will become a treasured partner
and serendipity a frequent guest.
They wish to be welcomed and expected.
Trust in the process and courage are needed
to take action on their proposals.

Intuition invites you to seek to know and understand your essence, to release anything nonessential, to let go and make room for the next right things to show up.

Give yourself permission to trust yourself to make sound decisions. The right decision for *that moment*, regardless of whether a nanosecond later you have a better idea. Following through on decisions gives you the retrospect needed to iterate and find the next right decisions.

As you experiment and explore, the goal is to discover the kernel of truth where your wisdom resides. This is how you connect with that higher self and live from its truth. It's how you think, feel, and act in line with your true identity. That kernel *is* within you, and it is fully and constantly available for consultation.

EXPECTATIONS MANAGEMENT DURING FIT

Measuring progress and success is based on the premise that it's the *number of things you try*, such as new beliefs, habits, or activities. It's about doing, not how deep you go or the results you achieve.

While in liminality, you're not measuring outcomes. Everything is grist for the mill as you sort out what's important and what's not, what serves you now and what no longer serves you.

A practice masters of change use is the ability to shift expectations. They don't try to twist reality to how they want it to be but rather acknowledge what is. Then they do what makes sense in the moment and trust that next steps will reveal themselves on their own timeline. They accept it's wasted effort trying to push the river.

This is the magic that masters of change harness. They allow reality to be reality and for the future to unfold on its own timeline, in its own way. They don't resist change. They're ready to address change with the right mindset. They apply effective concepts and principles to overcome adversity.

Your job is to show up and put in the work, one day at a time, just like other masters of change. Your journey will make many twists and turns. With a unique combination of options, decisions, and serendipity, your path forward will emerge. You will access clarity and deep meaning.

James Clear, in his book *Atomic Habits* (2018), describes the Plateau of Latent Potential. This is where we expect certain results at a certain point in time. We like to think things happen in a linear progression toward the outcomes we seek.

Reality shows we may start off moving at a good clip, but then we tend to make less progress than we'd like. For a while, we can even go into dips and think something's wrong. But if we keep at it, at some point the progress heads up again and goes faster than previously (Clear 2018, 16).

FIT is a full-emersion experience in divergence—
hanging out in the dip
until convergence is achieved.

When we connect enough of the dots to make sense of where we're headed, momentum picks up. We leave the divergent state. One thing leads to the next. This is convergence. In the beginning phase of creativity, one thing doesn't always lead directly to the next. And many things need to be released once we realize they aren't a fit.

The important thing to keep in mind
is the endless variations of who you can become.

Like a couture garment, the sky's the limit. Give yourself the time you need to try on different designs. Nobody has a target date for transformation. Each person has their own unique set of things to consider. Try out and work through these before making commitments and becoming.

The catalyst that pushed you into FIT will likely have cost you tremendous losses. In macrobiotics a principle is the bigger the front, the bigger the back. This refers to the phenomena that opposite things exist or happen in proportion to each other. Everything has a complementary aspect that makes up the whole. You don't have one without the other, but often, the other isn't apparent in the moment.

Those who master change have faith this idiom is true, even if only subconsciously. It keeps them going until they prove it right. Many of the stories in this book show this to be true. New versions of you await that you've never yet come close to imagining.

KEY TAKEAWAYS

DOS AND DON'TS

- Don't seek a quick fix.
- Bold becomers don't seek alterations or patchwork solutions. They seek transformation. Transformation takes time. They're determined to level up. They seek to uncover and fuse their essence with all aspects of their life with no parts missing and no extraneous parts.
- Don't try to attain transformation from applying rote solutions.
- What got you here won't get you to your next level. You need to trailblaze. Thinking creatively and trusting intuition supports this. Give yourself the gift of time to iterate until the right solutions emerge. Seek next right choices. Avoid premature commitment. Don't settle.
- Don't avoid leaving your comfort zone.
- Do suspend judgment and learn to tolerate doubt and uncertainty. Thinking you already know what you need to know causes people to miss out. Acknowledge what you know is only part of the picture. Ignite courage and curiosity to explore the unknown. Take risks. Flirt with possibility.
- Don't let avoidance of pain defeat you. Don't let it rob you of your transformation.
- Learn to recognize the fears underneath pain. Once identified, you can find ways to soothe them.
- Do not heed urges to override intuition.
- Change and growth are the spice of life, not practicality. It's a choice to get trapped in logic and fear and avoid change. Use intuition, creativity, and shifted expectations

to lay the groundwork for the unexpected to appear and then follow its lead.

- Don't give logical excuses auto-approval to override your intuition.
- Our intuition begs us not to override it. Use this opportunity to embrace your intuition as the partner it's meant to be. It's designed to conjure up the *exact* combination of elements to configure the new, best you. The apprehensive *and* exhilarated you waiting to take to the stage. The you you've always been meant to be.

Intuition, combined with creativity and adjusted expectations, give you a holistic perspective. Harness this, and you will become a master of change.

RESILIENCE

When we feel like we've fallen off track, it's our job to run with it even if it might seem we're veering off course. Sometimes, "going off track" is the exact right thing in that moment. It's important not to be so determined with our goals that we miss out on serendipity (even less obvious forms of serendipity only labeled as such in retrospect).

At the same time, it's a delicate balance to stay focused. We cannot afford to run after every shiny object calling for our attention. We can always give ourselves grace because discernment in decision-making can only have twenty-twenty vision after the fact. Intuition helps with in-the-moment discernment.

So let's trust our decisions. Like an airplane that veers off course and then course corrects, we too will get to our destination. Going "off course" is grist for the mill. We can choose to hold uncertainty and doubt with care as we collect ideas and begin connecting the dots.

YOU FIND WHAT YOU LOOK FOR

Once, a surgeon and a physiatrist treated the same population—kids receiving specialty medical care.

The children had an array of problems and diagnoses. Many had cerebral palsy. Among other problems, this can cause pain and limited mobility from limb contractures. These sometimes require surgery. Many were severely disabled and confined to wheelchairs. They and their families would have a lifetime of interfacing with medical teams.

The eternal hope is more functionality, less suffering, and incremental, sometimes seemingly inconsequential improvements in quality of life.

Every week these two doctors left the hospital. Each went to their respective off-site medical therapy unit where children received occupational and physical therapy. The doctors and the therapy teams met with the patients and families and determined treatment goals and recommendations.

My last social work job was working with these families for the agency providing the therapy. I attended these clinics. My unspoken and accepted role was that of mediator/facilitator for these (often tense) encounters.

I found it interesting and disturbing that the surgeon's solution was invariably surgery when the physiatrist's solution was often not surgery. Again, these treatment recommendations were for the very same kinds of problems. They treated the same population of patients. All patients had access to the same resources for medical treatment.

It became clear to me that people find what they're looking for. While the surgeon might not have considered other less invasive solutions, the physiatrist did. The surgeon seemed to be stuck in a box with only one solution. The physiatrist was a holistic thinker.

This is the power of creativity—allowing
for different perspectives to enter the equation.

I'm unaware of different outcomes of their respective recommendations. Even though they were seeing the same things, the solutions were often predictably different.

Even highly trained and educated people miss out on different available solutions. They're not always thinking as creatively as they might.

We always have choices. We can think we already know what to do or we can face every challenge with a beginner's mind, open to possibility. We can be open to seeing it differently by not starting with a solution or outcome in mind but with exploration.

Bold becomers use every resource available to think outside the box. They come up with creative solutions that leverage their opportunity for change. Then they become the people they really like to be with.

They seize the day and channel their power with conviction equal to that of water cascading over a magnificent waterfall, fully into a new life. Bold becomers transform choices into a symphony of actions aligned with their values, aspirations, and full potential. They look until they find themselves.

INTUITION TUNE-UP CHECKLIST

If your relationship with your intuition is a bit rusty, here are a few things to help access, trust, and act on it:

✓ Start a journal. Document every quiet whisper, gut feeling, or soft nudge you have for two weeks.

✓ Follow up these notes with details on future events that prove your intuitive information to be spot on.

✓ Mentally review your past six months. List all the times you've recognized intuition communicating with you.

✓ Jot down how reality matched up with those intuitive hits.

✓ Be particularly aware of intuition coming through during the following activities:
  - Meditation.
  - Walking or running alone without listening to music or podcasts.
  - Bathing, dancing, doing yoga, etc.
  - First thing in the morning upon awakening.
  - Last thing at night before drifting off to sleep.

✓ With all the above, go beyond these intellectual exercises. Tune into the *feeling* the intuitive hits cause you to have.

The more you expect intuition to be available to you, the more it will be. The more you feel it (rather than think about it) and act on it, the more you'll trust it. Remember, your logical mind will show up to override it. Give both equal access to your life.

YOU'VE GOT THIS

Change is tough. It requires courage to let go, to pivot, to turn around in circles until you're *past* dizzy. The creative process requires releasing unnecessary elements. The change required of you involves boldly letting go of more pieces of you than what you've already lost, to release those that no longer belong with the new you you're becoming.

You know which ones they are. This is your chance to wipe the slate clean. This is self-transformation. It's a gift although it probably doesn't feel like it now.

You might feel stuck, but you're not going to stay stuck. Now it's time to learn the eight principles of mastering change. I'm celebrating as you harness these and put your creativity and intuition to work for you!

FIT AND THE EIGHT PRINCIPLES OF MASTERING CHANGE

How long are you going to wait before you demand the best for yourself?

—EPICTETUS

CHAPTER 3

Courage and Grit

*Shattering my ego to understand what's beyond that,
to find my life on the other side of it,
that was the hardest and scariest thing I've ever done.*

—JOSH PERRY, MINDSET AND HEALTH OPTIMIZATION
STRATEGIST, FORMER PRO BMX ATHLETE AND MULTIPLE
BRAIN TUMOR WARRIOR, SPEAKER, AND PODCAST HOST

...

Goal: Be willing to take risks and trust you'll figure things out.

IDENTITY UNDER FIRE JUST FOR WHO YOU ARE

In 2016, San Francisco 49ers quarterback Colin Kaepernick began sitting on the bench during the national anthem. Alone, he decided to use his platform to protest racial inequality and police brutality (Boren, 2020).

The third time he did this, he addressed his protest to members of the media: "I'm not going to stand up to show pride in a flag for a country that oppresses Black people and people of color. To me, this is bigger than football, and it would be selfish on my part to look the other way. There are bodies in the street and people getting paid leave and getting away with murder.

If they take football away, my endorsements from me, I know that I stood up for what is right" (Wyche, 2016).

After a conversation with a friend, Nate Boyer, who explained how soldiers take a knee in front of the grave of a fallen soldier to show respect, he changed his form of protest and began taking a knee. On September 1, 2016, Colin Kaepernick and teammate Erik Reid made national news by taking a knee. Over time, other players followed their lead (Martin and Boyer, 2018).

By 2017, taking a knee during the national anthem was so controversial the president of the United States took note. National television broadcast his opinion: "Wouldn't you love to see one of these NFL owners, when somebody disrespects the flag, say, 'Get this son of a bitch off the field right now! Out! He's fired! He's fired!'" (Graham, 2017).

Kaepernick became the enemy of many and the hero of others. All while being aware of the potential of losing his career because of his choice.

In 2017 he did lose his career. He opted out of his contract with the 49ers and became a free agent. He has not played in the NFL since.

In 2019, Kaepernick settled a grievance against the NFL, claiming the owners colluded to keep him out (Mangan, 2019).

Kaepernick's willingness to sacrifice his career is even braver considering how hard it was for him to get to where he was. In high school he was a star baseball pitcher and people pushed him to continue pursuing baseball. He pushed back, letting everyone know he was going to be a quarterback (DuVernay, 2021).

His Netflix series documents this journey. It was "all I ever wanted my whole life," he says. "You gotta play the game that's right for you. With football, I feel like myself. With baseball, I feel like an outsider" (DuVernay, 2021).

Being biracial and considered by society as Black held him back. As good as he was at football, he continually lost out. Coaches passed him over in favor of White players even though he was better than his competition (DuVernay, 2021).

He learned early he was always going to have to prove himself, and nothing could be taken for granted. With others telling him what to do with his life, he followed his heart. His baseball coach pressured him to stay with baseball, pointing out all the scholarship offers for that and zero for football. But Kaepernick stood his ground. He kept his options open (DuVernay, 2021).

He took the one football scholarship that finally came through from the University of Nevada, and by sophomore year he was winning many awards, all while maintaining a 4.0 GPA. He turned down a contract to play baseball with the Chicago Cubs, and after college, he signed with the 49ers (DuVernay, 2021).

When the time came for him to publicly take a stand on his race relations convictions, he was ready.

He put his passion and livelihood on the line.
He refused to betray his identity as a person
who will do what it takes to uphold
his fundamental beliefs.

In 2022, Kaepernick still kept in shape. He showed up for training in the hopes that one of the thirty-two NFL owners would hire him (DuVernay, 2021). It had been six years since he played. At thirty-five years old and with the controversial movement he started still in motion, it was still unlikely the NFL was going to pick him up. While he waited, he focused his work on nonprofit and civil rights projects (DuVernay, 2021). And he hadn't lost all his endorsements. He was the face for a 2018 Nike ad campaign that drew both praise and criticism. The ad was called "Dream Crazy." In it Kaepernick said, "Believe in something, even if it means sacrificing everything" (ADL, 2018).

BEING YOUR OWN EMERGENCY RESPONSE TEAM

This might be one of the scariest times in your life. Many people in FIT face challenges they've never had or imagined having.

You can never be totally prepared. Now that it's your turn, courage and grit can save you from despair and get you back in the game. An amazing new you is possible, but only if you fight for it.

FIT comes in many forms, and each one counts as much as the next. Catalysts can be both external and internal. Kaepernick's identity loss, cloaked as a choice, stemmed from an internal catalyst—his conscience. His ideals won the battle over his identity as a quarterback.

People in FIT struggle with many fears. Among other things, they're afraid of:

- Never feeling better again;
- Losing people as they change;
- Letting go of outdated habits and beliefs;
- How they'll manage with their new circumstances;
- The outcome maybe not being worth the effort;
- The amount of effort change requires;
- Not knowing what to do next;
- Making bad decisions; and
- Being alone.

Decisions are hard for different reasons, apart from the lack of guarantees and clarity. We're trained to ask for permission and avoid mistakes.

FIT is filled with uncertainty and doubt. Its hallmark is feelings of ambiguity and disorientation. Regardless of how discombobulated, sad, and scared we might be, we still have to make decisions. We cannot remain stuck, thinking others have the answers we seek. The answers are within us. Courage is a human trait built just for these occasions. It invites you to lean into it and trust you will overcome.

Making decisions is hard enough when we're *not* in a crisis. A lot of fear is involved in making decisions. We even avoid making them to keep from making bad ones or because we resist change. And right now, you have no choice *but* to make decisions. Courage makes that possible.

> Courage and grit are what turn a forced transition into transformation.

Bold becomers rely on them to level up in the face of adversity. FIT gives us that chance to reprioritize and move our goalposts, to vote for ourselves and be happy with who we are, regardless of what others think.

You might be a novice with courage now, but after working your way out of liminality, it's likely nothing will hold you back henceforth. You will master change.

This chapter helps unmask and understand your fears. It will equip you for the exploration, experimentation, and pivoting FIT requires.

It will help you have those conversations you're putting off and own up to actions, habits, beliefs, values and relationships that no longer serve you.

You'll build your courage skill (yes, it's a skill) so you can act on new ideals and commitments to yourself.

It will help you reconnect with your essence. The goal: Put your stake in the ground with a confident declaration of who you are.

1. What is your identity loss catalyst?

2. What habits, values, and beliefs have come into question as a result?

3. What habits, values, and beliefs might you need to shift?

...

COURAGE

Here's my definition of courage:

> Courage is making a scary decision
> and then figuring out how to follow through.

This implies we make decisions without all pertinent information. We commit in the face of fear and when success is not guaranteed. We leave the familiar zone and take risks. This might lead to being worse off, or at the least, no better off than before.

We don't know all the steps needed or how to take those steps to achieve the outcome we're after. It can include, especially in FIT, moving forward without a clear target of where we're headed.

Only through taking action do we develop competence, which results in confidence. And the more confidence we have, the more likely we'll stretch and gain more competence.

This is the confidence-competence loop Brendon Burchard, personal development trainer and high-performance expert, teaches in his seminars and book *High Performance Habits:*

How Extraordinary People Become That Way (2017, 330). Confidence and competence are antidotes to fear.

But before being confident and competent, we need courage and grit. This begins with acceptance of the following:

- Life isn't fair.
- It's okay to be uncomfortable.
- We're responsible for how we respond to life.
- FIT has significant degrees of uncertainty, doubt, and fear.
- It's okay and expected to take imperfect action.

A theme in Brendon's teaching is *honoring the struggle* (Burchard 2016). A key to acceptance is honoring the struggle. We do this by lowering our resistance to reality and surrendering to discomfort.

Your job is to wallow in liminality and not to prematurely commit to something just to get out of discomfort or because you're afraid to boldly become who your soul is waiting for you to become. Listening to and acting on intuition is critical. Intuition won't let you settle, and rather than force you, it invites you to respect and act on its judgment.

GRIT

Grit is a combination of passion, perseverance, fortitude, direction, and courage. It plays a major role in harnessing passion and perseverance to achieve specific, long-term goals and is a psychological factor in determining success (Duckworth 2016, 291). It is the fuel that sustains courage over time.

Courage, on the other hand, can be independent of perseverance and passion. The fundamental characteristic driving courage is dedication to a particular need for yourself and/or others.

Purpose (passion and direction) gives courage its *raison d'être*. Without purpose, the grit needed to commit and follow through with a decision is a moot point. It doesn't require grit or courage. (I discuss purpose in the next chapter.)

Grit is the glue that holds things together
and gives us the ability to keep going after failure
and loss and not to jump ship when things fall apart.

Bold becomers keep grit on the front burner. They understand the nonlinear creative process and go the extra mile when goalposts move.

Angela Duckworth says in her book *Grit: The Power of Passion and Perseverance* that grit isn't about being the best or better than; it's about *getting* better. It's the constant drive to improve, where process is as important as outcome. It's about being satisfied being unsatisfied, and it's about knowing what you want (2016, 8).

FIT is filled with pivots. We keep changing what we want. This is normal, expected, and necessary. This is the iterative, creative process. It's done through compare and contrast. Only through iteration does the creative process produce satisfaction or masterpieces.

Grit, Duckworth informs us, directly impacts life satisfaction and well-being. Grit and courage are the formula for overcoming life's setbacks, as well as achieving one's greatest ambitions (2016, 8). Masters of change harness grit and courage to get the most out of what life serves them.

THE THREE TYPES OF FEAR

While courage is part of grit, I separate it because it involves managing fear. This is a huge topic on its own. Brendon

Burchard found that courage is one of the six habits that distinguish high performers from others. We face three kinds of fears in daily life (Burchard 2015).

Here's what you need to think about as you face any fear other than a dangerous situation threatening your physical health (Burchard 2015). When you're aware of these three fears, you can have more confidence when fearful. You can make better choices based on a more accurate evaluation of your situation and options.

    1. We fear *loss pain*—that by changing or advancing in our lives, we will lose something important to us (Burchard 2015).

For those in FIT, we've already lost something important and fundamental to who we are. This means it's not a fear but a reality. We must do what's necessary to honor our loss pain. (I discuss grief and loss in chapter 5.)

At the same time, change involves loss and gain, so we face the fear of losing more as we explore new options to replace the void our losses produced. With each new decision we make, we risk losing something else because of the nature of change.

Sunk costs (money/time/effort/emotional investment spent that cannot be recovered) and seemingly endless pivots are inherent in the change process. It's hard to see how things are adding up when new decisions often involve letting go of things. This is particularly true at the beginning of the journey.

> Awareness of loss fears buoys
> psychoemotional weight while on
> an uncertain, nonlinear path forward.

Awareness acknowledges the reality of our fears. It lessens the angst from taking necessary risks. It doesn't matter how many pivots you make, how many sunk costs you let go of, or how many things you find that aren't for you. What matters is seeking, finding, and then making informed decisions through taking action.

2. We fear *process pain*—that the mere act or process of changing will be too hard for us (Burchard 2015).

Especially for those in FIT who didn't vote for change, this is a bitter pill to swallow. We're in a change process whether we like it or not. Some are more agile than others for a litany of reasons. Regardless of qualifications, this is the boat we're in.

This is where courage and grit come into full force. Courage is a skill you can develop. You can become more courageous through a habit of awareness and intention.

This transition process is your tarmac where you *get to* develop more courage. You're leveling up as you transform into a new, higher version of yourself—a version you likely never imagined possible because you have no alternative but to level up. By applying the concepts and principles of mastering change, you can access strength, abilities, and degrees of grit and courage previously untapped.

3. We fear *outcome pain*—that all the effort we put into changing may not lead to a better outcome in our lives, that the grass might not be greener on the other side (Burchard 2015).

For those not choosing to level up but pushed into change without a vote, this might feel like a great indignity. Still, you've been positioned to surge forward through exploration, experimentation, and continual decision-making. You might not know exactly where you're headed, but bold becomers do not let that stop them from engaging in the change process.

Of particular importance to those in FIT is the need to avoid premature commitment. This means that finding, testing, and rejecting new pastures are imperative. The more you explore, the more you discover.

You don't know what you don't know.
Making informed decisions involves
rolling up your sleeves, taking action, and discovery.

We cannot learn and grow the way we need only through reflection and planning. In the actual doing we find our path forward. We must hop many fences before finding the right pasture for us. Bold becomers do not let impatience, weariness, fear, or doubt cause them to settle.

Changing *how you measure success* helps lessen the blow of any outcome pain you're faced with. It doesn't matter if the grass isn't greener. Like dating, we lower our expectations knowing most won't be what we're seeking. We don't let that stop us from putting in the effort.

...

Bold Becoming Prompts

1. My top three fears are...

2. Two bold actions I can take in the next ninety days to start moving through each fear are...

3. For each fear, why is it important to address it?

...

SCARIER THAN A BRAIN TUMOR

Source: personal interview.

At seventeen, Josh Perry had achieved his dream of living life on his own terms. He'd escaped his abusive home by becoming a BMX athlete. In his junior year of high school, he turned pro. Dropping out of school, Josh moved from Massachusetts to North Carolina, got his GED, and started competing around the world.

He finally had what he'd always needed. "I was seen and heard and validated."

Success, however, was only a veil. It covered the ongoing psychoemotional effects of growing up in a hostile environment. It didn't release him from his core insecurities and feelings of inadequacy. He still believed he was dumb and undeserving.

Josh also described a side effect of competition. "It kept me in a holding pattern." Every time he lost, it fueled his belief he wasn't good enough. That was the cost of living his dream, and it was the only life he knew how to live.

A typical young adult, he was partying, drinking alcohol, not sleeping much, and eating junk food.

"Nothing but processed and sugary foods—candy, ice cream, pizza, fast food, and then wash it down with soda because it was cheaper than water."

He didn't realize what he ate and drank became his body's cells and tissues. He thought he was just consuming calories and burning them off. And because doctors (erroneously) told him he was healthy, he didn't think twice about lifestyle choices.

But Josh wasn't healthy. Doctors misdiagnosed his symptoms for a year and a half before finding his tumor.

Suffering from chronic pain in his head, he was in and out of urgent care and emergency rooms. Doctors gave him painkillers and denied him any scans. They'd say, "You're twenty-one, you're a professional athlete, you have a six pack, and nothing is wrong with your bloodwork, so just take these pills."

The brain tumor diagnosis happened when he got an MRI after hitting his head biking. They rushed him into surgery and saved his life. That mortality moment kicked him into high gear.

"Auditing [his] life and becoming accountable for [his] choices," Josh began choosing accountability over victimhood.

The more he learned, the more he found out he needed to learn. He consumed content from all the top thought leaders and health experts. As he learned, he implemented what he learned.

He learned about nutrition, exercise, and mindset. He found out what he was doing with nutrition and exercise had been harming his brain and his health. He learned about the effects of stress, and he learned to become aware of and reframe past emotional memories. What had become beliefs became part of his personality.

He intentionally created a new identity as he discovered cause and effect and approached health from a holistic angle.

Using neuroscience, he rewired his thought patterns. He also used different emotional release modalities. He didn't recognize all the benefits until, in retrospect, he realized his efforts paid off.

But his most profound learning came from looking inward. For Josh Perry, surviving a brain tumor diagnosis wasn't what took all the courage he had. That made him look inward and thoroughly evaluate his life, and yes, that took courage. So did his subsequent tumors and surgeries.

What took all the courage he had was choosing to give up the identity of a BMX athlete. He needed to find out who was there without that. "I knew I couldn't act my way into a new self while still *being* my old self."

By now he'd already been retired from BMX for a few years and had a successful coaching business. But he was still training like a pro.

Accepting the role BMX had served in his life was complete, and that this identity was now holding him back "was the hardest and scariest thing [he had] ever done."

Acceptance happened because of a simple question during a conversation at a conference. He asked his friend Jimmy, a retired NFL player, "When was the last time you ever played competitively since you retired, even just flag or tag football, not just throwing a ball?" Jimmy said, "Never."

That was the catalyst that released Josh from his BMX identity. And in so doing, it opened his new path to freedom.

Josh found out he was still driven, creative, and resilient without BMX. He still had "purpose and passion and grit to get up and continue going," no matter what was thrown at him. This started the process of letting go of old, ingrained beliefs. "I morphed into my new personality and what I was going to allow to be acceptable or not."

BMX gave Josh a framework. It taught him how to chase his dreams and keep his vision alive, to keep creating plans as new visions continually moved the goalposts.

Josh believes suffering is a choice. He dedicates his life to helping others discover they, too, can choose. He helps them see life is not defined by their circumstances and they should pay attention to what each moment can teach them.

The brain tumor provided a catalyst to start looking within. The conversation gave him the tipping point to dare to embrace himself *from* within, value internal over external validation, and be himself.

KEY TAKEAWAYS

DOS AND DON'TS

- Don't allow the lack of a logical plan to keep you from making decisions.
- The only constant in life is change. Pay attention to those inner whispers. Allow passion to copilot with logic. Sometimes, allow passion to fly solo and see where you land.

- Don't let fear of being a quitter keep you from pivoting.
- Pivot to realign with new goals based on updated versions and understandings of you and your reality.

- Don't let yourself decide you can't do or have something you desire.
- Trust that life's got your back and you can figure things out. Commit to learning to master change.

RESILIENCE

When courage feels out of reach or you're too overwhelmed to have any semblance of grit, start with focusing on self-care. (I cover this in chapter 7.)

Check in on grief. On a scale from one to ten, how much are you avoiding feeling your pain? Be aware of your coping mechanisms and make sure they're not adding new problems (e.g., numbing substances or activities). Chapter 5 provides guidance on processing grief and loss.

WHO ARE YOU WHEN YOU ARE SMOTHERED?

When I was little, I lived on the offensive. I spent my first decade at war with my family and the world. I had two older brothers who were often cruel. They excluded, teased, and belittled me. They beat me up. My father hit me. A lot. His mother, who frequently babysat me while Mom kept my eldest brother alive, hated me. School was no escape. I was always in trouble there too. I had to fight for much of what I wanted because of gender discrimination. As a tomboy, I didn't fit in.

I learned early on I couldn't expect support; my life was up to me. Trying to be "a good girl" was never a role I played. That saved my sanity. I had no room for people pleasing. I needed to be me. I was too far away from being able to please people, and I wasn't going to let unfair societal rules and norms control my biography.

In elementary school I fought gender discrimination every single day. Grandpa once said I was more boy than my three brothers combined, but that didn't change my social rank. When boys tried to keep me out of "their" recess games, I'd beat them up to force them to let me play. My sweetest memory was in second grade when I beat up the most macho of them all. Out on the kickball field, I had him under my control—pinned on the ground, helpless, and humiliated. Violence was effective because I got to play in those games, but it was a reluctant inclusion.

Most of the time I was angry, mean, hurting, and with one poor girl, at times a bully. Tired of this antagonistic stance, in fifth grade I stopped fighting at school. I wanted more friends, but it wasn't a great fix. It didn't get rid of the anger, and without the threat of violence, boys succeeded in excluding me.

One day, waiting with the boys behind the softball backstop as captains picked their teams, I wasn't picked. For the millionth time. Because I was a girl. Lacking authority or tools to negotiate my way onto a team and without resorting to violence, I went to the yard duty man for help. He knew the drill. My cause was chronic. Standing by my side, his arm across my shoulders, we watched the boys play. Then he turned and asked, "Julie, why don't you just let the boys play their game?"

I was speechless and in shock. He betrayed me. I finally got the message: I was fighting a losing battle. In society's eyes, I was undeserving. My dream identity of being a fully fledged human was nipped in the bud, suffocated by misogyny. That day I acknowledged being a second-class citizen. His sentence was the impetus for repressing my rage. It changed the arc of my life's trajectory in ways I'm still discovering and reconciling, over five decades later. It sent me into a kind of immobilization that caused my first and most damaging identity loss.

That day, I left who I was behind on that field.
I accepted defeat. I gave up hope. I shut down.
My attitude became "I don't care"
because caring hurt too much.

To deal with this schism within myself, I did what people do when they can't be right: I internalized my oppression. I aimed that righteous anger against injustice, point blank, at myself. I learned self-betrayal. In a weird twist of logic, I transferred hating mistreatment and discrimination to hating myself. I came to view myself as an undeserving, bad person. Thoughts about myself became cruel and demeaning.

By sixth grade, as a result of stuffing my rage and my voice, I became depressed and withdrawn. I became meek. I started doing things against my self-interest. I was afraid to speak my mind because I didn't want to make people mad. I silenced myself and stopped loving myself.

I'd changed. I lost access to that strong, self-assured little girl who stood up to anyone. The real Julie Browne died in fifth grade.

I was no longer a person totally certain about the legitimacy of my desires and decisions. I started doubting myself, and I became a person who would dissociate, watching myself as if from the ceiling looking down. I'd watch myself saying and doing things I didn't want, or not saying and doing things I did want. It was so confusing. But one thing wasn't: I always knew I was *not* that person.

I knew my truth and when I betrayed myself. I knew when I was being me and when I wasn't, and I knew that someday, some way, I'd escape that hell. We always know who we are, even when we're not living that truth.

The word for this is incongruence. I was suffering from incongruence, from living a lie, from being split off from who I really was, from putting up with who I wasn't. For almost a decade I lived in that liminal space. I wasn't who I'd been, and I didn't even have a glimpse of who I was becoming. But I never stopped taking action. Without knowing my destination, I made choices I believed would deliver me back to the whole me. I trusted my inner knowing of who I was and wasn't and let that guide me.

I kept taking the next right step. Even when it meant going backward. Action gave me something tangible, and it created momentum. I was on a quest to regain the me who acts congruently with my beliefs, values, and desires—the me who answers to self-love rather than self-betrayal. I *had* to get back that little girl I knew and loved, the one who always had my back, knew her truth, spoke her truth, and lived her truth.

Two big, audacious leaps got my voice back and, with that, I could live more of who I really was.

My first intervention to get my voice back came in junior year of high school when I arranged to do my senior year abroad. I would live in a foreign country where no one would know me and I'd be forced to speak.

People in Colombia were curious and friendly, and everyone wanted to speak with me. Young, old, people in my neighborhood, strangers. Being *la gringa*, I was unique and intriguing. Through endless and often exhausting conversations, whether I felt like speaking or not, I got my voice back and learned Spanish. Immersed in a different culture, I became super clear on my values. Through contrast and comparison of two countries, it solidified me as a person. It validated who I was and what I stood for. I felt whole and happy with who I'd become.

But returning stateside, I regressed for many reasons. I lost my voice again, worse than before. This time I silenced myself because I thought I was dumb because of choices I was making. I couldn't let people know the real me because I was ashamed of who I'd become, and I hid out as much as possible. Self-loathing and self-betrayal returned with a vengeance.

It was more than five years of living as someone I wasn't before I got back to being more myself.

When I was twenty-five, I volunteered on a crisis hotline. Yes, I'd get serious mileage out of my expensive life lessons from that super yucky previous life chapter. But the real motivation was to get my voice back again. Like Colombia, fielding calls on a crisis line would force me to speak. I found out I excelled at saying helpful things. When callers described their problems, I connected dots in ways they weren't seeing. Drawing from my experiences and the well of empathy I had for others' suffering, I combined strategic planning with my voice.

Now that I was making a concrete difference, I loved using my voice. This time my intervention worked and stuck. I found my voice and, with it, my calling—my therapeutic voice—helping people access personal agency.

My struggle to reunify with my true self was worth the work. Through it I learned our true self will never abandon us. It's always communicating through our intuition.

It's our responsibility and within our capability to regain access to it. But that requires change—moments of stillness, stretching, leaps of faith, perseverance, and courage.

I learned not changing hurts more than changing. The "comfort zone" is often only a "familiar zone." Unless we acknowledge we're not comfortable, we may never summon the courage to change nor access the grit to make that change.

I found out how easy it is to slip into self-betrayal rather than stand my ground and how damaging that can be. Wrestling with this, I found a way to embrace life's adversities and to give myself grace in difficult times lest I annihilate myself with self-loathing.

I learned mistakes are choices, ripe with learning and growth... yours for the taking.

Over forty years later, I learned I was my fifth-grade teacher Ev Bryant's "favorite student of all time." I reminded her of her own free-spirited self at that age.

THE COURAGE/DESIRE CONNECTION

Choice

Courage

Desire

Self-Love

Inner Voice — Soul's Voice

© 2016 - Current Courage-Ignite Breakthrough Institute, LLC

Framework goal: Develop and use courage to make the choices you desire.

PERSPECTIVE

We have the choice of whether to let fabricated psychological limitations keep us from making the change we seek to make. Many feel undeserving and make decisions from this vantage point. They believe they are not enough and not enough exists to go around and others more worthy deserve. Developing an abundance mindset to replace a scarcity mindset helps people receive what they desire. This shift is an act of free will, free of charge, available anytime, anywhere, to anyone. Actively evaluating and changing our perspective to better serve us is our greatest superpower.

SELF-LOVE

This framework is about recognizing and acting on the validity of self-importance. It's about taking steps to revitalize and reclaim our birthright to sovereignty over what we desire. This begs the question, why are many of us cut off from self-love and negating our deepest desires?

Whole books address the lack of self-love. My nutshell view is this: It's about convenience and necessity. Since parents need their kids to mind them and others, they teach them to suppress emotion to fit in. Kids have little power in families, so their needs and desires are easily overridden. Feelings of not being enough come from not feeling seen and heard, being unsafe, and feeling insignificant and unimportant. To manage these conditions and belong, we disconnect from and let go of pieces of ourselves.

In adulthood, desire suppression as a coping mechanism continues, even now when we have choices we didn't as a child. Often, we don't even recognize we're overriding our ability to choose what we desire. It's done subconsciously, on autopilot. As a child, this is a positive coping mechanism. As an adult, it's self-betrayal. Complicity in this cycle of learned self-betrayal is passed down through generations.

COURAGE

Courage begins and ends with changing how we think. To act on our desires, we must make choices. Choice implies some sort of change, and change requires courage. To have freedom of choice, we need courage.

Creating a transformation in FIT requires digging deep into desire. This requires courage. We need to unlearn the bypassing of our desires for convenience. This is not to dismiss that sometimes we suppress desire out of necessity. But without connecting to what we deeply desire and making a commitment to go after it, remaining stuck in status quo, or at best incremental change, is the likely outcome. What is available to everyone—transformation—may remain out of reach.

DESIRE

We all have the capacity to untangle mixed desires, those that are ours and those that serve mainly to fit in. And we have the capacity to develop courage. These capacities come from a commitment to act on your soul's desires—a belief in the validity of your desire, where you know you'd betray yourself if you acted otherwise. When people are stuck, they may lack the courage to act on their soul's desires, so they settle. This is why developing your courage skill is paramount.

THE COURAGE/DESIRE PYRAMID

The bottom three tiers are necessary to develop courage. With courage, you can make decisions that allow you to choose what you really want. Without courage, you're making decisions based on incomplete assets. That's what settling is. Your courage asset is inadequate (unless you're acting out of necessity, where choice isn't available, such as Lena's situation in chapter 10).

The following illustrates how all tiers of the pyramid are interrelated:

- To choose, you need courage to change.
- To have courage, you need a deep desire. A desire strong enough to assuage fear and resistance to change.
- To respect your desires, you need self-love.
- To connect with self-love, you need to heed your soul's inner voice and accept the reality of self-importance.

Everything is interrelated and interdependent. Those who aren't making courageous choices are likely neglecting the bottom three tiers of the pyramid. Paying lip service to these parts of the human experience makes for mediocre, frustrating, and disappointing lives. To have exceptional, satisfying lives that access and enjoy our full potential, all tiers of the pyramid must be activated.

WORKSHOPPING THE FRAMEWORK

Answer the following questions in a notebook:

1. A choice I'm stalling on making is…

2. The fear stopping me from making it is [loss pain, process pain, or outcome pain], and it looks like…

3. The choice I desire to make is important to me because…

4. When I listen to my soul's inner voice about this decision, it's telling me…

5. The best outcome that could happen from taking this action is…

6. The worst outcome that could happen is…

7. When I think about my level of self-love, as it manifests in relation to stalling on making this choice/decision, I rate myself a number from one to ten, with one being leaning way into self-betrayal and ten being acting with pure self-love.

8. Now, finish this sentence: One thing I can do to have more self-love is…

9. Now I've examined what's going on, I [am/am not] ready to take action on my decision because…

YOU'VE GOT THIS

We can all level up our courage skill. The courage to know your truth, speak your truth, and live your truth is everyone's birthright. You can learn to hear, respect, and take action on your higher wisdom to guide you. Today, you can commit to making choices based on self-love. As you act on your soul's whispers, your courage will grow exponentially.

I honor your commitment to self-improvement. It takes courage to even delve into this topic. Reading this book and resourcing yourself with its content is a major step forward and a special gift to yourself.

CHAPTER 4

Purpose

I just feel like I'm an extra in my own movie. I know there's a different path that I should be on... I remember the moment clearly, when the thought crossed my mind in the law library: Bandz, there must be something more to life than this.

—BANDZ MABUSE, COACH AND PERSONAL GROWTH TRAINER

...

Goal: To live with deeply satisfying purpose and clear intention.

WHEN WAR CHALLENGES WHO YOU ARE

"On January 14 [2003], my life changed forever" (C-SPAN 2003). Abdul Henderson was twenty-eight years old and a full-time student when called for duty. A few weeks later he was on a plane to Kuwait. Mr. Henderson sustained a moral injury from acting and witnessing actions and behaviors against his values and moral beliefs. As he put it, he helped invade a sovereign country that had not attacked his. He watched men die over a cause he didn't believe in. He participated in missions where "people who were no threat to [him or his] country were killed." And in less than six months, he realized "the war in Iraq wasn't worth it" (C-SPAN 2003).

This bothered him so much that once back on US soil, he began speaking out against the war. The quotes above were from a speech in a 2003 meeting on Capitol Hill, not long after Mr. Henderson's tour in Iraq. As part of a panel with a group of House Democrats and military families, he spoke about the role of US troops in Iraq. While still an active-duty corporal in the US Marine Corps, he spoke eloquently, graphically, bluntly, and courageously about his experience in Iraq.

"I had reservations going into this war, and I still have them now. And I don't think we should have been there" (C-SPAN 2003).

One of documentary filmmaker Michael Moore's people was at that meeting. At the time, Moore was filming *Fahrenheit 9/11* about the Bush presidency, the war in Iraq, and media coverage. Moore's person recruited Mr. Henderson to be in the film. He would be an actor, but not for the reason many others are. This would be an act in full alignment with his newly clarified conscience. It would serve his underlying purpose—a life of service to his country and the world, quite possibly at the expense of his military service.

The day for his part in the film arrived. Again, his life was going to change, but this time he knew it. It was still 2003, and he and Moore were going to disrupt a normal day on Capitol Hill. They'd be asking members of Congress, as they walked into work, if they'd agree to send *their* son or daughter to war in Iraq. Their goal was to get those with the power to end the war to put some skin in the game. Corporal Henderson, in uniform, risking his career, filmed alongside Michael Moore doing just this. *Man, this is crazy*, he thought. *I'm gonna get my ass in some serious trouble* (Moore 2021).

Mr. Henderson knew showing up in uniform that day would end his military career advancement plans, but he had a purpose and mission larger than himself (Moore 2021).

The moral injury had produced an identity shift.
It forced him to rethink
who he was, who he was going to become,
and who he was no longer willing to be.

Out of that came the clarity and courage needed to pay the price of acting on his conscience. He spoke out on that panel and then with Michael Moore.

"If called, would you still go back, after everything you've seen in Iraq?" Michael Moore asked him that day on Capitol Hill (Moore 2004).

"No."

"Do you want to say that on camera?"

"Yes, I do, because it's the truth. I'm not going to go back and participate."

Up until that moment he hadn't thought about that option, but he knew how he felt. So when questioned, the answer was there. "I was not going to go back and participate in that illegal, immoral war because what I saw, Iraq posed no immediate threat to America. What we were told was all false" (Moore 2021). He would rather face a court-martial and possible jail time than go against his conscience. He would no longer do what he'd been called to do, even though in 2003, "90 percent of people were in support of the war on terror" (Moore 2021). Only one member of Congress, the honorable Barbara Lee, voted against that war.

Abdul Henderson did face an investigation after the filming event. Nothing came of it. He completed his remaining service time "under the radar as much as possible" (Moore

2021). Honorably discharged, he went on with life. After finishing his studies, he worked in some high-ranking roles for different political officials. This included serving as the civilian executive director of the Congressional Black Caucus (Moore 2021).

Mr. Henderson currently runs a mental health nonprofit in Georgia—Mental Health America of Georgia. He was recently instrumental in getting legislation passed to ensure enforcement of the health care parity law. His life mission is to get people to hold elected officials accountable, to challenge the system to do better, to work toward diversity and equity, and to inspire people to become well-informed, speak their truth, and stay engaged with the political process (Moore 2021).

Abdul Henderson lost his identity from a moral injury. He could not continue as a command-obeying serviceman. He retooled his identity to be a servant of his conscience, at any price.

RECALIBRATING EXPECTATIONS FOR YOUR LIFE

Forced identity transition cracks people wide open. The earth beneath your feet is no longer stable because you question the meaning of your life. Often, your sense of value as a human being seems to go up in smoke. You doubt things you were sure about and must reevaluate every aspect of your life. Things don't make sense like they did before, and you're filled with ambiguity and disorientation. You're in a state of divergence and a place of liminality. You may have or may be:

- Lost hope in future happiness;
- Clueless about who you are, now the catalytic event changed how you define yourself;

- Terrified of the prospect of or unsure where to start rebuilding your life without your once-familiar supports;

- Too exhausted, overwhelmed, or discombobulated to dig deep and examine who you are and who you wish to become;

- Afraid that by changing, you will dishonor the memory of who you once were or those who helped make you that way;

- Indignant and resistant to change just because circumstances changed. You worked hard for what you had, and you're not ready to let go of it; or

- Grieving too much to think of the future and what you want going forward.

This is a time of catharsis. It's a sacred rebirth. Your time in liminality is a gift of forced self-repositioning. It's a chance to retool your identity. It's your *job* to boldly become that person who was always in you but swayed out of reach because of outside forces: demands to fit in, the need to belong, or life circumstances. Self-redefinition is our greatest power. How we perceive ourselves is one thing under our control and *the* game changer.

You get to choose your new direction as you realign with your soul's calling, take back all your power, and courageously accept whatever will follow from being your most powerful self—both on personal and professional levels.

When you reconnect with your power, your purpose becomes clear, and vice versa. Things line up and make sense. Purpose gives life deep meaning despite, and often because of, your loss. Your loss catalyzes meaning into a previously unknown and enhanced caliber. It will make it possible to think and do things currently beyond your wildest imagination.

Reconnecting with your power, finding purpose, and letting go of self-betrayal habits allow you to find fulfillment and access joy. It's my belief that you have a mission to complete and only one chance for this—your short lifetime. Your purpose gives you the direction you need to face each day and carry out that mission.

Connecting with your purpose spares you from frustration, boredom, and distraction. It gives you laser focus and energy to keep going. Living congruently with your beliefs, values, and desires is the lubricant that reduces friction. Purpose and congruence make it possible to honor the struggle. Your purpose is your accountability partner, asking that you live a life in flow, congruent with, and connected to your soul's vision.

To be sure, self-transformation is a tall order. The goal of this chapter is to help you reframe your situation, to see it as an opportunity for exponential personal growth and self-improvement, to harness the challenges you face and forge new meaning into them, to find a reason for living each day at your peak level of performance and satisfaction, and to avoid settling.

...

Bold Becomer Prompts

1. My ideal life, lived on purpose, is one in which...

2. I'm reinforcing my intentions to consistently live in alignment with this ideal life by...

3. Personal, spiritual, and/or career activities that bring me deep meaning, joy, and fulfillment include...

...

HARNESSING PURPOSE

Purpose is a treasure chest filled with
a kaleidoscope of your dreams.

These concepts—vision, purpose, mission, and goals—help
you more intentionally design your life. Periodic evaluation
and updating of your purpose ensure on-target activities. Our
identity exists in service to our purpose. These four concepts
are contained in, and manifested through, our perspective.

Life Purpose Elements

Perspective
Decision-making lens directing choices

Goals
Manifestation of tactical actions to fulfilling mission

Mission
Practical strategy to work towards manifesting vision

Purpose
Conceptual ideal and commitment behind mission

Vision
Soul level knowing of our life's work

© 2022 - Current Courage-Ignite Breakthrough Institute, LLC

- A vision is something grand, out of reach, and unquestion-
ably worthy but unattainable. It would exist in a perfect
world. It's what you're ultimately striving for. It's your soul's
signature message and the driver of your core values.

- Your purpose is why you exist.

- Your mission is what you do with your existence. It aligns with your purpose. Together, they answer the question, *What's your life adding up to?*

- Goals are specific targets you must reach to achieve your mission.

- Perspective is the daily operating system driving decisions.

Vison makes your contribution in life worthwhile. It connects you with something important and bigger than yourself. Its size doesn't matter, but rather its sincerity and taking consistent action to manifest it. This is what feeds our soul. In return we get joy, fulfillment, and a deeply meaningful life.

Our gift to the world, and most important asset,
is our perspective.

Sharing our unique perspective is the fundamental contribution the world needs from each of us. It drives how we fit into the big picture of life and find satisfaction.

We manifest our perspective through taking action. Life gives us all we need to function at full capacity of our potential—attainment and disclosure of our true, highest self. When we express that self through our perspective and actions, we live in alignment with our truths and make the most of our existence.

FIT is a time to reconnoiter the shape and contours of our purpose and how it aligns with our vision, and to check in and see if we've been on track. Then, reconcile where we're falling short. This way we make sure that, going forward, we're in alignment with what we feel called to do with our lives. We commit to making the most of our precious life.

While our disruptive catalytic event likely caused great pain and loss, it also gave us a gift—an opportunity to step back and assess our lives in a holistic way we've likely avoided up until now for any number of reasons. These may include fear and the belief we're not qualified or worthy of chasing our biggest dreams or able to handle the new demands those dreams might impose on us.

DIFFERENT KINDS OF GOALS AND MISTAKES

We have the choice to set audacious goals that push and challenge us to move toward a worthy vision. SMART goals (specific, measurable, achievable, realistic, and time-bound) don't help us plan for our vision or purpose. They hold us back from dreaming big. SMART goals are the steppingstones needed to achieve a mission.

For vision and purpose we must set *stretch goals*. These are high-risk, high-effort goals, intentionally set above normal standards. These are not expected to be achieved one hundred percent but rather to inspire growth. And they often deliver exponential results. These are the goals bold becomers set.

A common mistake is to stay attached to sunk costs.

Sunk costs wreak havoc on goal setting. The narrow meaning of a sunk cost is money already spent that cannot be recovered. They tempt people to remain beholden to investments already made. Sunk costs go beyond money. They also include things such as time, effort, emotional labor, and any number of other categories in addition to money. When we are beholden to sunk costs, it can cause us to avoid setting goals we desire. They're some of the greatest barriers to making powerful, *best-choice-right-now* decisions and setting audacious goals.

Bold becomers don't measure choices by what they're going to lose but rather by what they intend to gain. They also do a full assessment of *opportunity costs*—what they might lose if they *don't* make that choice. They find ways to cut their losses, pivot, and invest their time, energy, and resources into new ideas and ventures. To do this, they're constantly on the lookout for decisions based on sunk costs and a limited vision of opportunity costs.

Mr. Henderson let go of sunk costs. He didn't have a clear vision of where he was headed or probably even what opportunity costs he might miss out on. But he gave up his career for his moral convictions when his worldview changed. In FIT, masters of change summon the courage to make decisions with incomplete information.

OUR CALLING

I see our *calling* as the vehicle through which we manifest our purpose. It has both an elusive and searing quality. In his book *The Soul's Code: In Search of Character and Calling*, James Hillman talks about the phenomenon of a significant moment that leads to a feeling and conviction about what you must do with your life, a call you must heed (Hillman 1996, 14). This happened to me when I discovered my therapeutic voice on the crisis hotline (see chapter 3).

Sometimes the call is not so vivid but rather a gentle, persistent pushing. It keeps landing you at the same conclusion—a place where you know you belong, even though you likely feel far from ready to be there (Hillman 1996, 17). This has been happening to me with my thought leadership direction and happened in my reentry story below.

Hillman says these callings determine our biography while at the same time we tend to put them aside. As every acorn is destined to grow and turn into a magnificent oak tree, so too are we predestined to become the best version of ourselves (Hillman 1996, 5). But we have free will and can succumb to fear. Hillman suggests that because this option is audacious, we dull our lives. We accept mediocrity rather than honoring the struggle to manifest our best self.

Marc Gafni, in his book *Your Unique Self: The Radical Path to Personal Enlightenment,* says the answer to following our calling begins with changing how we remember and interpret our life's stories. In doing so, we discover our *innate image* and live with a sense of purpose because of that destiny (Gafni 2012, 26).

FIT is a time when we renegotiate with ourselves and realign our life based on new variables. Like Mr. Henderson, we set new goals based on examination of all we now believe to be true and important.

> We're forced to stop cherry-picking and wearing blinders to our truths. We let go of these defensive tactics that have kept us in our comfort zone.

In FIT, we're in the perfect position to heed our inner whispers, the inner knowing we know are true. They won't disappear, so why not act on them?

THE GIFT OF CRISIS

The Chinese word for crisis is two characters: danger and opportunity. The English origin of the word means crossing over a line. Masters of change harness the opportunity a crisis presents. They know how to step back, take stock, and redirect. They make time to do this in an intentional way, and they recognize the danger of not doing this—settling and getting stuck in an unhealthy psychological place.

Those in FIT are given this chance without signing up for it. When I interview people about their journey, they talk about being stripped down to their core. They're in a place where they must assess who they are, now they're not who they were and from there, figure out how to rebuild. Their world is often so ruptured they no longer know where they fit in or even where they want to fit in.

This is the gift of an existential crisis. Clarity and focus (which I discuss in chapter 6) are the gears driving you to keep striving when you feel like giving up. Purpose is the fuel that makes it possible to put those gears in motion and keep moving forward. Our calling is the vehicle through which we actualize our purpose.

LIVING ON PURPOSE

Happiness isn't dependent on outcomes. It's not dependent on anyone giving us accolades or even support. We can be deeply happy because we're living aligned with purpose. We're being true to ourselves while connected to and contributing to something larger than ourselves.

At the same time, a full life is in relationship with others. Brendon Burchard teaches us to ask: Who most needs you to live the best version of yourself possible? Who needs you on your A-game? Daily motivation comes from vision and purpose. It's also highly influenced by relational bonds to those expecting excellence from you. Apart from your community, your team, and beneficiaries of your mission, who most needs you role modeling your best self? Tap into this emotional connection daily to boost motivation (Burchard 2017, 152).

Living fully engaged in a life where we create meaning and feel congruent with our beliefs and actions is where happiness lies. When we find the unique intersection of our interests, passions, and skills and put this to use for ourselves and others, we create a life of living in flow. This is where we experience joy and happiness.

...

...

WHEN MONEY AND MEANING ELUDE EACH OTHER

Source: personal interview.

Bandz Mabuse, a banker in his early twenties in South Africa, was having an identity crisis but didn't know it.

"Banking lured me in. It felt good. You're getting paid a decent amount of money and treated well." He was successful but soon became restless.

He only felt any zest for life on weekends when he made videos for Instagram. In the videos he explored personal development while doing his own self-improvement live on camera, figuring out how to be happy.

While researching the word "identity," he found his restlessness and unhappiness in his job were signs of being in an identity crisis. It became crystal clear he wasn't a banker. Successful yet unfulfilled, he didn't feel himself. Knee deep in liminality, he'd slipped into two versions of himself and was not fully either one. With his heart no longer in banking, he wasn't the successful banker in a business suit nor was he yet the inspirational speaker who motivated and helped people online.

Trying to figure out who he was, Bandz read personal development books, watched videos, and went to seminars. With friends, he was the "wise one" counseling them. At one point he thought, *Maybe there's something here for me.*

He didn't yet have the word coach or trainer—just the inkling that this was his milieu.

Then a friend said, "You know, Bandz, I could actually pay to have you talk to me. You're so good at analyzing the situation and helping me." That led to thinking maybe he could do more outside of his banking role.

A mentor told him that even though you don't know your destination, you know enough to take the next right step. Each video, book, and seminar gave him more clarity and assurance that pursuing personal development was right for him.

But while continuing to develop his platform, his dad fell ill and passed away. Because he left the family nothing but debt, Bandz thought about what kind of person he wanted to be.

He realized he needed to follow his passion "to make a decision about what [he'll] bring to the world." But because he'd now become the man of the household, he had to follow a practical plan. He couldn't just do what he wanted.

Shortly after his father passed a sister died and then another sister. He realized his sisters didn't live full, meaningful, purpose-driven lives. They lived by default rather than by design. Bandz decided he wasn't going to leave that kind of legacy. Mortality motivation allowed for "inconvenient and essential ideas." He began choosing his identity on different terms than just financial.

"I started to relinquish my identity as a corporate guy."

People were connecting with his videos, and this fed his "other self." As traction increased, he envisioned himself as the next Tony Robbins.

A poor evaluation at work provided the tipping point. Okay with the worst that might happen, he quit without a plan. He ignored sunk costs—all it had taken him to achieve success. Releasing the job status, friends, income, cars—"the guy who's got it all together"—he replaced it with the guy who doesn't have a job, struggling to figure out his life.

What he kept in the equation was future potential. He knew he wanted to keep helping people. He still didn't have a name for it or know what it looked like, but he knew and trusted how he felt.

Bandz left banking and became a coach. He created a program, the Purpose Frequency. He teaches people to tune into their intuition, follow their soul's whispers, and live in alignment with their purpose. He believes your soul is always yearning for more. You can resist, but it will find you in the end.

KEY TAKEAWAYS

DOS AND DON'TS

- Don't allow sunk costs to sway your decisions. Don't overlook opportunity costs.
- Accept sunk costs by remembering they were the best decision *in that moment* (without the aid of retrospect). Evaluate opportunity costs thoroughly and take into account things you'll miss out on by *not* taking certain actions.

- Don't avoid your power because of fear of what will follow when you embody your most powerful self.
- Trust that you can skill up and meet the needs of your future best self.

- Don't let instability, uncertainty, doubt, and lack of clarity keep you from making decisions.
- Do heed your inner whispers. Trust that next steps will reveal themselves when you're taking action. Dare to enter new doors of opportunity with, at best, only half-baked plans.

RESILIENCE

Sometimes you may feel you're not making progress or are lacking clarity, motivation, and a sense of purpose, especially in the beginning. Make sure you're taking enough time to grieve your losses. Make sure to identify and acknowledge all that's changed. The more you acknowledge reality, the faster clarity will arrive. With clarity, it will be easier to regain a sense of purpose and direction. Remember to honor the struggle and trust that transformation is happening on its own invisible timeline, if you're putting in the work.

SLOGGING THROUGH REVERSE CULTURE SHOCK

Colombia changed me forever. I was eighteen when I returned from my year abroad. I'd gone to Colombia, South America, to learn Spanish and because I wanted an intense experience. I'd gotten my money's worth, and then some. It had been the hardest and most profound year of my life. But I was utterly unprepared for what happened upon returning stateside.

I was in a pickle. In Colombia I'd felt stronger and more confident in who I was than I'd felt in years. But once back home, that evaporated. My sense of self fragmented, and I became directionless and miserable.

In my own country, I was now a fish out of water. I no longer knew who I was. I wasn't who I was when I left and didn't yet know how to fit who I'd become back into my own society.

I spoke a new language that I didn't want to give up. I'd even forgotten how to speak English properly, putting words in the wrong place and using wrong words. At Macy's, when I went to buy a new bra, I asked where the interior clothing department was. The lady stared at me. I'd forgotten it's called lingerie. I also had a very thick foreign accent. People who knew me laughed. Strangers asked me where I was from and then didn't believe me when I told them. Most importantly, I'd picked up new ideas and values. My worldview had drastically deepened and widened.

In Colombia I'd witnessed untold poverty and suffering and learned firsthand what privilege was. Privilege guilt now had me on my knees praying for release.

I'd spent the year constantly realizing I was no more deserving than the most destitute Colombian with nothing to hope for. Yet I had access to food, clean water, housing, health care, education, and employment. My opportunities were endless in contrast to many people I knew and cared for in Colombia. I could never unsee that. I struggled to understand why I was the lucky one instead of one of them, and once home, I couldn't squander this coveted status.

How could I be happy when others were suffering and I was able to do something about it? Because I have privileges they didn't—access to education and choice of employment.

But I was so discombobulated from reverse culture shock that I was in an aimless state. For the first time in years my mom made a decision for me. She told me I needed to sign up for school. In her turquoise Volvo, she drove me to the community college where I signed up.

I had no idea what my plans were. But lost and drifting,
I did have an intense sense of duty
I couldn't shake.

I'd concluded my life was more than just for me. It was connected to a bigger purpose. I couldn't yet see what that looked like or how to go about it, and I knew that to be true. I also knew getting an education would be part of this mission, but I didn't think I was smart. I only knew I was good at sports and Spanish, and neither of those connected to a life in service of others less fortunate.

Even though I still had a damaged sense of self from childhood traumas, I now knew I was important. I mattered. I knew unknown people counted on me being all I could be. I was in a position to help those who could not help themselves and needed me to step up to the task.

I'd gone to Colombia to get things for myself. I returned with a pledge to live my life in service to others. Without seeking, I'd discovered a purpose for my life. I trusted my inner knowing. Now I needed a concrete way to put that into action.

It had to be a career that would help without hurting people; "right livelihood" is what Buddhists call it. Now an undergrad at UC Berkeley, a teaching assistant told me about a public health course. I took it and then a few more. This is how I discovered the field of public health—preventing rather than treating disease. Apart from the practicality of prevention, public health takes a multidisciplinary approach to addressing problems that come with poverty. Deeply connected to social justice, it fit my purpose criteria on many levels.

Discombobulated and pressured to perform, I could have never guessed where I'd end up. Trusting my inner knowing and having a purpose larger than myself was my lifeline. It got me out of the liminal space reverse culture shock had landed me in and through school. It led me to discovering a place where I belonged and could make the difference I needed to make.

REVERSE ENGINEER YOUR LIFE PURPOSE

Our job is to manifest our unique perspective through taking action. Who we are—what we do and our intention behind all this—goes into defining our life purpose.

A definitive formula for discovering and/or defining a life purpose does not exist. You can start by identifying the top five or so things that constitute your unique perspective. This is likely the driving force behind your intentions in life. Then, list why these are important to you. This will get you in the life purpose ballpark.

Discovering and/or defining your life purpose is a life-long, iterative process, not a once and done manifesto. Some themes may never change, but the strategy, tactics, and even direction may. The goal is to keep crystalizing your purpose so you live a life guided by deep intention, which leads to deep meaning. It's your litmus test for decision-making.

Start by writing a rough draft manifesto for your life. Then keep tweaking it, as if you were editing a paper, adding and deleting as your values and belief system change over time. During FIT is a perfect time to start this practice. Then continue honing for relevancy. We continue to change and thus so does our purpose. Don't worry if you can't figure it out. Just start and stick with it, periodically evaluating and iterating.

Trust what your higher self whispers to you. Capture it in writing. Allow intuition to guide you and logic to play second fiddle. You don't have to know *how* you will manifest your purpose. Once you begin to allow the vision to surface, next steps will reveal themselves showing you how.

I like to use my vision to build my life purpose definition. It serves as a guiding north star. At least once a year, I do a deep dive assessment.

Here's my current thinking:

- If my vision is world peace, then a purpose of helping people smile more at themselves would indicate progress toward my vision. (When people are happier with themselves, they treat others better.) Work toward this can be carried out in many ways and change over time. Broad statements describe my strategy and tactics.

- To achieve my purpose, my mission is to change how individuals think about themselves so they gain more personal agency, self-compassion, and make better choices. This leads to more satisfaction.

- Being more satisfied, individuals will be more likely to treat others with dignity, equality, and respect. This brings more smiles to themselves and those around them. Most importantly, it helps individuals raise happy, kind, and generous children.

With this clarity on where I'm headed:

- I put a stake in the ground about who I intend to be to carry out my vision.
- I add to my strategy by listing specific tactics to use to work toward this vision:
    - I list specific, broad actions that, when taken consistently, will make me that person.
- I list the outcomes I'm after, resulting from activating and staying true to that person who's taking intentional action.

This becomes the blueprint for living on purpose and guides my decisions. It doesn't matter if it's "correct." It matters that I'm making a conscious choice about how to live and thinking of how that impacts others.

- The person I wish to be:
  - A positive force for change in people's daily lives.

- Actions that will make that happen:
  - Relieve pain and suffering.
  - Bring people together.
  - Bring them closer to themselves.

The changes I seek to make from living on purpose are helping people to live more courageously, leverage more opportunity, and become who they wish to be. When this happens, they'll smile more at themselves and be more inclined to treat others well.

Here's my (ever-evolving) life purpose statement:

- The purpose of my life is to be a positive force for change in people's day-to-day lives, to relieve pain and suffering, and to bring people together and closer to themselves so they can live more courageously, leverage more opportunities, and become who they wish to be.

Now it's time for you to put your stake in the ground. State your vision, deconstruct it, and build a life purpose statement that can keep you focused and motivated and remind you of what's important.

YOU'VE GOT THIS

I applaud you for your effort to find meaning and purpose during this time of immense difficulty. While disorientated, filled with angst and ambiguity, and with clarity in short supply, working on life purpose is both extremely challenging *and* rewarding. You are a bold becomer because you take the necessary steps forward to master change.

CHAPTER 5

Grief and Loss

God gave me crystal clear, divine instructions: "Live!" You've always lived for other people. Now it's time to live for yourself.

—ARLETHA ORR, AUTHOR, SPEAKER, GRIEF COACH

...

Goal: Reduce the impact of emotional and psychological triggers related to the catalytic event.

WIDOWHOOD RULES AREN'T FOR ANYONE

Source: personal interview.

Jill and Linda were a happy couple. One day Linda got the diagnosis from a routine mammogram—breast cancer. It was small and undetectable by palpation, and she had fourteen positive nodes. This was July, and the prognosis was that she'd be dead by Christmas. But Linda was "a fighter beyond all fighters," and Linda had Jill.

It was 1998 and they lived in Florida without legal protections heterosexual married couples had. For example, Jill wasn't allowed into Linda's hospital room after the mastectomy or to see the doctor's pathology report. None of this stopped them from thriving. Linda was an extremely independent and strong person, and during the cancer treatment, they each made valiant and dramatic role changes.

"I learned to become a caregiver,
and she had to learn to become a patient.
It was a bit of a culture clash."

People who weren't legally related didn't have family leave, so Jill had to keep working. She couldn't provide all the caregiving Linda needed, so Jill's dad, who also had a serious health condition, drove Linda to chemo appointments. He also did home care two days after treatments when side effects kicked in.

After Linda recovered and was cancer free, they hightailed back to California. They married during a quick window of opportunity and lived with quality of life top of mind. They also began adopting their three children from foster care.

Jill and Linda both knew about grief and loss. Jill did grief therapy and hospice grief work. Linda was an emergency room nurse. So when Linda got diagnosed with pulmonary fibrosis (a 100 percent terminal illness) shortly after her cancer went into remission, they knew the drill:

- Anticipatory grief work;
- Planning for the inevitable future; and
- Squeezing every last drop of life out of each and every day they had together.

With no time for denial, they got straight to work preparing themselves and kept it up until the very end. Pulmonary fibrosis eventually took Linda's life. Unknown at the time, it was a side effect from one of the cancer drugs. It was the price they paid to get ten extra years from the breast cancer.

Jill and Linda knew about death and dying, but applying that knowledge wasn't completely smooth. Jill knew Linda needed help *and* wanted to respect her independence. It was like walking a tightrope—easy to get off balance judging when and when not to step in to help. Linda, a highly competent and capable person, didn't take well to needing help. She was reluctant to ask for and accept it.

Jill's dad was critical during their initial role shifting phase. Seeing them struggle, he sat them down and said, "You know, when somebody's ill, everybody has to adapt. And you need to be careful to always be gracious to each other. As a dependent person I have to be extra grateful for the time I have and the care I receive and not resent the hell out of life for what's happened."

That talk was gold. For the next three and a half years, Jill and Linda made the most of the process, redefining quality of life as it shifted. Jill kept people updated through a blog. Linda lived as a survivor, working until her last six months. "Littler things started counting for more."

They packed everything into that time together. They created happy family memories and took the best vacations. Linda got a Spyder motorcycle. With her oxygen tank in the front, tubes in her nose, and kids on the back, she didn't quit until it was over. The adaptation process changed as needed. Jill started taking over paying the bills and getting the kids everywhere. They all started eating dinner together in bed instead of at the table.

Linda died at age fifty-eight. Now Jill had to figure out life as a single parent. She had to decide when to go back to work and other things you can't figure out ahead of time. She no longer had someone to bounce ideas off about the kids.

Other people didn't understand about being a young widow, and Jill needed to talk with someone who did.

That's when Jill and Casper started getting together at coffee dates. Toward Linda's end, Casper, a hospice nurse, entered the family's life. Then in a surprise twist, Linda told Jill and Casper they needed to get married once she was gone. Linda, seeing how the children had developed a relationship with Casper, insisted the adults do the same. Neither Jill nor Casper initially agreed with Linda, but they did it anyway.

"I broke all the widow rules. I married Casper. You're supposed to wait this magical year before remarrying. I scandalized a bunch of people, and a lot of people voted with their feet. They decided I wasn't doing grief properly. That I shouldn't have done it. That I smiled too much, laughed too much, and looked too happy. And you can't look too sad either because it will make others sad."

Jill had already done most of her grieving. She'd spent six years caregiving and had done anticipatory grief not once but twice—with the breast cancer and then the lung disease.

"We'd already said goodbye every which way you can and talked about everything possible related to her death."

Once Jill and Casper got together as a couple, Jill had to figure out how to:

- Let go of being the person calling all the shots now that she was no longer in a caregiving role;
- Allow the other person to make their own decisions, do their own things, have their independence;
- Be in an equal relationship with a new partner; and
- Help the kids adapt to a new adult in the house.

Another role challenge after Linda's death was at Jill's job, where she started to have a hard time. Everybody knew her as Jill and Linda—a blended identity—and now she was Jill and Casper, which didn't go over well. She decided to change her job because she "needed to change and reclaim who [she] was going to be" and because she was tired of people telling her how to grieve. "They were exhausting me and invading my space and my process."

Not yet forty-five and a widow with three teenage daughters, she was evaluating what really mattered and what she'd been putting off and reviewing plans she and Linda had made for her future. When Linda died, a lot died with her. *And* she left a lot behind.

> "With grief, you take them with you.
> You take what they wanted for you."

"Linda wanted me to get my social work license and open my private practice." So that's what Jill did. She passed her license a month after Linda died and, right after that, opened her private practice.

Jill knew what Linda wanted for her and was living that life. That's how she processed her grief; doing what they'd agreed would be good for her future. They'd talked about and planned it, and now Jill implemented the plan. Having had the tough conversations made the transition easier.

But Jill's life wasn't finished with unexpected twists. Shortly after Jill transitioned from a caregiver role to a partnership role, Casper got sick. Jill went back into caregiver role as Casper died. After Casper's death, Jill married Stacey—once again, someone who helped with end-of-life care. And again, she transitioned from caregiver to partner (and is still happily married). "Married three times and widowed twice."

> "The gift from this journey has been refining
> what's important and then leaning into it."

Jill entertained many options. She zeroed in on training therapists and others on how to do grief better. She's on a mission "to make grief and loss a force for change as opposed to a place to live and inhabit and create an identity around."

Jill trains and speaks internationally about grief and loss, end of life, and dementia. Her latest of many books is *The Rebellious Widow*, and she's raising awareness about different kinds of grief:

- *Anticipatory grief*, the Kübler-Ross five-step framework that many people know of; and
- The *grief after death process*, when we move into our new life.

Jill has stayed true to her caregiver identity, apparently branded into her for this lifetime. She is also her mom's caregiver, who has Alzheimer's.

NAMING IT TAMES IT: TAKING GRIEF AND LOSS BEYOND END-OF-LIFE PARAMETERS

During FIT, our losses cause significant psychoemotional pain that needs to be acknowledged. Losing or gaining major status roles is a contributing factor in this pain. Identifying and naming the specific contours of grief and loss helps us process it.

Ideas for this section draw heavily from Leech and Singer's book *Acknowledgment: Opening to the Grief of Unacceptable Loss* (1988) and are adapted to address FIT.

This pain applies equally to all catalytic events creating identity loss, not just when we lose loved ones. Grief and loss produce the same effects, regardless of cause.

These are (Leech and Singer 1988, 19):

- Stress/shock
- Loss/sadness

- Hurt/anger
- Guilt/shame
- Fear/vulnerability

This is the landscape of grief. Grief doesn't only affect psychoemotional health. Its impact is holistic. It affects everything from physical health to relationships to our faith to job performance. And all kinds of loss live on this terrain.

While grieving takes time and is uncomfortable, trying to avoid or delay it causes more problems. The best choice is to face it head on. This is paramount to overcoming your struggle. When we adequately process grief and loss, we release pent-up feelings. This allows our bodies to expend energy in more productive ways. It moves us away from a state of low energy to higher energy.

Processing grief and loss decreases suffering from psychoemotional pain. It might prevent depression. It can help prevent physical problems associated with unresolved grief. Most importantly, it may prevent a weakened immune system and the myriad problems that can cause (Leech and Singer 1988, 23).

Processing grief improves cognition. When we allow ourselves to feel the pain and process those feelings, it helps clear up our thinking and make better decisions. This impacts relationships and job performance. And when we're clear on what we've lost, we're also able to be clear on what we have left, what we carry forward with us.

The hallmark of FIT—feelings of ambiguity and disorientation—is connected to grief and loss.

The larger the loss, the deeper the grief and
the more ambiguity and disorientation
we experience.

Since society makes little room for processing grief and loss, it's up to us to be committed to our efforts not to push it under the rug—even while being expected to put up a front because grief makes others uncomfortable.

Processing grief and loss is a major task on your identity reconstruction journey. Spiraling down because of grief and loss is normal, but staying down longer than necessary can negatively impact every facet of your life. The intention of this book is to help prevent that from happening.

Intentional, committed navigation through
grief and loss can lead us out of our quandary.
As it did with Jill, it can even give us direction.

I've struggled with many forced identity transitions. None related to losing a loved one. Recently I realized my identity transitions' common thread is grief and loss. I discovered a label—identity loss. Since I didn't have that label when it was happening to me, I struggled to acknowledge and respect my grief. I didn't have a container with a common language to understand my experiences.

Because of this, I both missed out on growth and suffered more than necessary. I didn't grieve as thoroughly as I might have had I understood more about what was happening. I stayed stuck in psychoemotional pain longer than needed.

Entire books and courses are devoted to grief and loss. The scope here is limited to outlining a few important topics and concepts. The goal is for you to be able to identify and grapple with grief and loss in real time. Below are tools to handle it more effectively.

...

Bold Becomer Prompts

1. The social or personal pressures keeping me from processing my grief and loss include...

2. My response to the pressure(s) is...

3. A different response that would better serve my future is...

...

GOING FROM STUCK TO PROCESSING GRIEF

Below are areas to address to process grief and loss. The goal is to identify and *feel* your feelings. This compilation is slightly different from the Kübler-Ross five stages of grief framework although the two frameworks overlap. The Kübler-Ross framework addresses *anticipatory grief.* This is when you've been handed bad news and must come to terms with it while it's happening.

The below concepts, adapted from Leech and Singer (1988), are for grief *after* a loss has occurred. Jill Johnson-Young calls this the *life recreation process.*

1. Feelings are natural and designed to be expressed rather than held in. Make time to allow yourself to feel everything happening inside you. Know your feelings will not annihilate you.

2. Grief and loss exist to be thought through *and* felt, not simply thought through. Only intellectualizing this facet of life that is only partially rational won't get you to the other side of grief and loss.

3. Sustaining a loss includes losing many things attached to that loss. Some aren't apparent until later. You have a *primary loss*, which resulted from the catalytic event. And you have a cascade of *secondary losses* resulting from the primary loss. Every loss counts, no matter how seemingly small or insignificant (Leech and Singer 1988, 13). As you allow yourself to feel what comes up in relation to each separate loss, identify and categorize your feelings in writing (Leech and Singer 1988, 49).

4. The loss of life as you have known it can take many forms. The feelings associated with this loss are legitimate. They won't be neatly packaged for you to process. Allow for it to be messy. Trust the process.

5. It's common to feel confused or troubled about your inability to accept your loss (Leech and Singer 1988, 3).

   a. You have permission to never accept your loss.

   b. You don't have to pretend you didn't lose anything important or that you're not terribly affected by it.

   c. You don't have to suck it up.

   d. You don't have to ever start liking the fact you've sustained this loss.

   e. You don't have to get over a significant loss.

6. Instead, by acknowledging and processing your thoughts and feelings your relationship to the loss will change. It will cease to be the primary preoccupation in your life. You'll grow to a new acceptance of yourself and the event(s), as a survivor of a catastrophic loss (Leech and Singer 1988, 5). Acceptance does not imply we stop working to create positive change, but in the Buddhist meaning of simply accepting reality as it is. We don't try to push the river.

7. You can either choose to *respond* or *react* to life circumstances. Reaction bypasses important information. Response takes into account critical and fundamental information that helps you. When you acknowledge your feelings by allowing them to exist, you make better choices. They help you respond rather than react. Feelings are connected to your intuition. Intuition knows your truth more accurately than your mind.

...

Bold Becomer Prompts

1. My loss is impacting my sense of meaning in life in the following ways...

2. My loss is making me question the following beliefs and former certainties...

3. The following levers that create deep meaning in my life still exist...

...

FROM UNIMAGINABLE LOSS TO HAPPINESS

Source: personal interview.

It was almost the end of a normal workday. Arletha Orr, her husband, and their two kids lived in a small town in Mississippi and had a "pretty regular life." It revolved around work, church, and family. Arletha was planning to leave work to pick up the kids when her husband called and said he'd do it. So Arletha stayed late at work. On her way home, she got the call. "Your husband just got hit by a train."

Arletha's first thought was, *He has my babies with him.* They were one and seven years old. The caller gave Arletha the location and she went there immediately. It was five minutes from their home. In shock, looking at his red truck on the track, she asked herself, *Is this really happening?* In that moment, through her tears, the only thing she could do was pray.

When somebody gets hit by a train, you immediately know no one can survive. But as a mother and wife, you still think maybe somebody will survive. In the forever it took for the ambulance to get there, different versions of the same scenario coursed through Arletha's mind:

*Everything's going to be fine. They may need to stay in
the hospital for a few days, and eventually,
we'll get back to our normal lives.*

The emergency personnel pulled her husband out of the truck, laid him on the ground, and "did some stuff." Arletha thought he could be alive. A lot of people were gathering, and she was still thinking, *Maybe somebody will be okay. Maybe this isn't happening. Maybe this isn't reality.*

The chief of police soon informed Arletha that her husband and two children had passed. "I just stood there and looked at him." He asked what funeral home he should call. Not in any state to answer that question, an aunt gave a name.

They wouldn't let Arletha see her children. Arletha said, "I stayed until the bodies were picked up by the funeral home. I couldn't leave them until I knew they were being cared for properly. I couldn't leave my babies outside at night on the train tracks. I needed to make sure they were safe. I still had to care for and protect them."

Once the bodies were taken from the scene, Arletha went to her grandmother's home. Lying on the couch, she cried and cried on her father's shoulder. "I didn't know what else to do," she said. "I was just torn apart."

Family and friends showed up, and at one point, they all started singing. This helped "lift the burden off just a little bit." They also prayed. Then she got some sleep, but reality kicked back in the next morning.

Wow, this is actually my reality?
She went to her mom's house knowing
this is the beginning of a new life for me.

The grief hurt so much she'd never felt that kind of pain before. It was like piercing a knife through her heart. As she lay on the couch crying, she asked God, *What do you want me to do now?* The Spirit said something profound. "He spoke the word 'Live.' He gave me permission to live and be happy."

Needing more detail, she asked, "How?" God repeated, "Live." She was being asked to go out of her comfort zone alone, so she asked for more instruction. He said, "You've always lived for other people. Now, it's time to live for yourself." After she got the same message a second time, she got up, dried her tears, and went about her day starting her new life.

God's message gave her the winning inner attitude
she needed when she could never
go back to normal.

She started living differently, knowing it was okay to take care of herself and pursue her own happiness. She could be at peace, even happy, in the face of tragedy.

Arletha had always worked for somebody else, and since the tenth grade she'd wanted to work for herself. So she started her own business. She became a coach, helping people go through grief. She came to understand the reason she's still here is to help others have their best life, to show them they have permission to be happy and not to give up on themselves, to help people heal and be at peace and smile again. She wrote the book *Live!* In it, she talks about overcoming pain and grief with faith, love, forgiveness, acceptance, courage, and humor. She believes that fateful day when her family was taken from her was ordained "to get her on purpose."

Arletha has taken to heart God's message and is a servant carrying out his plan. She accesses happiness despite tragedy and lives a full and vibrant life. With Him by her side, Arletha shines a light for people whose lives are consumed by darkness.

KEY TAKEAWAYS

DOS AND DON'TS

- Don't try to force yourself to accept your loss. Some losses are unacceptable.
- Acknowledge your loss by expressing your grief and finding what you still have left to bring forward with you.

- Don't think that accepting what happened is the same as accepting the impact of what happened.
- Explore the nuances between accepting what happened and accepting its impact. The former helps us move forward regardless of circumstances. The latter can cause us to shut down our feelings because some things are impossible to accept. This is where replacing acceptance with acknowledgment can help us heal. We can be truthful about our nonacceptance.

- Don't try to fool yourself that you can't bear to feel the pain.
- Give yourself enough time and space to move through and transform your experience by processing grief head on.

- Don't downplay grief because it's invisible and makes you and others uncomfortable.
- Treat psychoemotional health as seriously as physical health problems that can be seen, measured, and treated with accuracy.
- Don't spend your time in resentment, rumination, and remorse.
- Spend your time processing grief and understanding exactly what's causing your pain. Pain is proportional to the importance of the loss. It's natural and necessary to grieve.
- Don't think what you lost is all gone.
- Find what parts of the past you can carry into the present in a different form. Transmute what still is into something that gives you meaning and purpose.

RESILIENCE

Sometimes, it feels like it's all too much. It's important to remember the process takes longer than you expect and want it to. Grieving your losses (primary and secondary) follows neither plans nor timelines. During these moments temptation invites you to stop too soon, to settle, to seek a quick solution to end the grief, to cut out early on the exploratory journey you're on toward finding and building the best possible new version of yourself. Every day is a chance to use your power to renew commitment to yourself.

WHO ARE YOU WHEN YOUR SOURCE OF PRIDE DISAPPEARS?

My identity centered around my athletic prowess for the first two decades of my life. Organized sports for girls came to my town when I was in seventh grade. We had softball and soccer, and I played both every season all the way into college. I was a star athlete. I lived for that flow state. Having the power, precision, and presence to get the results I was after was euphoric. Nobody could tell me I wasn't good enough in that department.

My first love was soccer. I preferred playing midfield because I could always be part of the action. I had a hero, Pelé, and wore Puma cleats just like he did. I remember watching a movie of him showing the bicycle kick at soccer practice. Had the opportunity existed back in the 1970s, I would have been an Olympic or pro athlete.

My high school didn't have a women's soccer team, so I played on the men's. When I did my senior year abroad in Colombia, South America, girls didn't play soccer there yet. Luckily, my exchange sister Dora did. We played with the men in some of the most fun games of my life. At age eighteen, being a star athlete and speaking Spanish "perfectly" (fluently and with a good accent) were the sole pillars upholding my identity. Such was the state of affairs with my otherwise mangled self-esteem.

In 1980 I went to UC Berkeley because, at the time, it and Stanford had the two best women's soccer teams in the country. I was twenty-one. I relished this pinnacle opportunity where I'd finally "make it" and reach my highest level of athletic achievement. I'd play with my equals and go out with a bang.

My dream ended on the first day of practice. I'd sprained my ankle in a pickup game a few months before starting at Berkeley. My ankle swelled double its size by the time they carried me off the field. It landed me in the emergency room, and I went home on crutches.

So before practice that first day at Cal, I had my ankle taped to protect it. Then halfway through practice the coach asked me, "Julie, how's your ankle?"

"My ankle's fine, but my knee's *killing* me."

He told me to go over to the bench, put ice on it, go to Dr. Garrick (a top sports medicine surgeon), and not return until I was better. Dr. Garrick did arthroscopic surgery. He cleaned up the edges of the meniscus. But that wasn't the cause of my symptoms, and he didn't know what was. I never returned to competitive sports because my knee never fully healed.

But I didn't know that yet. It was scary and confusing because according to the expert, nothing was wrong with my knee, yet something was. To keep in shape, I started swimming. I got recruited to the water polo team, but my heart wasn't in it. So I quit. I went out for crew. My heart definitely wasn't into getting up at 5:00 a.m. for that. Months passed, only to have my other knee start hurting the same way. I freaked out.

Nothing is wrong… yet something is became the story of my life.

Silently and alone (because doctors had no answers), I embarked on my journey. I was learning to live with chronic pain and severe fatigue. Accommodating an unpredictable and delicate body would become the focal point of my life—a life of fighting an uphill battle against fatigue and protecting an ever-growing list of hurting body parts.

But the immediate task at hand was finding out who I was, now that I was no longer an athlete.

So much of me depended on my identity
as an athlete that when it died, I felt like I died.
The me I knew no longer existed.

I was angry at my body for betraying me. I was terrified of growing old, as much pain as I was already in. I was angry and sad about losing what gave me joy and pride. I didn't know what would take its place to support my self-esteem.

I felt guilty, thinking I could do something to change my situation. I was also completely stressed out, struggling with school, and now my source of stress relief was obliterated.

Fortunately, being in college and needing to find a career softened the blow. That task filled the void from my identity loss as an athlete, as discussed in chapter 4.

But over the next decade a cascade of new chronic pain issues afflicted me. My constant questions were: *How much more pain can I hold? Which body part will fail me next? How soon will "next" be?*

Unfortunately, my grief never ended because my health challenges became chronic. That landed me in *complicated grief* because it is ongoing, which makes healing complicated.

Losing my identity as an athlete morphed into a story of losses that have vied to define who I am—a series of health problems that, to some degree, thwarted who I could become and losses that would lead me to becoming versions of myself I never would have envisioned or become had my health not gotten in the way.

I went from being a physically strong and healthy person to a person letting go of all kinds of activities and dreams. Pain and exhaustion cut me off at the knees. The person who did anything she pleased was in my past. I could no longer count on my body. As my life crumbled away, one body part at a time, and doctors denied my reality, I powered through.

The opportunity I missed in my twenties at the first signs of chronic pain was that I didn't take time to grieve since I didn't even know what I was grieving. It was confusing and messy. Closure was impossible, not having answers about what was going on with my knees and the litany of new things popping up. Turns out I'd endure lifelong, ongoing grief around this.

I knew I needed to grieve the loss of
my athleticism, but it got eclipsed with
each new health problem.

Rather than grieve my losses, I lived in fear of more losses.
I delayed grieving and didn't end up grieving anything in a
coherent or effective way. I never properly grieved my losses
since I never saw an endpoint with my health issues. Rather
than grieving, I adopted the habit of settling—living in a
kind of holding pattern—just getting by. It would take a few
decades before I finally integrated my new reality about being
an athlete into my psyche. My son astutely corrected me one
day: "Mom, you *were* an athlete." That was an important
step—acknowledging reality.

I learned grief and loss are not limited to death and dying.
That identity loss, regardless of the cause, can be as significant
as losing a loved one. The grief I experienced over the loss of
my identity as an athlete and my general health had all the
same characteristics. And it needed the same time, space, and
attention to adjust.

I found some grief has no resolution. And that's okay.
Grief is a symptom of losing something important, and some
losses are never going to be resolved. Some things aren't fix-
able. We adapt. That's where healing happens. We cannot
always fix or end the pain associated with our losses. But we
can learn to understand it, and this transforms it.

I've learned being healed doesn't mean the pain is completely gone. Being healed means we can move forward and
feel whole again. We will have a new configuration of who
we are while remembering, embracing, and shepherding with
alchemy what's left of what we lost.

The mourning part of ourselves gets integrated as we build a new identity while releasing, yet not letting go of the memory of the old identity.

Former identities continue to live within us, witnessed through occasional mourning. Yet that is no longer who we are. They become integrated into our historical self. They remain part of us in a transmuted state, continuing to infuse and inform our current self in ever changing ways.

LEECH AND SINGER'S
ACKNOWLEDGMENT FRAMEWORK

Below is an abbreviated grief processing method from the book *Acknowledgment: Opening to the Grief of Unacceptable Loss* (Leech and Singer 1988).

1. Write these five headings at the top of five pages in a notebook (Leech and Singer 1988, 19):

   a. Stress/shock

   b. Loss/sadness

   c. Hurt/anger

   d. Guilt/shame

   e. Fear/vulnerability

2. Allow an image of your primary loss, or a secondary loss, to come into your mind (Leech and Singer 1988, 19).

3. Write specific and personal "I" statements (Leech and Singer 1988, 49):

   a. What I feel; and

   b. How each of my feelings impacts me

4. In your process, distinguish between thoughts/beliefs and feelings. The goal is to move from the mind to the heart and to allow yourself to feel the body sensations and then be curious and accepting of them. This is how to heal grief. Just using the words "I feel," without feeling, won't do the trick (Leech and Singer 1988, 3).

5. Do these steps separately for the primary loss and every single secondary loss connected to the primary loss (Leech and Singer 1988, 50).

YOU'VE GOT THIS

While circumstances weren't of your choosing, this may be one of the most important times in your life. Opportunities you may have never considered will become available.

If we treat this as a time of renewal, the costs from our pain and losses often result in unexpected benefits. As you rebuild who you are from the ground up, nothing is set in stone. You have the potential to spiral down into depression or up into a new level of personal potential. It's your choice. You *can* transform your grief and your life.

This is our chance to be as courageous as children. They acknowledge, respect, and act on what they're thinking, feeling, and wanting. Let your feelings guide you to what matters most. The pain from your losses reveals the meaning they once held for you. When identified, you can transfer this meaning and express it through new avenues. You *can* create these new avenues. It's your time!

CHAPTER 6

Clarity and Focus

*I'd planned out my life so carefully—happy family, white
picket fence. It was all safe and calculated, and then suddenly,
everything looking forward became a blank slate. I never had
a plan B, and now I was stuck in an abyss of fear, uncertainty,
and overwhelm.*

—JANE DOE

...

Goal: Learn how to be more intentional and make better
decisions while under stress.

A MIRAGE ON STEROIDS

Source: personal, confidential interview.

Jane Doe thought she was in a happy, supportive, equal partnership marriage... until she found out her husband was
living a double life.

To avoid legal ramifications, Jane told me very little of
what she discovered about her husband. Suffice it to say, the
life Jane thought she was living never existed. The divorce
wasn't your garden variety trauma either. It was trauma on
steroids, and everything fell apart. The impact rippled out into
every aspect of her life for years to come. Overnight, she went

from "happy-couple-and-white-picket-fence kind of life to alone, scared, and confused." She started her new life with no plan B. She'd never envisioned being single. Now here she was, afraid of how she'd support herself, having visions of being out on the street, homeless.

In a daze about how she got into this situation, Jane wondered how she could ever trust herself to make another decision. The kind of situation she went through creates *reality ego fragmentation*. This is where your world turns upside down and everything you thought was true is fiction. She doubted her ability to keep herself safe. She questioned whether she could trust herself again, even for the smallest decisions. She spent the next few years figuring out how to get out of where she was and into the new self she had to find.

Jane availed herself to anything that would possibly help her stabilize and recover. For many years, she worked with a therapist specializing in complex trauma. She did yoga and became part of a supportive community. Her yoga group was also a lot like coaching; they listened to affirmations and questioned how they were thinking. She did group and one-on-one coaching programs, read books, and listened to podcasts.

Through all of this, she became increasingly aware of her thought processes, belief systems, and self-talk. She started recognizing how she told her story to herself. She paid attention to what that meant and how to change what stories she was telling. With awareness came agency. She stopped telling herself untrue things. Her life was like a horrible movie, with one hit after another, for years. But she began reframing things. She started asking herself, *What am I going to learn from this?* This mindset shift continues to take a lot of suffering out of her experience.

Still, everything in her life was out of control, and stability was elusive. Although she didn't even know where that endpoint was or what it looked like, it turned out to be a gift "because having everything structured is limiting."

The biggest gift was becoming clear on what she was feeling. She began allowing herself to feel it and trust it. She started recognizing feelings and understanding what her gut was telling her. She used this when things came up and she needed to make a decision.

She started to remember little feelings she wasn't conscious of at the time, things she had no context for at the time that, as horrible as they were, validated her experience. *Okay, so when this happened,* she would realize *this is what was really happening.*

Now, her feelings are a real-time tool
and they move her in the right direction.
"This is ultimate safety," she says, "when it's from
within you and nothing external matters."

She harnesses it in a conscious way. She's attuned to her inner knowing with:

- Increased awareness about how she's thinking;
- How her thoughts are working;
- What her belief system is; and
- How she interprets circumstances in her life.

What's always been there became accessible. This adjunct thinking challenges her beliefs. It pushes her to decide if her thoughts are actually true. It is her clarity barometer.

"Since so much of our thinking is unconscious,
access to our inner knowing is critical."

Jane no longer runs on autopilot. Her experience jolted her out of that. It forced her to learn much about herself she might not have otherwise. She learned how strong and resilient she is. She didn't know that about herself before. She changed jobs to one that's a better fit and she loves. She learned how much we can be responsible for our own experience, regardless of what's happening around us, and how to reframe challenges with curious questions rather than going into despair or overwhelm.

Jane eliminated that extra layer of suffering that we add to our experience. She puts space between herself and what's happening to her, but not in a pathological way like with dissociation. She has awareness of what's happening and commits the intuitive and mindset tools to scale back the suffering. She takes a breath between stimulus and response, and she's a tiny step back from what is happening rather than consumed *in* it.

"When you're in the middle of the intensity, you can lose sight and hope the chapter will end. You think your circumstances define you, but they don't."

Instead of operating from the primitive brain that reacts, she operates from the prefrontal cortex. This is where we have agency and capacity to evaluate and make choices.

> Beliefs are things we've thought over and over
> so many times we decided they're fact.
> But they're not.
> Our stories of our lives are just that—stories.

"Out of that pain and struggle grew the resilience, perseverance, and strength, turning me into a warrior. All of this came out of the survival phase and has now flourished with the realization that the stories I believed about myself—that I haven't ever questioned and just took for granted that's who I was—weren't true. And because the overall barrier had been broken down, everything became possible again. I didn't realize there were limiting beliefs around those things and so now, I just get to choose who I am. And the world is pretty big when you come at it from that angle."

CLARITY IN THE FACE OF UNCERTAINTY

Many in FIT lose trust in their judgment and decision-making capacity. First on the recovery agenda is managing grief and loss in a supportive and productive way. Improving clarity and focus is second in importance. They are fundamental to making good decisions. Without this, we wallow in liminality longer than necessary or even spiral down into more crisis.

Daniel Kahneman, in his book *Thinking Fast and Slow*, explains crisis-induced stress decreases our capacity for good judgment. Our brain cuts corners when we're tired, overwhelmed, or stressed (2011, 64). In the thick of forced identity transition, when we need our strongest, most creative thinking, impaired judgment holds us back. This is when we most need to avoid making rash decisions and premature commitments.

> Bold becomers level up by asserting
> what they stand for.

To do that, they make new decisions stemming from a solid sense of who they are becoming and based in reality. Three things help them achieve this that are fundamental to mastering change and harnessing its value:

1. Becoming more aware of how they think.

2. Reducing the influence of bias on their perceptions.

3. Correcting erroneous beliefs about themselves and their situation.

When you're clear on where you're headed and why, your actions follow suit. You start living in alignment, acting congruently with the best of who you are. You're able to boldly become that version of you yearning to reveal herself. Since this transition takes much longer than we expect or want, techniques to handle distraction can be a shortcut to clarity and stability.

> Clarity and focus help you identify
> what's important and worth chasing after.

When you understand what you value and why, it makes decisions possible or easier. It helps you let go of what no longer serves you. It boosts your courage to pursue things you might have thought were out of reach. When you know your *what* and your *why*, the *how* often becomes accessible.

We use statements such as "achieving clarity." However, it's more of an ongoing process. We maintain clarity through taking consistent, intentional steps. Tactics and strategies to increase focus, which support clarity, make the transition process smoother and more effective. With more clarity and focus, your actions will be more intentional. This decreases frustration, doubt, unease, and time in liminality. It doesn't eliminate the need for exploration and experimentation, but it helps you recognize when to pivot and do it sooner.

Clarity and focus are a struggle for those in FIT for many reasons:

- People are unprepared. Nobody asks to be in forced identity transition, and the crisis element clouds one's thinking.

- The need to generate new options through exploration, experimentation, and inevitable failures involves unwelcome stress and discomfort.

- Taking action despite discomfort requires courage we may not yet have or believe we can have.

- We must move forward regardless of fear, doubt, and uncertainty.

- We must make decisions without the benefits of clarity.

- Our comfort zone is demolished, and our mind and heart aren't ready for the journey forced upon us. Our focus is on the past and our present pain rather than on the future.

- We must move forward while we're still holding on to what we lost and while grieving our losses. Clarity while in grief is elusive.

Spiraling down in crisis is an option. So is bouncing beyond. This chapter offers concepts to prevent discomfort avoidance from holding you back.

...

Bold Becomer Prompts

1. Of my daily activities over the past week, X percent were important, and Y percent were urgent. (You define important versus urgent.)

2. Of these activities, X percent were of my choosing.

3. Of these activities, what percent were new activities intended to build my new identity (exploration and experimentation)? Two things I can start or stop doing today, which will increase that percentage, are...

...

CLARITY, FOCUS, AND THE PACE OF CHANGE

Clarity helps you make the best choices. It stems from knowing yourself—your desires, beliefs, values, and ambitions. With clarity, you make decisions in alignment with your best interest, decisions congruent with your soul's calling. This requires clarity about what's most important and why. It makes it possible to spend more of your time on what's important and less on what's urgent.

Focus and clarity are interdependent. Focus benefits from clarity, and it requires reducing distraction. When taking focused action, you make faster and fuller progress toward your goals. Focus makes validating your clarity possible. Without focus, it's hard to have clarity because unimportant variables cloud your vision and disrupt your effort.

Clarity and focus help keep momentum going,
especially in times of uncertainty.
They are the steering wheel and gears driving you
to keep striving when you feel like giving up.
Clarity is the compass, and focus sets the
pace forward.

Nir Eyal, author of *Indistractable: How to Control Your Attention and Choose Your Life (2019)*, is an expert on focus. In a podcast interview, he talked about how the modern pace of change impacts our levels of distraction. Melancholy from boredom used to be a dominant clinical challenge. Now, with so much going on, distraction is our mental challenge. The abundance of choice gobbles up our ability to stay focused long enough to get substantial traction. Traction leads to satisfaction, and multitasking is the demon of satisfaction. It makes it impossible to be present, to do anything well, and when we don't do things well, we don't get deep satisfaction (Murray-Serter 2021).

Getting swept away in distracting thoughts is a natural human phenomenon, even though it may seem like modern-day external stimuli is the dominant distraction. Fortunately, we can use techniques to harness focus. Especially, Eyal points out, since most distraction doesn't actually come from external triggers. It comes from within—our thoughts and emotions (Eyal 2019, 22).

Humans reminisce, ruminate, and think futuristically. So to manage distraction, we must intentionally become the boss of our attention although the constant fragmentation of our time and concentration has become the new normal. An *Inc.com* article reports that two decades ago, a Harvard study on mind wandering found we experienced five-minute interruptions about every eight minutes and it takes about fifteen minutes to regain concentration (Klemp 2019). This means most of the time we're not concentrating very well. And interruptions aren't all we're contending with. The digital age gives us a never-ending landslide of ways to zone out and a wellspring of things to discover. Chasing unnecessary shiny objects and falling off track are more probable than ever before.

All this challenges people in FIT more than the average person. On top of everyday demands, they're juggling psychoemotional pain and fear from grief, loss, and uncertainty. And exploration, experimentation, and discovering new things require yet more discomfort. Therefore, this kind of situation is a setup for distraction because, as Eyal explains, internal discomfort (thoughts and feelings) are triggers that push us to seek ways (distraction) to move away from discomfort (Murray-Serter 2021). Because the hallmark of FIT is being in a state of ambiguity and disorientation, the need for clarity and focus is greater than normal.

Only when we have a sense of clarity is
taking focused action toward goals possible.

But we're up against formidable challenges because our goals are moving targets. As we approach them, we pivot and iterate. We're constantly redefining and refining what we're after. Clarity and focus help us iterate, pivot faster, and avoid committing to something that doesn't best serve us.

We're continually asked to make decisions based on only glimpses of clarity while trusting the process of life. When we understand where the locus of control lies, psychoemotional pain is more tolerable.

Planning versus action can be a distraction that may
move us away from discomfort when discomfort
is where we need to go.

Control is not in our circumstances; it's in our decisions. Our thoughts and decisions create much of our reality and emotions. Therefore, clarity and focus are how we regain control. Our power is not tied to what happens but in choosing where to focus and how to respond. Robert Pardi, coauthor of *Chasing Life: The Remarkable True Story of Love, Joy and Achievement Against All Odds* (2021), describes choice: "Choosing to see the ordinary moments as extraordinary meant, at least for us, that we did not define our life by the cancer, but let it grow us. We used it as a chisel to chip away the unnecessary and define what 'living' meant to us" (Pardi and Melhado, 173).

One of the reasons I loved crisis intervention as a social worker was because I could provide structure when spontaneity and in-the-moment decisions were not in the best interest of clients. They needed help to decrease their psychoemotional overload and gain a sense of control.

One of the greatest parts of my role was to normalize their experience. I knew the terrain they were pushed into and explained where they were and what they were up against. I guided them with next steps. They didn't have the burden of needing to figure everything out. They just needed to follow the path forward out of the thicket, and they were open to being led. They would pick up their personal agency once the initial crisis was under control. We need not have the end in mind to begin. Taking the next step in front of you is all that's required.

In the end, clarity emerges through conversation and taking action. We figure things out through dialogue and experimentation not thinking and planning. Transformation happens through taking action. Through gaining control over focus, we can formulate a new daily habit plan. We can influence ourselves by holding true to our commitments to ourselves.

...

Bold Becomer Prompts

1. On a scale of one to ten, how much have my values, beliefs, priorities, and dreams changed recently?

2. In the following situations I am compromising my values and integrity...

3. The top five attributes of the best version of myself I'm working to manifest are...

...

WHEN ADDICTION ROBS YOUR TRUE IDENTITY

I realized how serious my problem with addiction was on a Tuesday in 1986. I'd just arrived at the San Andres airport on my way home from mainland, South America. I'd been at that same airport a week earlier, missed my connecting flight, and had to stay overnight. A staff person gave me a thorough telling off because she thought I'd done it on purpose. (I *had* taken a spin around the tourist destination island.) When I got off the plane this time, the same lady greeted me on the tarmac as I stepped off the plane.

She had me identify my bag from the plane's storage area, we retrieved it, and we headed toward the building. She said she wanted to make sure the same thing didn't happen again. I followed her into the airport and waited with her behind the counter on the employee side while she took care of my travel arrangements.

While waiting, a man kept staring at me from the public side of the counter. I was used to that. Colombian men always looked at me. The *gringa*. A curiosity. But the instant I stepped over the baggage scale onto the public side, he and another plainclothes cop were on either side of me, escorting me though the airport. I asked what was going on. They didn't answer.

They brought me down a corridor into a room, closed the door, and asked me a few questions. A policewoman frisked me but didn't find the bag of weed I had in my underwear like a Kotex pad. Thank God they didn't have dogs. President Reagan's War on Drugs had already been four years in the making. It was the middle of the Pablo Escobar era. I was returning home from Medellín, Colombia, of all places, with drugs! What was I thinking?

I didn't get thrown into a Colombian jail that day. I caught my flight to Costa Rica and, getting high on my hotel room balcony, went through some soul-searching moments. Why did I risk my freedom over a bag of Colombian gold?

I threw all the weed away, except one joint's worth. Was I *really* going to do it again? Yep. I wanted to have something as soon as I got off the plane once back in the United States. This made no rational sense. That's when I understood addiction had hijacked my sovereignty.

I was no longer in control of who I was. Something way stronger than my rational mind was in charge, and I didn't know how to take back my power.

Marijuana doesn't even cause physical withdrawals. How was it that I couldn't keep myself safe until I got back home? I soul searched and never did find the answer—other than further confirmation about how messed up I was, which stoked the flames of my self-loathing habit. I wouldn't learn until decades later that trauma and addiction were connected. And I'd had my fair share of childhood trauma.

Self-loathing proved to be an ineffective change stimulus. I continued with my addiction, living with the shame of having so little control over my thoughts and impulses. I was living a lie because this wasn't the real me. I tried for about ten years to quit. Every time, I would say to myself, *Okay, this is the last time I'm gonna get high. I'll just get high this one last time.* And that one last time never worked.

That's what addiction looks like. It doesn't have to even be a drug; it can be a behavior. Addiction takes hold of who you are and puts what you need to do on the back burner, servicing this obsessive and insatiable urge that negatively impacts your life. My thoughts and life centered around the next high. Addiction pushed other things aside to get its way. It was *never* satisfied, incessantly asking for that next time to hurry up while feeding self-contempt.

Fast forward to 1991. Because of a decade of chronic physical health problems, I'd finally followed my friend's advice. I gave macrobiotic eating a try. I got immediate and dramatic results:

- Increased energy;
- Laser focus;
- Decreased anxiety; and
- Improved immune system functioning.

I was hooked. I'd found a way forward that eluded doctors. But two years in, I'd stalled on making further progress. I still suffered from fatigue, and chronic joint pain had hardly let up. I wasn't doing everything perfectly with macrobiotics, but I had no doubt this was the path for me. One day I asked my macrobiotic counselor a question: Did he think smoking marijuana was holding me back from healing?

"You're still doing *that*?"

At that moment I realized how ridiculous it was. I was putting all this effort into cooking and being really careful with what I ate. Yet here I was, still putting an unnecessary substance into my body.

I was at a crisis point with my health. I felt I had no choice but to continue following the macrobiotic path to health. Since returning from my year abroad, I had a pact with humanity. I *had* to use my privilege to help those who couldn't help themselves. I had to get well so I could do that more fully.

I found out when necessity and purpose marry,
you get clarity on how to resolve
intractable problems.

I had a clear path forward to healing through macrobiotics. I trusted it to get me there with the tremendous change it initially gave me. So it was a no-brainer to give up smoking pot. It was such a no-brainer I don't even remember the exact date I quit.

All those other years I tried to quit I didn't have the clarity I needed to be able to make that change. I didn't have enough of the puzzle pieces to fit the picture together. I realize now, when we're trying to make a really hard change, it's not going to happen unless you're crystal clear on why that change is important. Mastering great change is driven by necessity and purpose. You must be clear on what those are.

You also need enough of the puzzle pieces in place to see a path forward, which always exists. You cannot abandon the search for answers to what next right steps are needed. Life is about piecemealing it back together when it all falls apart. This is how we create our masterpiece mosaics—what all the struggle is meant to become.

For me, it took clarity on how that decision to quit smoking was critical to my overall plan. Clarity about why I was an addict didn't help me change. Clarity on why I needed to change wiped addiction off the map. The desire to get high vanished. I needed to be fully myself to be the service worker I was built to be. Addiction stole that from me. It stunted self-realization, so it had to go. Now with a way to recover my physical health, I had enough of the pieces to make that happen.

KEY TAKEAWAYS

DOS AND DON'TS

- Don't amplify suffering by resisting it.
- Trust the journey of life. Create agency to counter resistance by grieving and seeking clarity.

- Don't lose faith in yourself.
- Without clarity, the impossible remains impossible. With clarity, you can do things you previously never imagined possible.
- Don't lose hope for a better future.
- Focusing on who needs you on your A-game can help create hope. Hope is intertwined with the amount you value your dreams and aspirations. Seeking clarity about what is truly important resuscitates hope.
- Don't try to push the river.
- Life happens on its own schedule. With clarity, things can change on a dime. With clarity, the need for will and determination melt away. Use focus and structure to support discipline and intention.
- Don't focus on what happened.
- Reality is what it is. How you respond and what you choose to focus on is how you access power, freedom, and happiness.

RESILIENCE

Even though the ground is shifting beneath you, and sometimes you're caught in quicksand, know important change is happening. Life is not linear. Wanting things to be different causes more suffering than necessary. Allow for feelings and reality to be as they are. You're in liminality. Things aren't expected to be easy or straightforward. Trust this tension. Discomfort is necessary and will end when the time is right. Everything resolves.

NIR EYAL'S INDISTRACTABLE FRAMEWORK

Source: *Interview with Nir Eyal (Murray-Serter 2021),
based on his book: Indistractable: How to Control Your
Attention and Choose Your Life (Eyal 2019).*

*Being indistractable means striving
to do what you say you will do.*

—NIR EYAL

Nir Eyal's framework helps distraction not derail us from doing what's important. He teaches how to harness clarity and focus by turning time into values. We do this through *time blocking* our life. Below are the bare bones of his model tailored to forced identity transition.

Here's how to begin using the framework to boldly become:

1. Reframe your relationship to FIT from a problem to get rid of to the project that it is—self-reinvention.

2. Schedule time to work on it. You need two kinds of time blocks:

   a. Grief processing; and

   b. Bouncing beyond activities.

The principal concept behind *Indistractable* is that we take action to relieve discomfort. Based on this assertion, *distraction* is an action we choose to relieve discomfort. But distraction moves us away from other desired goals, what we really want and what's important. *Traction* is what we need—actions that move us toward our goal. We live in the intersection of these two choices.

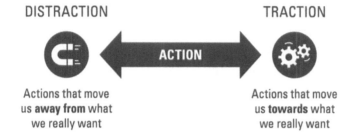

DISTRACTION | TRACTION
ACTION

Actions that move us **away from** what we really want

Actions that move us **towards** what we really want

Used with permission from Nir Eyal.

Add *triggers* to this model—things inside and outside of us pushing us to choose distraction.

The Indistractable Model

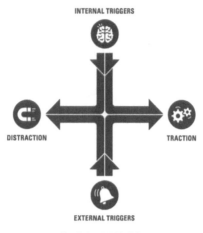

INTERNAL TRIGGERS

DISTRACTION   TRACTION

EXTERNAL TRIGGERS

From "Indistractable" by Nir Eyal

Used with permission from Nir Eyal.

Most people believe *external triggers* are to blame for not making progress—activities we can measure to see how we use our time such as work expectations, kids, phones and social media, and television.

But science proves otherwise. Distraction is almost always caused by five categories of *internal triggers* that cause discomfort. These drive us to seek external triggers to self-soothe. Distraction helps us escape unpleasant feelings while undermining goal achievement. Triggers prompt us to compulsively look at our phone or read just one more email.

Eyal identifies five main internal triggers at the root of distraction:

1. Boredom: lack of enjoyment in process.

2. Loneliness: process not fun to do alone.

3. Insecurity: not feeling qualified to do it (e.g., become who inner whispers are suggesting).

4. Fatigue: doing too many different things and not blocking off dedicated time for (e.g., healing/growth/transformation).

5. Uncertainty: not knowing where you're headed or what to do next.

Eyal's model suggests that if you're struggling with making progress, step back and explore internal triggers first. Find out what you're afraid of or nervous about. This is key to addressing what's holding you back. Until you're clear on your main internal trigger, you'll be susceptible to distraction hijacking your progress. You'll likely blame external distractions rather than the cause—what's going inside you.

Once you've identified your main internal trigger, you can harness these same feelings to create traction for your important goals. You can't stop fear, but you can get positive traction instead of negative distraction.

Eyal's four steps to turn feelings you have into *traction* instead of *distraction*:

1. Name the beast: identify internal triggers (see my example of this step below).

2. Create time for traction:

   a. Change perception from being "too busy" with being "distracted."

   b. Dedicate time on calendar (appointments to show up and work on FIT project).

   c. Follow through with appointments. Put in the time. Measure time working on what you said you were going to do, not outcomes of your efforts.

3. Make pacts with others. Create an accountability engine. Move from "me" to "us" to improve motivation:

   a. Involve supportive people in your process through informal agreements.

   b. Promise to deliver input to them by certain deadlines (actions taken, not outcomes on actions taken—e.g., I went to that networking event. I had a three-hour grief processing session with myself. I researched that new thing.)

   c. Talk about momentum toward your goal. Use structured five to thirty minutes of consistent check-ins. Socialize your learning by talking about where you are, what you did, where you struggled, where it went well.

   d. Reverse roles. Listen as the other person shares.

4. Hack back. Once you have the first three tactics working...

   a. Create rules for yourself that hold you accountable to your plans.

   b. Create clear boundaries for others to decrease interruptions.

   c. Control tech by turning off notifications, etc.

The indistractable model is perfect for people in FIT because both the indistractable model and the FIT process focus on measuring success differently than we're used to. Rather than measuring *outcomes* (results from actions and effort), we measure *input*:

- Did we take the action we said we'd take?
- Did we work on the task we scheduled into our time box?
- Did we do it for the amount of time planned *and* in a focused way?

It's not about finishing or even how far we get. It's about doing—not planning, not thinking about, but taking action. Period. That's what's required to make it out the other end of FIT. Creativity comes alive through motion not speculation. Creating the next version of yourself depends on:

- Taking one step at a time. Each step is the next output toward your dream.
- Deciding on the next right action and completing that action.
- Trusting next steps will reveal themselves.

APPLYING STEP ONE OF NIR EYAL'S FRAMEWORK:

FINDING THE INTERNAL TRIGGER

Though I'm not applying the exercises at the end of every chapter, I want to offer an example because it's not always obvious how far you need to dig to find your internal truths. Once you get something out of your head and into writing, your mind opens for new information to surface.

Below, I dig deep to figure out the cause of my discomfort and distractions to bouncing beyond, out of liminality, and into thought leadership. The example is from my identity loss story in chapter 7. I lost my social work career, trained to be a couturier (maker of fine clothing), realized I was still in liminality (that new identity didn't fit properly), and finally landed in thought leadership, a term I didn't even know existed.

Salient factors of the story:

- Career loss led to fulfilling repressed dream of becoming a couturier.

- But that was no longer who I really wanted to become.

- But I didn't know how to become a person aligned with my desire to be of service using my therapeutic voice—helping people heal and increase personal agency—or even what that version of myself could look like. I had no desire for public speaking. I had and have no desire to be famous. I cannot return to "regular" work because of a disability.

- The clothing gig kept me stuck in liminality until I took a major step away from it.

- I took a marathon online seminar (Seth Godin's altMBA) because I wanted to see if I had any intellectual capacity left in me.

- That opened new doors via more courses. Exploration and discovery of personal development and thought leadership began.

- But I kept myself busy, still on the clothing track, not knowing where to go or how to get into thought leadership.

- I kept taking actions that took me away from thought leadership goal (more sewing classes, after knowing it wasn't what I wanted to do; wrote a book on personal image and couture wardrobes; and spent over 250 hours editing videos to make an online bespoke jacket making course).

- I stayed distracted from the goal of creating a new way to use my therapeutic voice in a thought leadership venue while inner whispers continued telling me that was the right direction to go.

Rational reasons I kept going with the clothing gig when I knew it wasn't for me:

- I wanted to make it work after all the effort and investment I put into it (decision based on sunk costs).
- I wanted to hurry up and work and make a living again.
- I needed to be able to answer the "What do you do?" question in a way that satisfied myself and others.
- I wanted to make my teachers proud of me and not feel their efforts were in vain.
- My mom and son needed to see me succeed with my wild plan.

What was *really* holding me back? I was afraid of:

- Not finding an answer, a way to use my talents, skills and passion to help others;
- What finding the answer would require me to do/become;
- What my full power might unleash;
- Not having anything to offer that would make a difference;
- Wasting my life;
- Not being enough to fill that role;
- Being in the spotlight where haters could hurt me;
- Being called a showoff;
- Being authoritarian like my dad and telling people what to do; and
- My own power.

ANALYSIS

I've been afraid of my own power and what I would be responsible to do once I embody it. I've been suffering from insecurity.

Without digging deep I might have blamed uncertainty because I didn't have a clear roadmap or vision of where I was headed. But insecurity was the real block.

I let myself stay distracted in a project I knew I didn't want to succeed at (clothing gig). Insecurity around my power, not uncertainty, caused me to seek external triggers (continued efforts with the sewing gig).

This distraction kept me from the discomfort of working toward my real goal of finding a topic and avenues to become a leader around that. I let myself get distracted by external triggers because I was scared of my own power. When I used my power as a little girl, I would get in trouble. I would get ganged up on. People would make it their business to block me. If I never showed up now, nobody would know. I would stay protected.

YOU'VE GOT THIS

You might feel like you'll never regain a sense of normalcy or like your ambition and dreams are impossible or not that important. You might believe uncertainty, doubt, fear, and lack of clarity will remain at these heightened levels. Hang in there because the change you seek is within reach. Even when you're backsliding and moving in too many directions at once, you're actually bouncing beyond. I honor your trust in the process and faith that life has your back. You're stronger than you recognize.

CHAPTER 7

Self-Care

I finally feel like myself again. I'm using more constructive coping strategies and now I'm a healthy human being.

—LENA CEBULA, SERIAL CHILD RAPE SURVIVOR,
FORMER HEROIN ADDICT AND ALCOHOLIC, SEX SLAVE
SURVIVOR, HUMAN TRAFFICKING AWARENESS LEADER

...

Goal: To create habits that generate abundant energy and restore a sense of well-being.

WHEN A JOB REQUIREMENT CHANGES WHO YOU ARE

Source: TEDx Talk: Self Care: What It Really Is
(Winters 2019).

Susannah Joy Winters, "self-care made simple" expert and former Olympic kayak racer, wasn't always a self-care expert. In her TEDx Talk "Self Care: What It Really Is," she talks about her before and after journey. She knew physical and emotional stress is one of our greatest threats to health. But in 2017, when a coworker asked what she did for self-care, cringing, she said, "I eat and I sleep, and that's enough."

Susannah knew she wasn't doing herself justice. She was managing a high-volume retail business in Washington, DC. She and her husband were also starting their own company while raising their two-year-old son. Susannah started every day with coffee and a scone. She went to work, took very few breaks, and finished the day watching Netflix and scrolling on her phone. "I was in complete denial about what I needed to do to take care of myself."

Predictably, she burned out. Susannah quit her job and started listening to her heart. Following her passion, she became a labor doula and childbirth educator. This forced her to put self-care as a top priority. Much of her new job was teaching pregnant women to be as relaxed as possible during what could be a stressful event. She realized she was living at odds with what she was teaching. She knew to be effective, she had to be a relaxing presence.

This is when she discovered what self-care really is. She began to learn the difference between self-indulgence and self-care. "What the industry sells is not what restores us. It's not self-care." More often than not, it's only self-pampering. It's passive and may be a good start but doesn't have the potential to revitalize and restore.

Self-care is proactive—taking responsibility for your health and responsibilities.

Susannah's journey into self-care began with a diet rich in whole, plant-based foods. Then she added three restorative activities:

- Moments of stillness and silence;
- Movement; and
- Time in nature.

In the end, Susannah's motivation to become a relaxing presence did much more than help her relax. It improved her mood, energy, and joy while *also* protecting her health and well-being. Susannah asks us, "What would be possible for you if you showed up for yourself?"

SELF-CARE IS NOT OPTIONAL

Forced identity transition generally starts off as a crisis. Crisis management involves triage decision-making. This involves deciding what the most critical things to address first are. Things other than self-care become priorities so self-care often gets pushed aside. Things like finances, where you're going to live, what options you're going to choose around a health challenge, or how you're going to manage shared parenting take precedence.

Self-care is needed now more than ever.

Being in a situation against your will, you're likely experiencing psychoemotional duress. Self-care helps you manage stress. It also supports the immune system, which is impacted under circumstances of grief and heightened stress (Leech and Singer 1988, 23).

New, unfamiliar, and urgent demands make self-care routines harder to prioritize. Adjusting to the ground falling out from beneath your feet impacts every aspect of life. Focus is scattered. Many things you need to get out of your predicament are thwarted—in particular, good judgment. And for many, even in the best of times, self-care is not as straightforward as we might think it should be. Now with FIT's extra demands on executive functioning, this challenge may become yet another source of overwhelm.

Apart from the normal difficulty, people struggle to keep up with adequate self-care during FIT for several reasons:

- Daily routines are disrupted by urgent things needing to be stabilized as fast as possible. This takes time away from activities that (theoretically) can wait.

- Triage decision-making requires critical thinking, cognitive skills, intuition, and experience (Smith and Cone 2010). But stress negatively impacts judgment (Kahneman 2011, 65). Because of stress from your situation, your thinking, intuition, or trust in your intuition are not at their best.

- You likely don't have experience with many things life is now demanding of you. This is new terrain so you're on a learning curve, taking time away from other priorities.

- You are now both the triage decision maker and the "patient" being triaged. You might not have professional help and you might lack the constellation of support you need. You may not even know who or what kind of help you need.

Maintaining, and especially now, doubling down on self-care, helps your psychology, emotions, and physical health. It reduces the impact of stress and uncertainty brought on by your situation.

It supports clarity and focus. This creates space
for a sense of direction and purpose
to emerge from the confusion, fear, and pain.

Self-care is also preventive. It can keep the crisis from spiraling downward by preventing new physical ailments and unnecessary psychosocial problems (Leech and Singer 1988, 23).

Self-care goals go beyond physical wellness. This chapter broadens the definition to include things that help us feel alive: a life filled with energy and pop, a sense of vibrancy, presence, and spirit that creates a new level of aliveness.

...

Bold Becomer Prompts

1. My routine activities that create energy include...

2. The top three things most impacting my sense of mental, emotional, and physical vibrancy in a negative way are...

3. Three things I need to start doing and three things I need to stop doing to generate twice as much energy include...

...

WHAT IS SELF-CARE?

Susannah's definition of self-care is "deliberately taking care of your well-being through restorative activities" (Winters, 2019). I'll add to that—restorative *and* preventive activities.

The ten-billion-dollar self-care industry, says Susannah, would have us believe it's a complicated process filled with novelty, expense, and out of the ordinary activities. It's not. It's everyday regular activities and practices that reduce stress and restore, maintain, and enhance our short- and longer-term health and well-being. Examples include (Winters, 2019):

- Getting sufficient sleep;
- Taking time alone and away from screens; and

- Eating food that doesn't make you crash.

Self-care is activities that improve mental clarity and emotional stability and help you feel more energized and vibrant. It helps you push aside discouragement, be more likely to feel grateful for life, and experience more meaning, flow, and fulfillment.

Self-care isn't about "getting it right, it's a practice" (Winters 2019). It's about showing up consistently for yourself. Self-care is neither selfish nor self-indulgent. It's the way to maintain a healthy relationship with yourself, and it enables you to share good feelings with others.

> Self-care is a practice fundamentally about
> being nice to yourself—self-compassion.

Its payoff is becoming tougher, calmer, and more resilient. It's the driver behind optimal effectiveness and success in every aspect of our daily lives. I see it as the undercurrent to our energy—physical, mental, emotional, and spiritual.

In the words of the fourteenth Dalai Lama, an esteemed scholar of compassion: "For someone to develop genuine compassion toward others, first he or she must have a basis upon which to cultivate compassion, and that basis is the ability to connect to one's own feelings and to care for one's own welfare... Caring for others requires caring for oneself" (Mills and Chapman 2016).

SELF-CARE AND FIT

During FIT you're searching for new ways to be, belong, and perform. Your social and/or professional roles have changed dramatically. You're reevaluating desires, beliefs, values, and aspirations. You're re-establishing new fundamentals around what you do, how you connect to and influence others, and where you're headed. This all happens while feeling upside down and inside out.

People in FIT generally lack clarity on many levels. Their mental health may be affected. They may be depressed because of a snowball effect from losses caused by the catalytic event. Answering simple questions like "How are you?" or "So what do *you* do?" are often filled with a barrage of painful emotions. These can connect to a sense of chronic overwhelm. Lack of clarity, overwhelm, and depression impede normal decision-making and taking action, and depression strains the immune system (Leech and Singer 1988, 23).

Self-esteem and self-compassion correlate with levels of self-care (Nelson et.al. 2017 and Mills and Chapman 2016). After your identity loss, these can all get knocked off balance. When you no longer know where and how you fit into society, you're living in limbo. Your sense of value and belonging is tested to the core. This impacts self-esteem. In turn, your willingness to take good care of yourself can waffle or even tank. Catalytic events causing identity loss are generally quite stressful. Many are traumatic. Add to this the grief, disorientation, and ambiguity inherent to FIT. Now it's easier than ever to let go of self-care routines right when you need them most.

This is the time to build a solid and intentional self-care routine. It will help you:

- Stabilize energy, emotions, and thoughts as you tumble along.

- Think straighter and better weather the blows from your losses.

- Brace against criticism (yours and others'), making it more likely to make the many pivots necessary to find your true north.

- Get the energy needed to feel good enough to show up and partake in exploratory activities needed to discover your next steps forward.

Without the trio of self-esteem, self-compassion, and self-care, you're at risk of making premature commitments. You're at risk of selling yourself short and settling on who you are becoming. You're at risk of doing what's easy instead of what's worth it.

This is your chance to implement a holistic and consistent self-care practice, one that supports you as you put in the time and effort needed to harness the full benefits of FIT so you can live a life congruent with your best self. FIT offers you this opportunity. Your catalytic event gives you a choice for a makeover. Amping up self-care is the ticket to deliver on this opportunity.

TYPES OF SELF-CARE

Self-care activities and practices fall into six categories (Planned Parenthood 2022):

1. *Emotional:* activities that help you connect, process, and reflect on a full range of emotions, e.g., seeing a therapist, writing in a journal, engaging in creative activities such as knitting, throwing pots and other arts and crafts, and fly fishing.

2. *Psychological:* activities that stimulate your mind and spark interest and curiosity, e.g., reading a book, solving puzzles, going to a museum, playing chess, participating in a mastermind group, or an exciting project.

3. *Physical:* activities that support your physiology, e.g., good nutrition, regular exercise, staying hydrated, getting enough sleep, avoiding stressful relationships as much as possible.

4. *Spiritual:* activities that nurture your spirit and allow you to think bigger than yourself, e.g., meditation, yoga, religious

services, being in nature, self-reflection time. Spiritual health is one element of the World Health Organization's definition of health: "living in a way that leads to realizing your meaning, purpose and full potential in life" (2022).

5. *Social:* activities that nurture and deepen relationships with people in your life, e.g., going out with friends, going on dates, calling or texting important people on a regular basis.

6. *Practical:* doing things to ensure core aspects of your life are taken care of and don't create future stress, e.g., being responsible with your finances and employment, keeping your home clean and orderly (as works for you, not defined by others), meal planning and prep, enrolling in growth activities such as professional development courses, time boxing tasks to ensure a balanced life, practicing self-care.

Time in nature has long been recognized for its positive effects on physical, mental, emotional, and spiritual health.

- My own great grandfather, Colonel Charles B. Wing, knew the inherent value of time in nature. He and others founded the California State Parks System in the mid-1800s. This prevented the most beautiful natural places from becoming private property. It ensured that everyone could enjoy the pleasures and restorative power of nature.

- In 1982, the Japanese Ministry of Forestry, Agriculture and Fisheries created the practice of "forest bathing" (Kaiser Permanente 2022). This was a preventive health care measure. Forest bathing is one kind of "nature therapy," or "ecotherapy." It's where you immerse yourself in a forest while focusing on the five senses (vision, smell, taste, hearing, and touch). The purpose is to improve immune function, prevent disease, and produce a relaxed state.

- Canada recently passed regulations so some doctors can prescribe treatments in nature (Pruitt-Young 2022). They give patients an annual pass to its national parks.

THE NEED FOR A HOLISTIC APPROACH

The heart of self-care addresses both physical and psychoemotional well-being. This includes stress management. Managing psychoemotional well-being is *as* important as what we eat, how we exercise, etc. It's sometimes hard to see and always hard to measure these contributing factors to our health. Because of this they can be overlooked, dismissed, or discounted. We can see, measure, and treat physical injuries and illness. We use Band-Aids, casts, blood tests, body scans, medicine, etc.

Addressing psychoemotional stressors is more elusive than physical health problems. They're subjective, generally invisible, and experienced differently by each person. But since FIT can involve extraordinary levels of stress, we might choose to be extra vigilant to counteract its effects.

It's best to approach self-care holistically. When one aspect is missing, it affects the balance of the whole. Like Susannah, many people don't have huge problems or emergencies. Because of this they risk putting aside proper self-care altogether. Others resort to extreme measures to cope as best as they can in impossible situations (e.g., addiction to cope with abuse and trauma). The rest of us fall in between on this spectrum. We give self-care more or less attention and may cherry pick our way into believing we're doing okay in this department when we're not.

Everyone practices self-care in their own way, but based on modern health statistics, many of us have lots of room for improvement.

- A National Institutes of Health study analyzed numbers of premature deaths caused by modifiable risk factors (Danaei et.al. 2009). They found:
  - One in five deaths were caused by either tobacco smoking or high blood pressure.
  - Obesity and physical inactivity were each responsible for nearly one in ten deaths.
  - Among the dietary factors examined, high dietary salt intake had the largest effect.
  - Alcohol use was responsible for premature deaths from cardiovascular diseases, other medical conditions, road traffic accidents, and violence.
- Ryan Romano, in his TEDx Talk (2020), gave some harrowing mental health statistics for Texas:
  - Someone takes their life by suicide every two hours. It's the second leading cause of death between the ages of fifteen and thirty-four.
  - Five to eight times as many high school and college students meet the criteria for major depression and anxiety than fifty years ago.

Each person manages their most important priorities first when it comes to self-care. And often, people neglect a holistic approach. For some, their psychoemotional health is paramount, and it's all they can do to stay alive. Others have a physical health challenge that motivates them. Others may put more focus on leveling up in the practical aspects of their lives. For example, they focus on fulfilling a desired status role at the expense of their health and relationships.

Committing to a balance in self-care activities
is more important than achieving excellence
in one or two areas.

WHAT HOLDS US BACK FROM PRACTICING SELF-CARE?

Self-care is challenging during regular times. The pull to do what's easy is profound, enhanced by endless advertising dollars molding and reaffirming our decisions. Like Susannah, it's easy to live on autopilot. Many let caffeine and sugar do the heavy lifting instead of creating energy from within through healthy lifestyle choices. It's easy to use things like alcohol and Netflix to deescalate stress and curb difficult emotions.

People tend to put more attention on convenience than on what brings them deep, lasting joy. Decisions about what they do with their time, who they spend it with, and what they put in their bodies are often an afterthought.

The goal with self-care is to make decisions based on well-considered and executed strategic intentions.

Something about life makes taking extra good care of ourselves seem unnecessary or superfluous—until something catastrophic shakes sense into us, like a serious disease, an accident, or hitting rock bottom.

Susannah had to change her self-care to succeed in her new career. Lena's story below shows how she had to change her self-care to the only thing possible at the moment—addiction. When she eventually got a chance for something safer and more functional, she upgraded. My story below is about being forced to change because of a health crisis. Motivation for self-care comes from both internal and external factors.

...

...

EXTREME SELF-CARE: IT CAN EITHER KILL YOU OR KEEP YOU ALIVE

Source: personal interview.

When Lena Cebula was eleven years old, the Soviet Union
dissolved and her country, Ukraine, "fell apart." Her parents lost
their well-paying jobs and became alcoholics. The same happened to many others. A power vacuum created social unrest.

"The country was destroyed and in chaos," says Lena, "and
morals were down."

Lena's home started filling up with "strangers bringing in
booze and drugs." When she was thirteen or fourteen, these
strangers started drugging and serial and gang raping her in
the basement. Her father was aware of what was happening.
One day some men broke down the door and dragged her

from her home by her hair. Her father, drunk, said from his armchair, "Just take her, as long as you don't bother me." That day Lena's heart shattered and filled with hatred. Neither her parents, the neighbors, nor the police offered any help, so she turned to drugs to cope.

"In a crazy way, drugs allowed me not to kill myself. I needed my brain to be checked out because it was tormenting me."

A month before Lena's fifteenth birthday, when she thought things could not get worse, she awoke with severe abdominal pain. She found out she was pregnant and in labor. She gave up her parental rights and left the baby in the hospital because she couldn't care for her. Three months later her baby died from health complications. Lena berated herself: *Now I'm just like my parents—neglectful.*

Lena's method of self-care was drugs and alcohol because normalcy was inaccessible. "They gave me relief from the anxiety, fear, and panic attacks," says Lena, "and anger became a coping mechanism because it made me feel in control."

Now eighteen and a "hopeless junkie," a friend connected her with a lady who took her under her wing and then sold her into human trafficking. She awoke one day hearing Muslim prayers in Cairo, Egypt. From there, she was shuttled to a brothel in Israel where she lived, imprisoned, for almost two years. During her time in the brothel her bodyguard shared the gospel with her—"the good news of God's love." Through this Lena found a new way to cope. She developed a relationship with God. Her extreme form of self-care kept her alive long enough to find a more sustainable way—faith in God. Eventually her bodyguard also helped her escape.

Fearing judgment and rejection, Lena stayed silent about her ordeals for twenty years, even to her fiancé (who declined to hear her story when she offered to share it). She thought her story was one of guilt, shame and condemnation. "But now I know it's God's story of salvation." Lena is now a speaker, a podcast host of *Love&BLoved*, the author of *Miraculous: My Journey from Hell to Heaven*, a coach, a wife, and a mother of three. She's been in recovery for fifteen years. She still gets help from a therapist to recover from trauma. Lena is on a mission, determined to break the chain of violence and dedicated to ending modern slavery.

KEY TAKEAWAYS

DOS AND DON'TS

- Don't overlook the importance of stress management.
- Make stress mitigation a top priority.

- Don't ignore the benefits of eating a more plant-based diet.
- Add more nutrient-rich foods to your diet such as whole grains, vegetables, and plant protein. Reduce processed foods and increase whole foods.

- Don't be a couch potato or tech slave.
- Add movement to your routine. Pick activities that work for you in this chapter of your life.

- Don't let others tell you what you need to do.
- What works for you isn't best for the next person. Take guidance from within.

- Don't strive for perfection.
- Embrace being human. Making sound choices and taking consistent action, not perfection, are what count. When you fall off the wagon, get back on it.

- Don't judge your destiny by your circumstances, and don't let your choices steal your destiny.
- Focus on choice over circumstance. If you meticulously and consciously take responsibility for your choices, you'll make better choices. Choices create your destiny.
- Don't delay implementing self-care practices.
- Allow yourself to take care of yourself now. Allow others to help you.

RESILIENCE

Everybody's doing the best they can. Reserve judgment. Cheerlead your own resilience, even if you don't see it and must force yourself to assume you have it. Have faith that you are your own hero.

WHEN SUFFERING LEADS TO SOLUTIONS

It was October 1989, two weeks before the Loma Prieta earthquake in San Francisco. I was thirty years old and in the worst physical pain of my life. On an internship in my last year of two graduate programs, my body had become almost unbearable to live in. I'd spent my twenties terrified about which body part would become my next chronic pain point. Each one limited me in new ways, increasingly cutting choices out of my life. Fatigue affected my social life, work, and school. Migraines required heavier and heavier medication, and nothing helped the joint pain.

I'd stopped seeking medical advice. Doctors didn't have answers. Not only was I freaking out about my health, but I was also scared about my career. I'd worked more than ten years to get to where I was. Upon graduation, my hope was to work in international public health. But now my own health wasn't going to let me go anywhere.

My friend Juan was worried too. I'd confided in him I was having thoughts of suicide. He'd begged me, for almost ten years, to try a special way of eating—macrobiotics. He claimed it would get me "back out on the soccer field," something I'd given up at age twenty-one when my health problems began (see chapter 5). But I never took him seriously. I thought, *If macrobiotics is so great, why is he still an alcoholic?*

Juan asked if he could cook for me for ten days so I could make an informed choice. Because I was in crisis, I let him. It helped, so much so that I've been cooking that way ever since. Juan gave me what doctors couldn't—hope and the keys to my destiny. These were a set of guiding principles, not just about food but about life and the challenge to take full responsibility for my choices.

Macrobiotics catapulted me into an identity loss for the better. At the same time as the Soviet Union, I underwent my own glasnost and perestroika—upheaval on every level, physical and mental, and a personal repositioning. The foundation of my thinking metamorphosed as I changed my eating. This metamorphic change forced me to let go of and replace beliefs about life's essentials and what was important.

I went from a person who felt scared, helpless, and vulnerable to becoming empowered, capable and confident.

My initial healing success was spectacular. It gave me a new lease on life. I regained hope in the possibility that I could decrease or end my physical suffering. My ROI (return on investment of effort) was at least ten times. Shortly after those ten days, my supervisor noticed a change. She called me into her office to find out what was going on. "Julie, what happened to you? What's your secret?"

In a few short weeks my energy doubled. My mental focus became razor-sharp. I felt grounded. My anxiety evaporated. Over the next few months I lost weight, and over the next year, my immune system improved dramatically. After two years, I stopped carrying painkillers in my purse for migraines. The joint pains were the most stubborn. They got better but never disappeared completely. I never made it back to competitive sports. But in a few short months, because my anxiety was gone, I made it home for Christmas. There, I had a metaphysical healing when hugging my dad, whom I'd disowned for two years. In that embrace, I felt a physical sensation. Thirty years of anger and hatred evaporated out of the top of my head.

After those ten days, Juan gave me a couple of cooking lessons and I started eating a diet of mainly whole and unprocessed grains, vegetables, small amounts of fermented foods (miso and macrobiotic pickles), sea vegetables, and mostly plant protein.

I didn't totally eliminate all unrecommended foods, especially sugar, but I loved the food and worked hard to eat mostly macrobiotically. I'm not a creative cook so it's not as much fun as it could be, but I keep at it because my health demands that I do. The hardest change has been my addiction to sugar. It's like being an alcoholic—all or none. I can't have just a little. Once I have some, the pursuit for more always follows. Sugar would turn out to be far harder to quit than marijuana.

But that initial success was coupled with
tremendous social rejection.

Many people gave me a hard time. They didn't like the taste of my food. They said it was weird. They were concerned with the weight loss. My mom thought I spent too much time cooking. People felt criticized. When I brought my own food to dinners and potlucks, it was like I was saying they were making bad choices. People would say things like, "Oh, so my food isn't good enough for you?" I traveled the macrobiotic path to health alone, and I hadn't felt better physically or mentally in years.

Later, when I became a parent, I stopped putting as much effort into my health, and I've been settling ever since. Twenty-nine years have passed, and that settling gets under my skin every day because half efforts help but aren't enough. I've continued with chronic health challenges, and the more consistent I am with macrobiotics, the better off I am. It is my most powerful form of self-care. At the same time, I've gotten used to not feeling great. Although I know what to do and like doing it, *doing* it is another thing. This is where a quote from Brendon Burchard really helps me:

"Our greatest personal power is in the ability
to take over our impulses and direct our minds
to choices and commitments that will serve us"
(Burchard 2016).

Another part of my self-care is stepping back from projects, even those I'm passionate about. I'm learning that powering through can't be an option. When I try, my body puts its foot down. Letting go can feel at odds with my spiritual self-care, but spreading myself too thin ends up serving no one. This is where each person must find their own self-care formula. While we all need a sense of purpose, each of us can only give so much. I have to check myself when I compare what I can accomplish to others or even to my past self. Those aren't valid measurements.

My conundrum is how to go as all in with myself
as I do for others.

Writing that last sentence sounds logical. Carrying it out feels selfish because of unresolved developmental trauma and social norms. Taking time to replenish to give myself permission to administer self-care to myself is a constant challenge. Work is never ending, and self-care is time consuming. To take better care of myself, I must let go of my settling habit and self-betrayal because functioning at less than my prime is a choice. To a great degree, I can avoid living suboptimally.

Learning to put myself first has been a long learning curve. I'm still looking for my off button. I cannot push myself relentlessly. I must respect my body by putting its physiological needs first. I didn't take time out to heal in my twenties when my body started falling apart, and now I'm in my sixties. If not now, with the extra need to be positive, empowered, and resilient against physical disease and societal vitriol, when? This quote from the late, great macrobiotic teacher Herman Aihara (1991) helps me:

"Macrobiotics amounts to finding our
physiological limitations and trying to live
within them. When we think that we can
do anything we want, we become arrogant.
This arrogance causes sickness."

I can look at my health challenges through a lens of loss or through a lens of privilege. Had I not become desperate, I wouldn't have changed my diet. A diet Western science, including my HMO, now promotes thirty years later (more whole, plant-based foods with intact fiber, less processed foods, animal protein, and sugar). I haven't done all I could to keep myself in tiptop shape, and my job now is to use my knowledge and intentional self-care structures (versus determination and willpower) to create a healthier body, psyche, and soul, one day at a time.

The macrobiotic path is work, as is any self-care activity worth its salt. While it takes time and effort on the front end, it has the possibility of giving more time and quality on the backend. That's what self-care is all about: taking responsibility to prevent, restore, and revitalize.

EATING BETTER:
A CRASH COURSE IN MACROBIOTICS

Macrobiotic philosophy and practices trace back to the dawn of civilization in East Asia, as recorded in *The I Ching (The Book of Changes)* and *The Nei Ching (The Yellow Emperor's Classic of Internal Medicine)*. Transmission of this knowledge was modernized by George Oshawa (1893–1966). Oshawa brought it from Japan to the West after saving his own life as a young man, when he had tuberculosis and implemented this lifestyle. Oshawa's interpretation of what he coined "macrobiotics" came from two main teachers: Ekken Kaibara (1630–1716) and Sagen Ishizuka (1850–1910).

The information below is from over thirty years of my own study with various teachers including Juan Fortín, Kaare Bursell, and Herman and Cornellia Aihara, and consolidated from a recent macrobiotic counselor training course with David Briscoe (Briscoe, 2020).

What is macrobiotics?

- Outcomes focused: What change are you trying to achieve?
- Nutrient dense.
- Health preservation and restoration focused.
- Mainly consists of whole, unprocessed grains; vegetables; plant protein; and some fermented food.

Main principles:

- Always think for yourself.
- Natural human qualities need to be honored and respected.
- Health and happiness are our natural state.
- Food is a primary contributing factor to our health.

- We can change our physical and psychoemotional conditions.

- Cultivate gratitude.

Main concept driving decisions: focus on alkaline-forming foods and attempts to live within the physiological laws that create an alkaline condition.

The past three decades of Western science validate two-thousand-year-old macrobiotic dietary beliefs/practices:

- Excess acidity promotes disease.

- Excess consumption of animal, animal products, and sugar can be detrimental to health.

- Adding significant plant-based food is a cost-effective, low-risk intervention.

How to achieve acid/alkaline balance:

- Decrease highly acid-forming foods.

- Increase alkaline-forming foods.

- Increase trace minerals, which are alkaline.

Plant-based, whole, unprocessed foods are less acid-forming than:

- Animal products.

- Processed plant-based products (e.g., flour products).

- Artificially made food.

- Sugar and other simple sugars (mono and disaccharides).

Foods to limit or eliminate, depending on health goals:

- Extreme yang (contractive) foods:
  - Meat, chicken, eggs, cheese.
  - Saturated fat (instead use sesame or olive oil, in small amounts):

      o Any fat firm at room temperature.

      o Coconut oil is 80 to 90 percent saturated fat.

   – Hard and/or baked food (e.g., bread, chips).

   – Overly salty food.

   – Food with a high sodium-to-potassium ratio.

- Extreme yin (expansive) foods:
  - Sweets.
  - Alcohol.
  - Drugs (including Rx).
  - Refined sugar.
  - All other refined carbs (flour products).
  - Simple sugars (mono and disaccharides):
    - Anything that immediately tastes sweet on the tongue.
    - Organic sugar, raw sugar, date sugar, etc.
    - Honey, maple syrup, molasses, rice syrup, barley malt, agave nectar, etc.
    - Soymilk, rice milk, etc.
    - Fruit juice and fruit (fructose, the sugar in fruit, is a monosaccharide and goes immediately into the blood stream faster than table sugar, a disaccharide).
    - Milk and soft dairy products (galactose, a monosaccharide in dairy, and galactose combined with glucose, which creates lactose, a disaccharide).
  - All sweetened beverages.
  - Foods with high potassium-to-sodium ratio (e.g., tropical fruit).

David Briscoe's *Acid/Alkaline Made Easy* framework (Briscoe, 2020):

A. Acid-forming foods:
   - Protein = amino acids
   - Fat = fatty acids
   - Simple sugars
   - Refined carbohydrates

B. Alkaline-forming foods
   - Whole plant foods are nutrient dense and rich in vitamins, minerals, fiber, and complex carbohydrates (polysaccharides):
     - Almost all land vegetables
     - Sea vegetables
     - Whole, unprocessed grains = complex carbs

The foundation of macrobiotic eating centers around whole, unprocessed grains, supplemented with vegetables and mainly plant protein.

Generally, the protein proportions are smaller than we're used to, and not necessary at every meal. Protein in any form, plant or animal, produces acid as a byproduct of digestion.

Whole, unprocessed grains with fiber intact is the foundation because the body's favorite form of fuel is glucose. Whole, unprocessed grains provide the blood stream with a slow and steady supply of glucose, an important tactic to maintain blood sugar stability.

Vegetables and trace minerals in macrobiotic condiments balance the slightly acid-forming whole grains (polysaccharides) and the acid-forming protein, while also providing other nutrients and fiber.

Diversification is key, which exists in a balanced macrobiotic diet. Just in the whole, unprocessed grain category, the main recommended ones include:

- Short grain brown rice
- Sweet brown rice
- Medium grain brown rice
- Barley
- Wheat
- Oats
- Rye
- Millet
- Quinoa
- Amaranth
- *Hato mugi* (job's tears)
- Buckwheat

In the vegetable kingdom, the four categories are:

1. Root
2. Ground
3. Leafy greens (especially dark ones such as kale, collards, mustard, bok choy, watercress)
4. Sea vegetables

Most common plant proteins:

- Beans and legumes
- Tofu
- Dried tofu
- Seitan
- Fu
- Natto
- Occasional servings of small, white fish (wild, not farm-raised) are often recommended.

Common sea vegetables available in the US (contain massive amounts of vitamins and trace minerals):

- Nori
- Wakame
- Kombu

- Arame
- Hijiki
- Dulse

Diversification of the four cooking elements:

1. Fire
2. Pressure

3. Time
4. Salt

Diversification of cooking styles, from yin to yang:

- Raw
- Pressed salads
- Steaming
- Blanching
- Water sauté
- Boiling
- Pressure cooking

- *Nishime*
- *Nitsuke*
- Long sauté
- Baking
- Deep frying
- Pickling

Miscellaneous, and no less important, macrobiotic practices:

1. Good chewing.
2. Finish eating three hours before bed.
3. At all costs, avoid overeating.
4. Develop appreciation for simpler foods.
5. Give yourself time to develop new tastes and to heal.

The following is my framework to help you implement the above ideas:

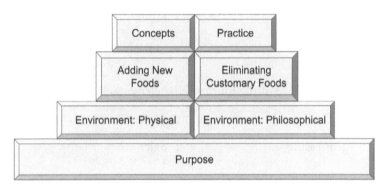

7 KEYS TO MASTERING HEALTH & WELLNESS

Concepts	Practice
Adding New Foods	Eliminating Customary Foods
Environment: Physical	Environment: Philosophical
Purpose	

Philosophical Environment:

- Am I living my truth?
- What do I need to believe about myself to fully be that person?
- Why is it important to change the way I'm eating?

Physical Environment:

- How have I prepared my physical space and the people around me to support my success?
- In my kitchen, do I have a place for everything to increase ease and decrease chaos?

Concepts:

- Am I able to make sense of nutrition advice and put it to use?
- Do I need to consult with someone for help?

- With all the contradictory and ever-changing ideas out there, how do I discern the truth?

- What's the foundation of my eating and why? Do I have a foundation to my eating?

Practice:

- Am I translating nutrition concepts into action consistently?

- Do I have a translation strategy, and if so, how well is it serving me?

- What would it take to multiply my good eating habits by ten?

- What are my eating habits? Is it a grab-bag approach, or do I follow a plan?

Adding New Foods:

- Am I actually adding what I believe I need in a significant way?

- How consistently am I doing this?

- What's keeping me from adding these new foods, and what's it costing me if I'm not?

Elimination:

- Have I eliminated or reduced the food I already know I need to?

- Do I have a replacement game plan to keep me on course?

- How well do my current thoughts about health and wellness serve me?

Health is built on our lifestyle choices.

Macrobiotics provides an identifiable path to steer us away from accumulating health conditions and toward personal freedom. These principles and practices hold true despite and regardless of tradition or culture. To attain better health, we need to let go of sacred cows regarding diet and culture. To do this we can learn to understand how we:

1. Contribute to what's making us sick;

2. Might create the change we seek; and

3. Might increase the likelihood of avoiding the condition from returning in the future.

If you'd like a starter course for macrobiotic cooking, here's the link to one I made with step-by-step instructional videos teaching everything you need: https://www.courage-ignite.com/offers/fdYZcu9t.

YOU'VE GOT THIS

Health comes down to luck and self-respect. Cultivating self-love and self-compassion leads to self-respect. I honor and celebrate all you do to take responsibility for the things you can control regarding your health. If you're reading this book, you have the power to control your mind and make decisions that give you the sense of vitality and joy you're after.

CHAPTER 8

Mindset

You're going to triumph and be a champion.

—DIANA GIRALDO'S DANCE TEACHER

...

Goal: Leverage choice in how to think.

FOCUS ON WHAT MAKES YOUR HEART BEAT FAST

Amy Purdy was nineteen, working as a masseuse in Las Vegas where she'd grown up. She dreamt of traveling the world, having adventures, and spending her free time snowboarding. One day, she left work early thinking she had the flu. Less than twenty-four hours later, she was in the hospital on life support with less than a two percent chance of living (Purdy 2011).

Doctors diagnosed her with Neisseria meningitidis, a bacterial infection. Penicillin usually kills it within twenty-four hours, but Purdy's case was different. Her body was shutting down due to a raging infection that had her white blood cell count at 103,000, when a normal amount is five to ten thousand. Her face was gray, and her feet and hands were purple. Remarkably, she survived (Sun 1999).

"I remember seeing a white light when I was in surgery for my spleen," Purdy said. "I knew at that moment I had a choice. I was going to stay or I was going to go, and there was no way I was going to die. I have my family and my friends to live for and so much to do" (Sun 1999).

Four weeks after being hospitalized, she had her lower legs amputated. When she awoke following surgery, Purdy saw her parents were disturbed. "I hated seeing my parents hurt," she said. "I felt I had to be strong. I didn't want my parents to be in pain" (Sun 1999). This was the beginning of her survival strategy—helping others. "It's so easy to get caught up in your own world with how hard it is and how unhappy you are," she recalls. "The only thing that really helped me in the hardest times was somehow giving back and helping somebody else" (Stanfield 2022).

In her TEDx Talk, she describes getting her new legs. A couple of weeks after leaving the hospital, her prosthetic legs arrived. When she and her mom first saw them—bulky metal calves with pipes bolted together for ankles and yellow rubber feet—they cried. They didn't know what to expect, but it wasn't that. When she strapped them on and stood up, "they were so painful and confining that all I could think was, *How am I ever going to travel the world and live the life full of adventure in these things? How was I going to snowboard again?*" (Purdy 2011).

"That day physically and emotionally broke me." Amy spent the next few months passed out in bed, escaping from reality with her legs resting by her side (Purdy 2011).

But one afternoon, she heard "a good song" come on the radio. "I wanted to dance. I got up on my legs, grabbed my dad, and had a little dance with him right there. It got me up because it was fun, and that little moment let me decide I could keep going on those legs." During this time, she knew she had to let go of the old Amy and embrace the new Amy, and she was determined to make that happen (Stanfield 2022).

Then she asked herself the question that changed her life:
"If my life were a book and I was the author,
how would I want my story to go?"

This question prompted her to begin dreaming again. She daydreamed and imagined herself walking gracefully, helping others *because* of her journey, and snowboarding. But she didn't just see herself carving down a mountain of powder. She actually felt the wind against her face and her heart racing. She brought the future into the present through thoughts and feelings. This moment began her next chapter of life (Purdy 2011).

Amy started focusing on the perks. She could now be as tall or as short as she wished. If she ever snowboarded again, her feet wouldn't get cold. And she could make her feet the size of any of the shoes on the sale racks!

Seven months later, she *was* snowboarding! But things weren't going so well. Her knees and ankles wouldn't bend the way she needed them to. At one point, she fell and her legs detached. Traumatizing everyone in sight, her legs rode the snowboard down the mountain without her (Purdy 2011).

Discouraged but by no means giving up, Amy soon discovered what authors Morgan and Barden talk about in their book, *A Beautiful Constraint: How to Transform Your Limitations into Advantages and Why It's Everyone's Business (2015)*.

She learned obstacles can only do two things:
stop us in our tracks or force us to get creative
(Purdy 2011).

She got creative. Purdy started looking for other prosthetics. When after a year of research she hadn't found the legs she needed, she and her leg maker began inventing. With new feet made from rusted bolts, rubber, wood, and neon pink duct tape, and with a kidney transplant from her dad, she rebooted her life. At twenty-one she was following her dreams again—snowboarding and back at work and school (Purdy 2011).

Over the following decade, she (Purdy 2011):

- Cofounded an organization helping youth and young adults get involved in action sports.

- Helped put shoes on thousands of children's feet in South Africa so they could go to school.

- Won two back-to-back World Cup gold medals, taking on the mantle of highest-ranking adaptive female snowboarder in the world.

In a span of eleven years, Amy went from having "no idea what to expect of her life to not wanting to change a thing." Her situation forced her to use her imagination in ways she wouldn't have otherwise and to believe in impossible possibilities. It made her see the power of the mind and believe in her dreams to live beyond limits. That's where innovation lives. That's where barriers end, imagination ignites, and the story begins. Amy challenges us to push off from our barriers and see what amazing places they might bring us. "If you can see it, you can believe it and you can achieve it" (Purdy 2011).

FIT'S SUPREME NEEDLE MOVER

Forced identity transition lands us in a place where *mindset*—the established set of attitudes held by someone—is everything. We're at a junction where we choose to be victim or striver. Our circumstances do not determine whether we spiral down into despair and stay stuck. Our choice of perspective does.

Humans have only a small modicum of control over what thoughts we think, and we have unlimited capacity to choose how we respond to those thoughts. Mastering change depends on becoming acutely aware of how you think and then leveraging it, like Jane described in chapter 6. This is particularly important for those in FIT.

Leveraging the power of mindset makes all the difference in how much you suffer. When you tell your story with different details—choosing some over others—it changes your experience.

We win if we develop a positive attitude around failure and uncertainty and if we adopt a "fail forward" mindset. Our world is full of unknowns, newness, and loss. This requires the courage to test, experiment, and fail on a massive and holistic scale. Test new beliefs and activities. Make new alliances and relationships. Let go of what no longer serves us. A victim mindset will rob us of the sweetness of life that is both within and beyond our present circumstances. Acknowledging and grieving what happened and how it impacts you is how bold becomers take control of the next chapter of their lives.

Individuals in FIT enter the process on an uneven playing field. Some struggle more than others to leverage the power of choice we have over our thoughts, options, and actions. Even those starting from higher ground face thoughts and beliefs that challenge them to their core. We all are thrust into examining every aspect of our lives.

Grief and loss magnify the challenge to achieve and maintain a positive mindset. The void caused by loss has the power to force even the strongest and most high-functioning individuals to the brink of hopelessness.

In my own case, since my health has continued to be a challenge, I keep my focus on what I can do rather than what I can no longer do. It's a delicate balance between acknowledging reality and my losses and continually bouncing beyond that. When I give my mind free rein, I go down unnecessary rabbit holes, which can be hard to extricate myself from. Psychoemotional energy is better used elsewhere. When I'm forward focused and curious, I find new and exciting opportunities to shape who I'm becoming.

This chapter will help you gain awareness of how you think and why this is of utmost importance. You'll be better able to harness the power of your thinking to benefit more and suffer less from your challenges.

...

Bold Becomer Prompts

1. The boldest version of myself looks like... My highest aspirations for myself are...

2. With this opportunity for change, I'm exploring these three new ideas about who I wish to become...

3. In order to gain more certainty about whether these ideas are dreams I'm willing to chase, I need to take the following first three steps...

4. The following thoughts and beliefs negatively impact my progress toward these dreams... The following new thoughts and beliefs can replace those not serving me...

...

WHY YOU NEED TO KNOW ABOUT MINDSET

In 2006, Stanford professor Carol Dweck published her groundbreaking book, *Mindset: The New Psychology of Success*. Dweck details differences between people with what she calls the *growth mindset* and the *fixed mindset*. These views people adopt for themselves profoundly affect how they lead their lives. These categories are not mutually exclusive. Both can be present at the same time to different degrees and in different areas of our lives. The important thing is to learn to distinguish between the two so we can use the power of choice to adopt a mindset that yields better results (Dweck 2006).

People with a fixed mindset, Dweck explains, believe their basic qualities—intelligence, abilities, and talents—are fixed traits, stable and unchangeable over time. They spend their time documenting their intelligence and talent instead of developing them. They need to prove themselves over and over because if they only have a fixed amount, they want to make sure they're seen as having a healthy dose of it. They fear feeling deficient in these essential characteristics (Dweck 2006).

They also believe talent alone creates success without effort. They generally fear challenge, devalue effort, and are risk aversive because of their need to be seen as smart. In their eyes, intelligence and failure don't belong to the same person (Dweck 2006).

> The problem with a fixed mindset is
> it leaves no room for growth,
> and growth is at the core of FIT.

With a growth mindset, people believe their most basic abilities can be developed through dedication and hard work; brains and talent are just the starting point. Intelligence, abilities, and talents are learnable and capable of improvement through effort (Dweck 2006). This means those with a growth mindset don't shirk frustration and failure, a crucial skill in FIT because of the necessity for the trials and iterations inherent in experimentation.

The growth mindset creates a love of learning and the resilience essential for great accomplishment. Dweck asserts that character grows out of one's mindset, and a growth mindset leads to acting in one's best interest by developing effective strategies. Mindset is the asset behind how people work hard and cope successfully with setbacks. Ability can get you to the top. Character keeps you there (Dweck 2006).

People with the growth mindset are those who love to exercise *personal agency*, even when it requires stretching beyond their ordinary abilities. Personal agency, or having a sense of agency, means having ownership—being the agent—over one's thoughts and actions and therefore having the ability to generate causation. People with a growth mindset sense they can influence their own actions and life circumstances or, more importantly, can gain that ability. This contrasts those who deny or overlook having agency, claiming they're unable to cause or generate specific actions (Dweck 2006).

The way through FIT is learning new things through experimentation, which involves taking risks. Therefore, if you don't already have a growth mindset, it's the first choice to make to take the reins and regain control of your life.

Without a growth mindset,
you are constantly undermined by the belief that
your circumstances control you.

A growth mindset is likely the key element behind those who cope successfully with an unexpected identity loss versus those who linger behind, suffering more than necessary. Amy Purdy had a growth mindset to start with. She could see she had the power to help her parents suffer less. This kept her from the jaws of despair. It also made it possible for her to discover new perspectives about her situation, such as the benefits of choosing her foot size. It gave her what she needed to rebuild her life and become the extraordinary person she might have never become, had the tragic catalytic event not occurred.

A person in FIT is already vulnerable. They're generally deeply questioning who they are and where they fit into the world as well as examining their core value as a human. They're thrown into a position of having to experiment and learn new things they weren't expecting to be facing. Through this process, they make many choices they'd likely never have made and take many risks they'd likely never have taken.

Because FIT forces you to make choices and try things outside of your comfort zone, having a growth mindset is the greatest tool available to navigate this uncharted territory. It makes it possible to take risks and pivot rather than get paralyzed from fear of failure.

THE POWER OF A VOTE

I first learned the power of mindset (and choice) taking biostatistics. It was a course for people getting PhDs in epidemiology, and I hadn't even completed college algebra. Statistics was a requirement for my master's in public health. I was flunking and mad I had to take that class. I was even ready to quit the program over that. A friend, the smartest student I knew, was dropping the course. Who was I to think I could manage it?

In an emergency meeting with my advisor, I told her my predicament. I'd worked years to get to this point and was ready to throw in the towel. I demanded to know why I had to take that class, and to my surprise, she said I didn't. I argued it was a requirement. She told me I'd already completed the requirement with a course I'd taken as an undergrad.

Stunned and not quite yet calming down, I asked, "Then remind me why I'm taking it?" She spoke of our planning session at the start of my program. We'd discussed what I wanted to do with my degree and why I'd chosen an advanced course in statistics. It was because to be a planner in public health, statistics was the language used to convince others to spend money on disease prevention programs.

Leaving that meeting, armed with the knowledge I'd chosen that course versus being forced to take it, I turned my grade from a D+ into a B- and went on to the second semester. That was all because of mindset. The difference between being forced to do something and voting to do it literally changed my reality.

> Mindset gives us a vote.
> It puts us in the driver's seat.
> It activates the power of focusing on
> choice over circumstance.

...

Bold Becomer Prompts

1. On a scale of one to ten, how much do I embrace challenges that come along?

2. Do I tend to fall into victim mode and make excuses for the undesirable aspects of my life, or am I more the type to jump in and embrace challenge? What makes me this way?

3. Do I embrace change and challenge differently when I'm not looking for it, not expecting it, and not wanting it than when I choose it? If yes, how might I harness the skills and mindset I have when choosing change in instances of un-wanted change?

...

NEVER LET ANYONE PUT OUT YOUR SPARK

Source: personal interview.

Three days before leaving Colombia to compete in the world tango competition in Argentina, Diana Giraldo broke up with her boyfriend. Her now ex-boyfriend was also her dance partner. She was so distraught she wasn't talking to him and had decided not to travel.

Diana was born with clubfoot in Cali, Colombia, the salsa dance capital of the world. Dancing is as ubiquitous in Colombian culture as drinking water. In house parties, people of every age—from children to grandparents—dance to the same music.

Apart from salsa and other Latin music, Colombians love tango. From the age of three or four, Diana remembers her father's birthday parties. He was a tango music collector, and his birthday was in the same month as tango's first superstar, Carlos Gardel. Each year her dad's birthday would last almost a week with other collectors and aficionados coming to hear his music.

Like many little girls, Diana dreamed of becoming a classical ballet dancer. From age three or four she told herself she was going to be a champion. She knew she would be great and powerful. But her legs and feet twisted inward, so she had a poor center of gravity affecting her balance. Because of her anatomy, she couldn't do the extreme leg rotations needed for ballet.

Her father supported her dream to dance, and at six, she started her first lessons. They were tango lessons, not so much because she loved tango but because she loved her father and it was a way to be closer to him. Her teacher, Marta Mejía, motivated Diana when she cried because she couldn't do things the way the others did. She accommodated Diana's needs and told her to never let anyone put out her spark. Marta called Diana her "champion" and told her, nonstop:

- "You're going to be great."
- "You're going to attain wonderful things."
- "You're going to triumph and be a champion."

When Diana was ten, she switched to classical ballet. This teacher taunted and degraded her in front of other students and said she was no good and couldn't be a ballet dancer. Because of Diana's persistence, determination, and goal, she endured two and a half years of abuse before she left, traumatized and giving up her childhood dream.

She took some time off and then tried other dance genres, but only tango moved her. So she returned to it when she was fifteen. Tango allowed her to fully express who she was without any predetermined structure. "It has rules, and you can break them."

Twenty-eight years after starting to dance, Diana qualified for the world tango championship in Argentina!

She and her partner, Carlos Paredes, were one of 485 couples who would compete during the two-week competition in front of an audience of ten thousand. But now her partner was her ex-boyfriend. They'd had a huge fight, broken up, and weren't talking to each other. Diana wasn't going to let anyone put out her spark. She'd dreamed of this moment her whole life. It was *her* time. It wouldn't happen again because she was going to retire from competitive dancing. So she put aside her pain and traveled with Carlos to Argentina.

Before their first dance in the semifinals, she told Carlos this was her life and she was going to do it—become a champion. She wasn't going to let anyone kill her dream. She asked him to respect her and share it with her. When it was their turn, they faced each other, hugged, and the moment her feet hit the dance floor, it was magic. She forgot everything and they danced their hearts out. They made it to the finals—one of thirty couples—then to the final five.

During their dance in the final five, Diana broke her big toe and didn't even know it. The energy was so intense, her nerves were on edge, and the crowd roared so loudly she only knew her toe was bleeding. She thought she'd torn her toenail. She made it through the dance, but they all had to dance again to break the tie. She pushed through, again, dancing the extra round on a broken toe.

The judges announced the second and fourth place winners first, and Diana's name wasn't announced. The first, third, and fifth place contestants were on tenterhooks. At that moment, Diana was already satisfied with making it to the final five. "It didn't matter where I placed; being in the top five was champion enough." They announced fifth place, and it wasn't her name.

At that point Diana was *sure* the other couple would win. She was telling the other couple they were going to win. The other couple said no; she and Carlos had been the best and would win.

When third place was announced and it wasn't her, she didn't believe she'd won champion of the world. When they finally announced first place, she repeated the name—Diana Giraldo, world champion—as if she didn't recognize it. She was in a frozen state, feeling so much pressure in her chest she couldn't breathe, and she had to hold on to Carlos because her legs no longer held her up.

As champions, they had to dance yet again. It was the most wonderful feeling ever, despite her toe and not feeling she had control over her body. Colombians from the audience jumped on stage from the crowd to hug them, and two hours later, after all the interviews, over two hundred people waited outside in the middle of winter to applaud and salute them. Diana and Carlos won the highest artistic and professional achievement of their lives. They were world champions! Diana had achieved her dream.

In the face of twenty-eight years of obstacles, Diana maintained a growth mindset.

She understood bullies are everywhere, but she didn't let them stop her. She navigated the emotional obstacle of the failure of her relationship as well as the physical obstacle of a broken toe, and she brought herself back from the brink of destruction.

Nothing could keep her from maintaining her identity: the dancer who would become a champion.

This story could have been in the Courage and Grit chapter, but it's here because behind courage and grit is mindset. The overcoming mindset knows where there's a will there's a way. This mindset allows people to dream big dreams, even seemingly impossible dreams. This mindset isn't afraid to set out toward an audacious goal and make wrong turns along the way. This mindset recognizes we don't all do things at the same rate, or the same way, or even the same things, and that's okay. This mindset embraces growth and change and knows you can figure it out.

KEY TAKEAWAYS

DOS AND DON'TS

- Don't shirk your responsibility to maintain a positive mindset.
- Mindset is a choice. Take responsibility to maintain a growth mindset regardless of upbringing and current circumstances. Be the one choosing your own thoughts through awareness and choice.
- Don't let outdated beliefs and habits run your life.
- Is the glass half empty or half full? Your answer determines your happiness and the opportunities you'll find in life. Your answers are up to you.
- Don't let self-betrayal have the upper hand.
- Self-betrayal is a choice. We're socialized to be considerate and help others. As children we must go against our will frequently to keep the peace and can develop a self-betrayal habit that can last a lifetime. As adults, we can choose to work to balance consideration for others with consideration for ourselves. As an adult, people-pleasing is a choice.
- Don't settle for lost integrity and living incongruently with your truths.
- If something feels bad, do something about it. Be vigilant of unacceptable circumstances and eliminate negative people from your sphere of influence. Avoid naysayers and surround yourself with people who support who you are and where you're headed.
- Don't commit too early to who you are becoming and end up settling.
- You get to choose how to define success. In FIT, success is measured by exploration, effort, and action, not outcomes. This is also how a person with a growth mindset measures

success. In FIT, the goal is to maintain a long enough iteration process so you reach your potential and avoid selling yourself short.

- Don't let lack of clarity and fear of failure keep you stuck.
- It's possible to make decisions without having clarity. In FIT, you're not going to have tons of clarity, yet you must make some moves. With a growth mindset this becomes possible. With a fixed mindset you may remain stuck because of aversion to failure. Failure and pivoting are the name of the game in FIT. Choosing a growth mindset gives you the option to win.
- Don't settle for a fixed mindset.
- Be willing to grow. The growth mindset harnesses opportunity. It recognizes serendipity and rides its waves into new and challenging experiences. Its foundation is built on knowing competence develops confidence, and more confidence creates more competence. This feedback loop fuels growth with the courage needed to overcome immeasurable obstacles in front of your happiness and potential.

RESILIENCE

When you feel you can't, direct your mind to ask:

- "How am I going to get that done?"
- "What's *one* thing I can choose right now?"
- "Is how I'm showing up enough to get what I want?
- "Am I lacking commitment because it's hard and scary or because I'm making an informed decision that I no longer want what I've been going after?"

A POSITIVE, UNEXPECTED IDENTITY LOSS

In my twenties, when my health had crumbled and my body was no longer dependable, my hope for life was tainted. My health problems put a damper on my attitude and outlook. I was demoralized. I'd spent a decade terrified of growing old, with the amount of physical pain I was already experiencing. At thirty, when I started practicing macrobiotics, I had the keys to control my health and my destiny. But having a clear path forward didn't automatically change my predisposition to see the glass as half empty.

I was still an angry and depressed person. My habit of self-loathing I'd developed earlier in life hadn't disappeared. I had horrible, demeaning self-talk. Now I was angry at my body's betrayal, even though I was on the mend. Enduring ten years of chronic pain and fatigue, with no help in sight, had worsened my attitude.

I was still tired all the time. Even eating better, I only improved my energy by fifty percent. I still had chronic joint pain. I complained about my problems incessantly. It wasn't any fun living in my body, and I wasn't fun to be around. I was also a highly critical person. My mom always said my paternal grandmother was the most critical person she'd ever known. My grandma half raised me during early childhood while my mom shuttled between hospitals and doctors' offices keeping my oldest brother alive. From my grandmother and other adverse childhood experiences, negativism was ingrained in me and now my health added to it.

But one evening, in my friend Juan's apartment, my attitude changed on a dime. In the middle of a litany of complaints, probably about how I was being mistreated on my job, among other things, Juan stopped me in my tracks. His exasperated yet not unkind statement "Julie, you are *so* negative!" lodged in my brain like a new set of neurons. It connected with what he'd been teaching me about macrobiotics, which went far beyond dietary choices. Macrobiotics teaches us to take full responsibility for our choices. For the first time, I realized I had the choice to release myself from my negative attitude.

I'd never known my outlook was a choice.
I thought it was a reality-based extension
of my circumstances—a cause and
effect phenomenon.

In that moment I realized I was suffering more than necessary. I realized while many circumstances might not change, I had the choice to be angry or sad about them, or not. That day I chose to stop equating attitude with circumstance. I even had role models to prove this was true—the many Colombians I witnessed accessing joy despite their suffering (see chapter 4).

From that day on I became aware of my language. Awareness became a tool to support my emotions. I took control of my thoughts by listening to and judging the words my mind was saying to me. By policing negative self-talk, I could nip negativity in the bud.

Depending on my self-talk, and what I did with it,
I could choose to feel better or worse.

We can't control our thoughts, but when I paid attention, I could change them. I started choosing not to engage with negative thoughts. When they arose, I'd replace them with something empowering (and often more honest). I stopped taking their invitations to go down rabbit holes.

My reality was still dealing with fatigue and pain. It took time to disengage this physical reality from having free rein over my thoughts. Through being aware of my thinking I worked hard to replace negative thoughts with positive ones. Change didn't happen overnight.

Freedom came with the realization
I didn't have to believe my thoughts.

I could choose to fill my mind with self-serving thoughts. My pattern of self-loathing became diluted with intentional injections of self-compassion. I became a more positive person even while facing unwanted realities. To this day, it still takes work.

I learned how to overlook certain facts and focus on the glass being half full. Before, I would have said that was denial. It's not denial. It's choosing empowering rather than painful perspectives. It's looking reality straight in the face. It's not trying to twist it into something it's not or letting it affect me one nanogram more than it must.

I learned facts and logic don't equal reality.
Choice over one's outlook is a variable that
skews everything.

Macrobiotic principles gave me the freedom to leverage choice over my mindset as well as nutrition. I can still address what I want to change while enjoying the good that's available each day.

That day in Juan's apartment, I started becoming a more emotionally healthy person because I began to see the glass as half full instead of half empty. This is one of the most important things I've ever learned. I have control over how I think.

Now I'm aware of this. When I give up that control and let thoughts live on autopilot, I'm choosing to betray myself. Thought control is my number one tool to nurture self-compassion. It's free. It's always available, and it always works.

MINDSET CHEAT SHEET

✓ Focus on choice over circumstance; acknowledge choice and the power of reframing.

✓ Prioritize self-care.

✓ Bring the future into the present. Think as if what you desire is already done.

✓ Make decisions from that vantage point—act "as if."

✓ Use "I can *now*" affirmations.

✓ Replace "I'm trying to..." or "I'm going to..." with the present tense "I am..."

✓ Replace "should" and "have to" statements with empowering statements:

   – "I could..."
   – "I get to..."
   – "I choose to..." (awareness and choice creates agency)

✓ If, after deep consideration, the above replacements sound untrue, reconsider *why* you're obliging yourself.

✓ Check yourself when you blame. Blame tells your mind you have no power to change. Pivot and see where you can take ownership.

✓ Let go of resentment. Focus on where you can take ownership. This is where your power lies.

✓ Replace "I can't" with more accurate words:

   – "I'm not yet ready."
   – "I don't want to."
   – "I choose not to."
   – "I don't yet have the skills I need."
   – "I don't believe doing that will give me the results I'm after."

✓ Replace judgment with curiosity. Options and solutions emerge from curiosity. Curiosity means you believe in potential.

✓ Be aware of abundance versus scarcity thinking. Challenge yourself to create new, empowering beliefs.

✓ Challenge yourself to entertain options that require sacrifice to change.

✓ Rethink your non-negotiables. Distinguish between what's most important versus what's comfortable and easy.

✓ Determine whether thoughts arise from the well of self-betrayal or self-love.

✓ Practice living in the moment and being fully present. Give your full awareness to that moment rather than the past or future.

✓ Practice gratitude—appreciating what you've been given, what you still have, and the potential that exists.

✓ Celebrate milestones as much as crossing finish lines. Awareness of process versus outcome builds gratitude.

✓ Keep the Serenity Prayer by Reinhold Niebuhr in mind (1943): "God grant me the serenity to accept the things I cannot change, courage to change the things I can, and wisdom to know the difference."

YOU'VE GOT THIS

I honor and respect you for your courage and determination to make this challenging time pay big dividends. When you position your mindset with that expectation, even though you're still slogging through the muck, you're setting yourself up for happiness and success.

CHAPTER 9

Productivity

As much devastation and crumbling of my life, it was also such an amazing rebirth, to rediscover myself, bring color into my life again, and have the freedom to live on my terms.

—LORI LINFORD, LIFE COACH AND
Single and Strong PODCAST HOST

...

Goal: To shift success markers from outcomes to actions taken.

WHEN WHAT YOU DO DOESN'T SUPPORT WHO YOU ARE

Source: personal interview.

Seven and a half years ago, Liz Bonny quit her job when her first child was born and became a stay-at-home mom.

Liz also weaves, and she spins and dyes a lot of her own yarn. She and I were in the Kaw Valley Fiber Guild together. The Guild is a place where knitters, weavers, spinners, dyers, and I, a couturier (designer and maker of fine apparel), gather to support, teach, and have fun with our textile passions.

At one of our meetings, Liz mentioned feeling frustrated and unprepared for motherhood. She felt let down that she hadn't been forewarned about the challenges she would face.

A few years later, after I'd identified my identity loss topic, Liz gave me an interview, and then another one a year later. I wanted to know what about being a mom wasn't working out, how it impacted her identity, and in the second interview, what she'd done to change her situation.

Liz described her transition to motherhood as "shocking" and said it "uprooted" her. She described everything changing so dramatically. Everything was "going out the window," and she didn't know who to talk to about it. She shared that suddenly "everything I was doing was so in the real world... experiencing the immediacy of living... feeding myself and another person. Just living." She couldn't find the answers she needed. She didn't know what parenting advice to follow. She couldn't figure out how to remedy the overwhelm that left her without time and energy to have any life apart from being Mom.

What is this strange new world I'm in,
and where's the guidance?

Liz and her husband had their ideas about how to parent, but with conflicting advice and with the uncertainty of outcomes regardless of methodology, she was confused and frustrated. The more time she spent researching parenting, the more she questioned herself.

What am I doing? Why am I so frustrated? Am I a horrible mom? Am I a horrible person?

This added to her mental stress, almost to a "level of crazy chaos." At this point she was angry she'd had no forewarning or preparation for this role.

Liz's plan was to stay home for the first year and then return to work. But when that time came, her plan no longer made sense. While motherhood was harder than she'd ever imagined, she also couldn't imagine going back to sitting in front of a phone and computer in an office. At the same time, she was asking herself, *What else am I going to do?* because motherhood alone left her wanting.

Around the time Liz had her second child, she shifted her research focus from parenting to fiber arts and joined the Fiber Guild.

"That was a *big* step, deciding to do something for me, outside of being just Mom all the time."

She attended monthly meetings, breastfeeding baby in tow, and that's when I met her. By then, Liz had been home alone raising children for five and a half years and was really struggling. She was desperate to have quiet time—time alone to sit and have her own thoughts and do what she wanted: read and do fiber arts work. But she could never get in the flow with artwork and was overwhelmed living with constant interruptions.

She was also realizing she didn't have to do motherhood the way she'd been told or the way she thought she should do it. She started embracing her individuality as a mother.

She began to regain that missing part of herself— the rest of her—apart from her mother role.

"I just want to be what I would think of as me—to be myself—but there's something being imposed on me, covering up the majority of who I think of myself as being, and I'm constantly questioning how the role of motherhood and I as a person can come together in a way that feels aligned… I can't even have my own thoughts because my kids are always coming at me and throwing me off."

Liz knew her life was unbalanced, and the stress was starting to affect her mental health. She wasn't living the kind of life she wanted. She wanted to support her kids *and* be herself. She needed time to calm down and relax and just have time to be. As she continued to fit time into her life to be herself, she produced more and more art. Every month at our fiber guild meeting during show and tell, she'd share taller and taller stacks of weavings. Impressed and curious, we asked how she managed to produce so much work.

"I'm honestly doing it to survive mentally. It's my mental health practice because without it, I'm not doing well if I don't get that time... All the work I've been doing, it's a terrible indication of how stressed I am. I had to make sure I didn't go into any kind of breakdown mode because to me, mom life is that hard."

Between our first and second interviews, Liz started to chase her dreams. She realized she couldn't go on doing things the way she'd been doing them, being Mom most of the time. The only thing she really wanted was her fiber art, so she took it to the next level. She started selling in art shows and online and teaching. She discovered she loved helping people find answers and sharing what she knew—introducing them to fiber arts and helping them have fun regardless of what it looks like in the end.

Liz wasn't looking for fame or fortune. She was after the process. Nevertheless, she turned her artwork into a business and set up an LLC. That helps her work feel more legitimate and provides boundaries. Instead of "just messing around in my studio, now I'm going to work." Her husband's doing his part by taking on more parenting responsibilities. By turning her work into a business, it's helped her frame it "into a real thing. It's my job."

On top of all this, the pandemic helped Liz find things she could let go of to create better balance, things she could let slide like house cleaning and some of the home cooking. She's even only doing some of what she could with her social media around her business: "I'm putting my energy in other places." She's allowing priorities to be fluid. She's also helping other moms "not get completely taken over by other people's needs and eaten alive from endless nurturing."

REDEFINING PRODUCTIVITY

Our job in liminality is to figure out where we are, what our new role is in the moment, and how to manage it—not where we're going to end up because we're in virgin territory and our destination is yet to be discovered. During this time new rules apply to productivity. It's no longer about milestones and outcomes. It's less about setting goals and more about exploring where we are and where we wish to go. The traditional definition of productivity—getting things done and producing predetermined outcomes—isn't what will best guide us now.

> FIT requires letting go of the old way
> of judging productivity and putting in time
> to explore, experiment, and pivot.

This is what qualifies as productivity while in liminality. If we keep the old standards in place, we won't have the breakthroughs we need to master change. It's important to have a new way to view what taking action means. In the context of FIT, action might be sleeping, crying, or any number of things specific to turning our world right side up again. We're used to equating action with work and productivity, and attaching our self-worth to it. In fact, our worth is dependent on neither action nor work nor productivity. This is a welcome, and often surprising, truth bold becomers discover, one of many gifts from FIT.

When you're able to let go of the way you generally judge progress and success and embrace boldly becoming, you're on track to discovering things you've never imagined. You're heading toward an unexpected and treasured version of yourself. Through harnessing hardship you learn otherwise out of reach, valuable lessons. Hardship gives you the opportunity to emerge as the person you were designed to be. At the end of the dark tunnel of liminality, some are even grateful for the journey. Hardship prepares you for a meaningful and fulfilling life unlike anything you'd ever envisioned.

People in FIT struggle with productivity because they're measuring against everyday standards. But they're in limbo and don't even know what goal posts they're heading toward. So they don't know what to measure and often feel like they're going around in circles.

They're also pivoting a lot. They might not want to explore and experiment and pivot. This can feel like failure. They're not always convinced this is integral to healing, growth, and success. And with lack of clarity, because of ambiguity and disorientation, their confidence is down. It's hard to feel confident when you don't know what you need to do, where you're headed, or how to get there.

Later in this chapter my story tells how I took a long time to adjust productivity expectations. Without that, I suffered more than necessary. I wasn't able to feel good about my progress. When I finally came to understand taking next right steps was all the success I was going to get, I began to honor the struggle. As a person with two master's degrees in planning I could let go of frustration over not being in control of the process and focus on gratitude for what I had in the moment.

The goal of this chapter is to replace your definition of productivity and success with different expectations by:

- Measuring process (actions taken, changes in thinking) regardless of outcomes;

- Helping you become comfortable with iteration;

- Guiding you to lower your expectation that you can plan your way out of this;

- Asking you to trust that next steps will reveal themselves, but only a few at a time; and

- Seeing that your main job is to make it through each day by taking next right steps without knowing exactly where you're headed. *That* is productivity and success. Take, for example, Liz (chapter 18), who started measuring success by whether she could get a smile on her son's face after he came down with schizophrenia.

...

Bold Becomer Prompts

1. Where can I change the focus in my narrative to tell a more empowering story?

2. What do I need to believe to trust that pivoting and iteration are successes rather than failures? Even if I cannot yet connect the dots, how can I allow myself to trust the process?

3. How can I put aside my previous goals and focus on self-care, including processing grief, as a top priority?

...

PRODUCTIVITY DURING FIT

After the initial shock of the inciting incident that plunged us into FIT, it's expected that we're in a hurry to get back to normal. But it's in our best interest to fight this urge to rush the process because we may end up settling.

Grief expert Jill Johnson-Young uses the term "grief card" (Browne 2022). This is where we get to do whatever we want, dream whatever we've held back from dreaming, explore with curiosity and delight, like children, and follow the whims life presents us. Later, many of us see our transition process as a gift. When it happens, we rarely wish it had happened. Yet what comes out of it can be hugely positive and something we could never have imagined.

During this transition, if we measure our day-to-day productivity differently, we'll have a better experience. We can measure it by:

- Generating new options;
- Leveraging new perspectives; and
- Finding purpose in suffering.

In the throes of FIT, productivity's a different animal. So you need to treat it and think of it differently because you're in a metamorphous and many things are unrecognizable. It's not about how much you get done or how well you do it. Even messy, "incomplete" work has power and value. It's all adding up and making sense, but you probably won't see it without a bit of retrospect.

As the creative process unfolds, dots that seem random start to connect. Somewhere along the way, you'll start to feel a flow and a sense that everything's adding up to become something that matters. Gifts and surprises beyond your wildest dreams await you. Allowing for pivots is how you avoid premature commitment. The moving goal posts might seem like you're looking at a mirage. This is normal.

The essence of mastering change
is embracing the reality of living in a fluid state.

It invites you to you summon, trust, and act upon your intuition and have faith that next steps will appear at the right time and not beforehand.

You will cultivate the stability and trust you need for these new approaches to productivity when you keep up a good self-care practice (see chapter 7) and control your mindset (see chapter 8).

Productivity for bold becomers is about pull, not push. It's about allowing desire and serendipity and vagueness to pull your future toward you—a future based on creating the feelings you desire versus a concrete vision of what will exist. Allow for what is in the moment, instead of powering through and pushing toward a predetermined destination. This is the creative process. It doesn't fit neatly into normal productivity standards and measurements.

How do we measure productivity and progress with a different measuring stick? We measure things like:

- Did I schedule my time?

- Did I show up and do what I intended in those blocks of time?

- How am I reducing distraction?

- How well have I implemented my self-care routines?

- Even though I don't feel like I'm making progress, am I trusting that I am?

- Am I trusting the process of life?

- How well am I managing the rate at which next steps are revealed?

- Do I really believe next steps will be revealed on the right timeline?

- How well am I making the most of each of these steps?

- Am I treating them as the gifts that they are, or am I side-stepping them, thinking I know better?

- Do I believe logic trumps intuition and serendipity?

- Am I limiting my decisions based on sunk costs?

- Or am I ignoring sunk costs and making decisions based on the present and future?

- Am I accepting, understanding, and integrating all I'm learning?

- Am I leveraging my struggle or resenting it?

- Am I open to receiving and relishing my precious life just as it unfolds?

- Or am I hellbent on defining success on my own terms, ignoring or downplaying what some might interpret as divine intervention?

- Am I letting circumstances define who I am?

- Or am I making the most of my circumstances by choosing how to interpret them and what to do with them?

- Am I rewriting my life's narratives to serve me?

- Or am I stuck on old narratives created by myself and others and integrated into my psyche?

These process questions are how bold becomers harness challenge. Rather than setting outcome goals, we confront outdated beliefs. We eliminate beliefs and activities that no longer fit with who we are becoming. This is how to master change and find treasure in the challenge.

...

Bold Becomer Prompts

1. What do I need to let go of measuring for the time being?

2. What beliefs do I need to change to trust those next steps that reveal themselves are the right ones to follow?

3. What is my greatest fear creating distraction from taking those next right steps?

...

SORTING OUT HER GARBAGE LED TO A REBIRTH

Source: personal interview.

Up until her marriage failed, Lori Linford spent her life wearing a mask of perfection. She was an overachiever. She succeeded at anything she did. Lori was a pro at knowing how to make things happen. A strategist, she calculated success probabilities and then reverse-engineered how to achieve those which guaranteed success. Evaluate, plan, implement, and succeed was how she lived.

She'd always been an overachiever—skipping from fifth to seventh grade, being a top athlete and team leader. Everything she decided to do she checked off the list: college, marriage, kids. She only did things she knew she'd succeed at.

But when she divorced, after discovering her husband's affair, she was faced with the novelty of failure.

She managed the hard days the only way she knew how—by winning. She won her mindset. She'd tell herself, *You can lie in bed for one hour and cry and feel sorry for yourself. But after that hour, you have to get back up and do something.* She wasn't going to allow herself to "get stuck in the darkness." She wasn't going to "let pain swallow" her. To allow for this she changed her success standards.

She threw off the mask of perfection and started
measuring her life on a completely different scale,
one that didn't leave out any variables.

One day, staring in the mirror, she realized she had no idea of who she was. So she set different goals based on one question: *Who do I really want to be?*

"I brought all my garbage out and spread it on the table to sort it out." Through therapy, self-help books, coaching, listening to podcasts, and sharing with friends, Lori began to see that who she was and what happened to her were separate. She learned her story was part of her but did not define her. She started releasing shame and revealing secrets as she let go of living to uphold an image. Lori found out what living for *her* looked like.

"That's how I got through this, by facing my truth, and then I could see what I wanted and needed in my life."

Lori stopped changing her "whole world to make everything work for everybody else." She stopped living for everyone else but herself. She started living on her own terms. She stopped planning things out. She found joy in the moment, regardless of outcomes.

Doing, rather than achieving,
became her new success measurement
and the reward was freedom.

Lori approached her new life—her rebirth, the gift from that devastation—as a sovereign woman who knew her truth, spoke her truth, and lived her truth. She shifted her understanding of what was important. She put that chapter behind her and based every decision on her own needs and desires.

For an overachiever, pivoting what success looked like was huge. Her to-do list and goals looked like a foreign language compared to before.

While she still had parenting and work roles to uphold, everything was tinged with a new value because adding herself to the equation shifted the balance. She now measured success by happiness and connection with those she loved, not looking good in the eyes of others.

Divorce forced Lori to find new perspectives and let go of previous definitions of success. She found that putting herself first wasn't selfish. She learned how to stay true to herself and trust her only job right then was to keep putting one foot ahead of the other. By letting go of control through planning, she allowed life to flow on its own terms. She learned a pivot is not a failure. Most importantly, Lori took the time and steps needed to heal and support the person inside who'd never had a chance to blossom.

KEY TAKEAWAYS

DOS AND DON'TS

- Don't hold yourself to the same productivity standards as usual.
- Allow your mind to shift with your world. Find out what matters most now that things have changed. Let your beliefs, values, desires, and aspirations evolve.

- Don't let fear of the unknown keep you from making decisions.
- If you make decisions without adequate information, you get unstuck sooner and suffer less. Once you see something's not for you, allow yourself to let go of it. Testing something out and changing your mind is not failing; it's required.
- Don't judge success on outcomes achieved.
- Judge success on consistency in taking action.
- Don't expect this process to happen as fast as you'd like.
- Transformation takes time. To gain new skills, put growth into your schedule to systematically and consistently figure which beliefs and roles fit and which do not. This includes scheduling downtime, where you're purposely *not* taking action.
- Don't worry if it feels like you're just spinning your wheels.
- Progress and growth happen over time, often silently and invisibly. Pay attention to your intuition and follow its lead, even when sometimes it feels like you're going backward.

RESILIENCE

Keep in mind the hallmarks of FIT—ambiguity and disorientation. This throws a monkey wrench into productivity. Even when you think you've gotten things figured out, you'll continue to pivot unless you settle. Be on the lookout for self-betrayal habits that tempt you to settle. Replace these with self-compassion and remember that action, not outcome, is what counts.

A PENCIL TOOK ME OUT

I read it in the local paper. A worker in Berkeley, after someone robbed her bank, quit to follow her dream. Mortality motivation gave her the courage to let loose and start the sewing business she'd always dreamed of. In the picture you could see all the colors of thread on the wall behind her. A crisis moment connected her head with her heart, and she took a gamble.

When I read that article, I'd recently lost my social work career. At 5:30 p.m. on December 29, my hand seized up writing notes in the middle of a client interview. Taken out by a pencil, a repetitive stress injury left me disabled, no longer able to write, type, click, or drag. Productivity as I knew it ended. Getting paid to contribute was how I defined my value. It was what I equated to productivity.

I was nine months out of work and in doctor and physical therapy appointments. Dr. Searcy said, in a casual, upbeat way, "Julie, just let yourself dream of what you'd really love to do."

Dr. Searcy's comment signaled her belief that I wouldn't be returning to my job. It confirmed my fear: *I had a new chronic pain problem, one that would severely limit options for financial independence.*

I needed a new career and had just one shot with my vocational rehabilitation training money. In shock and unable to think straight, I *had* to figure out a plan. But with what? What can you do without use of your dominant hand?

All my years of study went down the drain. So many things hurt my hand, I couldn't even be a grocery store clerk or receptionist. Feeling like I was blindfolded and in a straitjacket, fear invaded every moment.

I was inside the front gate of an uninvited and foreign next chapter of my life.

The worst part of any day was the question, "So what do *you* do?" My answer—"I'm on disability"—caused me to feel unprotected and unworthy. It left me managing the judgments a person with an invisible disability must endure. My goal was to have an answer that pleased both me and others, stat. I couldn't stand feeling like my life wasn't adding up to anything more than staying at home taking care of myself.

Until losing my career, I'd never realized the degree to which my self-worth was tied to it. As a social worker I'd discovered a limitless well of empathy and a use for it through my therapeutic voice. I'd gained mastery in my field. My clients trusted me with their stories. Every day I made a difference in the world. I answered that "What do you do?" question with pride.

Now here I was, a forty-one-year-old single mom with two master's degrees, who'd been working two jobs in my field to make ends meet, and I couldn't work. Anywhere.

I was disoriented, terrified, and at a loss because hoping for recovery was unrealistic. In my twenties I'd accumulated a litany of body parts that never stopped hurting once they started to. So I didn't have reason to think this new one would be different.

While my life was pending, I became depressed and judgmental about not being a productive member of society. I felt like, since I was "only" taking care of myself and my son, I didn't have the same value as when I was working outside the home. I even felt guilty having time to get enough sleep. I especially felt inadequate and horrible when nosy people questioned the validity of my disability. My situation was complicated in so many ways. Fortunately, my doctors trusted and understood me.

With the judgment of others and my own desire to make more of my life, I had a hard time accepting the need for disability retirement. I felt like a failure. But the reality was that disability caused loss of control over my independence I'd worked so hard to attain. It shut me out of every future professional career I could imagine. I still had so many skills, but now they were locked inside of me with no outlet, no way to make a difference in the world. I couldn't see the value of my existence. I no longer measured up.

It was back-to-school time in August when a part of me broke away from depression and fear. I came alive again when I took some fashion design classes at the community college. A passion I didn't know still existed reignited in full force. Much of this work used different, relatively pain-free hand movements, and I had unbridled desire to learn all I could. When I was a high school exchange student in Colombia, South America, I'd spent six months in heaven, immersed twelve hours a day in sewing school. But back in the US, unable to find a path forward with sewing, I gave it up for a "real career."

Now having lost my "real career," these classes set me on a trajectory to build a custom clothing business. Then, through pure serendipity, I found the perfect private teacher to get me there, Simmon, who taught haute couture patternmaking and sewing. But I'm a severe pragmatist. I'm a planner. I do assessments, analyze data, project risk, and then reverse-engineer viable strategic plans. This plan had *no* predictability or viability.

Client acquisition would be like finding a needle in a haystack. I lived in the wrong era for this vocation. Ready-to-wear was selling at rock-bottom prices and lasting quality, a hallmark of haute couture, was no longer a valued feature.

Nor did this plan reconcile with who I'd become. I was a specialist helping those with the least access to resources and personal agency, a humanitarian.

I was torn. Did I go with what's squarely in my lap, which included certain uncertainty? Or did I seek a practical plan, and one with at least a sliver of humanitarianism?

Trusting in something higher than logic,
I chose a fling. I followed my heart instead
of my head.

Temptation to study with Simmon was legions beyond rational control. Like the woman in the paper, I chose to live with the consequences of my choice rather than betray my heart. I leaned in. I learned design, patternmaking, sewing, fitting, and then marketing as well as how to run a luxury price point business.

But my journey was long and blustery. It was a series of iterations from one product and market to another. People around me got tired of me changing my mind. I felt discouraged. I wanted to make daywear and career wear versus formalwear. I could make jeans that fit, women's suits, and men's bespoke jackets. (I went back to Colombia to learn men's jackets.) I had a niche idea of making button-down blouses for hard to fit women. What I really wanted was to dress women leaders I admired. I even wrote a book about leveraging personal image to support your message.

But an inner voice kept telling me that *I* wanted to be one of those women making an impact, not the couturier. By now I'd figured out that while sewing is a passion, it wasn't my purpose. My destiny with Simmon was only a stopgap measure. In the end, I never connected with a market.

Toward the end, shortly before throwing in the towel, I met Dara Lamb in New York City. Doing exactly what I wanted, charging eight thousand dollars for a woman's suit, she validated my experience.

"Everything about it is hard and stays hard," she said, "from design, to sewing, to pricing, to client acquisition."

> During that entire life chapter, I felt like a failure because I was only measuring myself against a monetary yardstick.

I wasn't making money. Therefore, what I was doing didn't count toward answering the "what do you do?" question "properly."

And over time, something else became clear. This chapter was actually only about getting me to first base, and every chapter isn't about external measures of success. This chapter was there to hold me over. It kept me from the jaws of despair, keeping me going long enough to connect with what would come next and fit much better.

I learned that having value and being productive was so much more than getting paid or earning a living. That deep, sustained connection with pleasure was a different form of productivity. It had inherent value.

As I continued to feel ashamed, each time I answered the "what do you do?" question, I began to cancel out that shame. I redefined and expanded what being human really means. I redefined what needs to be included on to-do checklists. I came to embrace how life makes its own terms for each individual. Our job is to take what it gives us and figure out what it all means.

Productivity in FIT is about sifting out who you are and who you are not, who you will become and who you will no longer tolerate being. It's where you use creativity, intuition, and intentions in a self-realization process. Who do you need to step into *being* so you can be confident in doing what you choose to do? How do you do this?

Step 1

- Shift priorities: What's important now is different than what used to be important. Be willing to let go of beliefs, activities, and goals not needed in this moment.

Step 2

- Focus on what is instead of:
  - What you wish it were;
  - What you expected it to be;
  - What it could have been;
  - What it should be; or
  - What it could be.

Step 3

- Lower expectations: Match expectations with what's in the moment. Don't try to twist reality into something it's not.
  - Acknowledge loss.
  - Accept reality.
  - Maintain hope.

Step 4

- Step into new roles:

    - Identify new things you want now that you're forced to see things with a new perspective.

    - Do things outside your comfort zone so you can make informed decisions.

    - Stop doing things that no longer serve you.

Step 5

- Assimilate loss and growth as you allow yourself to step into new roles and create a new identity. Allow time for the creative process to unfold and produce a full metamorphous.

YOU'VE GOT THIS

Grief and growth require time, patience, intention, and action. Masters of change understand that to have the courage to change, self-care is their number-one productivity measurement. They double down on sleep, nutrition, exercise, and joyful and soothing activities. They understand others may be confused and concerned about their choices and release the need for external validation. They know only they can cheerlead themselves into the new version of themselves.

CHAPTER 10

Support

*I was trying to bury who I was under a persona I thought
would make me more lovable.*

—THOMAS H. EDWARDS, JR., AUTHOR, PLAYFULNESS
COACH, AND MEN'S RELATIONSHIP COACH

...

Goal: Ensure you have the right people to lean on.

THOMAS'S HEALING TRIFECTA: FEEDBACK, FELLOWSHIP, AND PROFESSIONALS

Source: personal interview.

Thomas Edwards, Jr. had international success as a professional wingman helping others find love. Suddenly, he found *he* was unhappy and lonely. He had to understand he needed support before he could ask for it himself.

At the peak of success, at an afterparty following a televised interview with Steve Harvey, Thomas had a panic attack and realized he wasn't happy. "Celebrating being one of the best in the world at what I do, something strange happened."

Restless, sweating, and short of breath, Thomas felt a profound sense of emptiness and a lack of fulfillment. He didn't realize he was lonely. "I was trying to bury who I was under a persona that I thought would make me more lovable." Not knowing how to handle these emotions, he was scared.

He realized this version of success wasn't his, and he wasn't going to keep living someone else's dream. Being a wingman wasn't who he was, but he didn't know what else to do.

Without answers to solve his unhappiness, Thomas started staying out late and drinking more. He added drugs to enhance the drinking, which no longer "did the trick" on its own. His marriage began to suffer, but he "didn't have the tools or resources or places to go to figure this stuff out."

Still working as a wingman, he didn't know who he really was. He stopped caring about his work and lived on autopilot. He needed to learn how to identify his emotions, find a safe place to express them, and get some feedback and guidance on how to talk about and reflect on them.

In the middle of this turbulent time, Thomas found out he was going to be a father. "I lost my shit when my wife told me she was pregnant," he says, calling it "the best worst day of my life." He wanted to be a dad, but in his mind that was incompatible with being a wingman. It meant he was done.

"Fathers aren't wingmen because wingmen need to be cool, hanging out with people, and dads need to be home."

His behavior went from bad to worse, continuing into the first year of his daughter's life. His wife tried everything until she announced, "This is not the marriage I want to be in. Something needs to change."

"That's when I took a hard look at myself and decided I needed help because I didn't have the tools to get myself out of that situation."

This was the first time he ever asked for help. Thomas's parents taught him not to ask for help and to do everything himself. Now, he went all in with help because he wasn't going to lose his marriage. He had a personal therapist, couples' therapist, addiction doctor, and a coach. He did leadership weekends, spiritual retreats, recovery programs, and brotherhood groups.

In therapy, he learned being a wingman had become "an escape hatch" from dealing with his feelings and finding true happiness. It kept him in a holding pattern. That identity kept him safe from the parts of life he didn't know how to handle—his emotions.

He got better incrementally and had backslides. He was still working as a wingman and didn't have an exit plan. His wife got really good at maintaining boundaries, not letting him in when he came home late. He had a couple of blackouts over a period of two days, and his wife held the boundary.

In a hotel room, blacked out, Thomas's higher power said, "You're done. You've had enough." And on January 14, that obsession to escape his feelings with alcohol was gone.

Thomas returned to his recovery program he'd left behind, tapped into his spirituality, and became unrecognizable. He realized he had a higher power that was better than his own will, and he didn't need "to be so in control of [his] life." He felt protected and he understood the universe had him here for a particular purpose.

Things he'd learned from his support team clicked in a different way. He now understood drinking was escapism from the emotions he couldn't handle. That desire to escape went away, and his drinking friends stopped calling.

As he worked the program, stayed sober, and incrementally got better, he felt strange and didn't know why. He realized he wasn't enjoying life. He wasn't having fun. He was still living out of obligation.

He allowed himself to spend ninety days finding out what fun looked like to him. With the first video game controller back in his hand since college, "an electric charge went through [his] body, like [he] went through a portal back to when [he] was thirteen and experiencing pure joy."

Thomas iterated on his newfound joy. He pulled from his professional experience as a wingman and from what he learned from his support team and combined it with what he learned about connecting with joy. He invented a business as a playfulness coach. His methodology is in his forthcoming book, *The 1up Effect*, and his latest venture is helping men save their marriages.

LIVING BY DESIGN RATHER THAN DEFAULT

Among the many losses FIT causes are relationships. You are no longer who you were. You're not going to get back to being that same person. You, and those close to you, are impatient for you to arrive at the new version of yourself.

The process of boldly becoming gives you chances to make different decisions than you previously might have made. This makes some people uncomfortable, so they stop showing up. Others may stick around and become obstacles to your growth, and you'll have a choice to let go of them. At the same time, unexpected new relationships provide tremendous value. Those who journey with us are fundamental to our transformation, even those chance and fleeting encounters. Dr. Ibarra's work on networks—"the company we keep"—reveals their monumental impact in our lives. Especially during an identity transition, "kindred spirits" are essential (Ibarra 2017).

We understand ourselves in relationship with
others. Our support systems help make self-
realization possible and give it purpose.

When we allow for the ebb and flow of relationships during
our time in liminality, we can be free to become who we are
becoming. When we seek the help we need, from traditional
and even what others may consider off-the-wall options, we
leverage our situation. We have unexpected breakthroughs, and
serendipity finds a way to deliver its goods. Solitude and going
within to hear and understand ourselves is half the work. The
other half is allowing others to help facilitate transformation.

Maintaining adequate support is critical, but many have
weak or inadequate support systems or they may not know
how to deepen and enliven valued relationships. Some people
disappear when times get tough.

People in FIT may try to hold on to what they have at
any cost. They may resist letting go of those holding them
back. They've already lost so much because of the catalytic
event and want to prevent more loss. They may fear they'll
find themselves alone when the opposite tends to happen.

When we let go of someone or something,
it opens space for something new and sometimes
better to enter.

Letting go can look like saying "no" more often and having
and maintaining boundaries. It can include stopping interacting with people and situations you deem unsafe. Letting go
basically means to stop doing one set of behaviors and start
doing something else.

I adjust my support system as new chapters of my life
create new struggles and realities. Allowing for fluidity in my
support system makes it possible to find answers I might not

otherwise find. This is where serendipity shows up. Through conversations I discover and explore options I would never find or consider on my own. Only in retrospect do I know which conversations were instrumental to my growth and healing. Therefore, each is as important as the next.

It's okay not to be okay. It's okay to ask for help. The purpose of this chapter is to help you think more expansively about support. You will become more aware of your relational patterns, and necessary shifts—seeking the help you need *and* letting go of what no longer serves you—will become more likely and timely.

Bold becomers explore and experiment with things that make sense in the moment. They're willing to break with tradition and habits. They take decisive, consistent action and are first and foremost beholden to themselves.

. . .

Bold Becomer Prompts

1. Which connections no longer serve me? (Indications include feeling worse rather than better after encounters with them, drained, criticized, belittled, undermined, ignored.)

2. What kind of support helped in the past that I'm not getting/using now?

3. What defines a beneficial relationship that gives me what I need? What am I doing to improve and deepen these relationships? Have I shared what my ideal relationship looks like with each person?

. . .

WHAT IS SOCIAL SUPPORT?

A *social support system* refers to a network of people—friends, family, and peers—that we turn to for emotional and practical support that provides us with a sense of security. As discussed on the University of Buffalo School of Social Work website (2022), those with robust social support benefit in many ways. They:

- Have better health;
- Live longer lives;
- Report higher well-being; and
- Are more resilient in times of stress, setback, or loss.

Social support also:

- Makes the good times even better;
- Helps you identify when you are stressed or distressed. In some cases, friends notice before you do. This may be particularly true in the case of depression;
- Provides you with information, advice, guidance, and tangible support;
- Bolsters you emotionally when you're feeling down or overwhelmed by listening to your fears, hopes, and dreams, and make you feel seen and understood;
- Helps you think through alternatives, solve problems, and distract from your worries when needed;
- Provides encouragement and lowers your stress and feelings of loneliness.

In FIT, all the above is needed more than ever. Masters of change often add professionals and others who help in specific and highly skilled ways that laypeople cannot. Ultimately, they rely on their intuition and trust the creative process to piece things together on its own timeline, in its own fickle way.

COMPANY AS WE JOURNEY

As hard as your transition process is for you, it's also hard for those around you. They don't like to see you suffer. But the truth is you, and you alone, hold the answers to piece everything together to fully align and live on purpose. Other people's help can only get you so far.

> FIT is a powerful time when, regardless of fear, logic, or best-laid plans, our instincts are pulling us back home to who we really are, who we've always been but strayed away from, and who we need to be.

FIT is a nonlinear process requiring patience and faith in the intelligence of life. Others belong on this path with us, and it can be a time of awkwardness as social networks change and evolve. Some of our connections will walk away. It might be because our situation makes them uncomfortable or we're no longer fun to be around. They may or may not return. We can keep the door open, or not, for choosing to return.

For others it will be frustrating as heck, and they'll hang in there with us even if it means by their fingernails. My amazing friend Diane is determined to keep up with me. She's never faltered. Each time we catch up it takes all her mental power to keep straight what version of my multitude of plans I'm working on. She's resigned to my life of pivots. She goes with the flow, respecting my intelligence and supporting my decisions. She challenges me when necessary and always supports my decisions.

Others seem to appear from nowhere—the right person at the right time—strategically placed on our path. It's as if a certain homing instinct brings us perfect, new connections to solve specific problems, like Simmon (chapter 9), Herminia Ibarra validating my experience by putting words to it, and

Brendon giving me the words "thought leader." And a chance encounter with a man resulted in me realizing my superpower is courage—something so easy I don't even see it and wonder why others struggle with it.

It's critical to discuss our journey with others—not to get their thoughts and opinions but rather to gain perspective from hearing ourselves.

The sacred job of our allies lies not in
serving as sounding boards but as witnesses
like Diane, stalwart observers supporting
our agency and protecting our sovereignty.

It will be a spectrum of less to more involved and supportive people. If we allow for grace, each person will have a chance to do their part.

At the same time, this is a chance to cull. In his book *The Charge* (2012, 129), Brendon Burchard talks about releasing the friends you no longer wish to keep in contact with—those who don't add much joy to your life and with whom it's not feasible to raise to a standard that serves you, and as Brendon posted on Instagram, "those who are consistently angry, drama-driven, and selfish" (12/4/22).

Brendon goes on to describe (2012, 126) that the quality of our immediate friendships (versus family or intimate) is one of the most important factors in determining our overall:

- Stability
- Mood
- Ambition
- Emotional range
- Growth
- Satisfaction in life

As we search to clarify and reach our future destination, it is a time to fully and frequently commune with ourselves. We're asked to listen to all voices within us and feel all feelings in order to sort them out and to process our grief and fully engage with what's left of our possibilities. In these times of self-reflection and acknowledgment, we reconcile what may feel like the futility of our efforts.

Often, the journey feels like it's either not getting us anywhere or we're going backward. FIT is different from what we're used to. It invites us to move from a place of constant motion, spurred by the painful desire to regain stability and certainty as fast as possible and to choose stillness, repeatedly, as we continually pause to evaluate and pivot. We heed our heart and inner wisdom. It's a time for being in the present instead of racing toward the future. This is a time to shed all we know so we may learn anew who we are and who we are destined to be.

FIT is a wild, internal journey. It's where heart, mind, inner truths, and loneliness coexist. When we take time and make the effort to bear witness to all of that, clarity around who we need to become emerges.

> Self-discovery requires a fierce independence
> in connection with others.

It's a delicate balance of knowing, speaking, and finding ways to live our truth while seeking, allowing, and using support from others, including the spirit world.

It's about both seeking and allowing others to influence our lives while measuring and acting on how that support impacts us. If support strengthens our personal agency and leaves us with a positive mood, it's the kind of support we need.

But if we follow advice from others yet their ideas don't resonate with us, it's an indication we should not invest in those ideas. Now's the time to trust those inner whispers like our life depends on it. People generally have good intentions, and their advice might be sound for *us*. They don't know our soul's code. They only see the tip of the iceberg. They don't know what we're built to do. We, alone, discover that.

SUPPORT WEARS MANY HATS

Support comes in many forms. In my own experience and that of the people I interview, it comes from God, family, friends, strangers, down to the last person you'd expect, like Lena Cebula's bodyguard whose job was to keep her captive as a sex slave but connected her to God and eventually helped free her (chapter 7).

Support can be a double-edged sword. It can help as much as it can harm. It can facilitate a swifter, easier journey or delay and derail us. This is why, when we're in our most vulnerable moments, we must always be the supervisor of those connected to our destiny. It's why, when we raise our hand to seek and accept help, we must also be the one to astutely evaluate its efficacy and take decisive action based on that information.

Support is often cloaked in unlikely steps forward that only make sense in retrospect. Also bombshell connections give you exactly what you need when you need it, which allows you to make huge leaps forward. An example is Leia Baez (story below) who, during my podcast interview with her, connected me to the book program that enabled me to write the words you're reading right now.

> Relationships and dollops of serendipity are
> the ingredients of a robust support system.

Adding intentionality and sharpening awareness of what we need and don't need facilitates the transition process. It can soften the blow from the catalytic event. It can flip a painful journey into one filled with eager anticipation and willful engagement, one where we honor the struggle.

...

Bold Becomer Prompts

1. When in the past have I found unexpected support that turned out to be an inflection point? What did I do to make the most of that opportunity?

2. What kind of help do I need right now that I'm not getting? What can I do to get it? When will I do this?

3. What potential am I overlooking right now? What decisions might I make to ensure I don't leave potential on the table?

...

WHEN TRAGEDY TURNS YOU INTO SOMEONE UNIMAGINABLE

Source: personal interview.

Leia Baez transformed tragedy into triumph by leaning on her support system, including her relationship with God and seeking professional support.

When she was five, she was sexually abused by a distant family relative. When she was thirteen, she learned about inappropriate touch, realized she'd been abused, and disclosed it to her mom.

By then, the man was dead. Her distraught parents asked if she was okay and if she needed anything. Nobody talked about getting therapy. In her culture as a Latina living in the US, "You're taught to be strong, pick your own self up, believe therapy's not for us, and just keep going at all costs."

Because of this, "Sometimes you won't even recognize when you have a problem." After her disclosure Leia started drinking to cope.

Always the life of the party, she was a straight-A student chasing ambitious dreams. But later in college, she "amped up" her drinking to cope with an abusive boyfriend. Her self-worth and mental health plummeted.

> She lost the confident, independent, courageous, strong-minded woman she really was.

"I just felt like crap all the time, yet I stayed. I drank to deal with the emotions from this terrible, abusive, narcissistic relationship."

She knew she wasn't herself anymore. Her parents told her to get away from him. She still loved him and, instead, stayed away from her parents.

By that time, he'd moved from "dabbling in cocaine to meth, and then things went crazy for [them]." On days when he was sober, he'd promise to get help and beg her not to leave him. Leia's self-worth hit rock bottom with his continued abuse and false promises. Right as she graduated from college, she called the police over a domestic violence incident. With him in jail, she finally kicked him out of her apartment.

After graduation she met her husband. They drank and partied together, argued a lot, and both knew alcohol was a problem. A bit jealous and controlling, he didn't support her ambitions. She wanted to get higher paying jobs and loved to work late and mingle at social networking events. He wanted her to be a stay-at-home mom, cooking and cleaning. Tension got worse after their daughter, Stella, was born because Leia started drinking more. They divorced when Stella was five, after a monumental crisis connected to her drinking.

Leia wanted to stop drinking. "Unfortunately, I didn't before a really tragic night and I lost my marriage and custody of my daughter."

> That forced her to reevaluate her life, habits, and the kind of role model she wanted to be for her daughter.

At the time of her separation, Leia started suffering from anxiety and having flashback nightmares from the childhood sexual abuse. Her daughter was now the same age as when she was abused, but Leia no longer had full control over where her daughter was or whom she was with.

"I knew the trauma was still lingering inside me because I could hardly sleep at night, and sometimes I'd wake up in a cold sweat." Fortunately, she had professional support from a therapist. In therapy Leia discovered her drinking was connected to early childhood trauma—the sexual abuse that had never been properly acknowledged or processed.

Now during the darkest moments of her life, she was thirty, divorced, and sleeping in her childhood bedroom. Trauma explained why she used alcohol and drugs to numb her pain. But it didn't give answers about how to quit. And all the while her physical health was deteriorating. Trying to cure hangovers, she'd eat poorly, which would make her feel worse.

During this time her parents were her backbone. They gave her a place to stay and helped her juggle single parenting. Her friend Maggie remained stalwart through the contentious divorce. She provided a calming presence with a nonjudgmental ear while rumors circulated on social media.

Still a successful professional—an award-winning journalist—but "now a defeated mom," Leia stared at the plastic glow-in-the-dark stars she'd put on the ceiling as a little girl. The light from those stars reconnected her with the hope each had represented. She realized how her choices and behavior were impacting not just her but those around her.

She started praying a lot, asking God for help to get sober and healthier. God answered by leading her into graduate school via an ad on television.

"I always felt empowered in the classroom." Her parents instilled in her the value of education, and she'd taken that to the moon and back winning scholarships, including a full scholarship for undergraduate studies. Leia knew education was a steppingstone to achieving whatever she wanted in life.

What she wanted more than anything right now was to quit drinking. Asking God to give her signs, a couple of other spiritual experiences happened back-to-back, convincing her to quit cold turkey.

When her favorite uncle, a drinker, died from cancer, she had a mortality motivation moment. She thought about her own death and asked, *Am I really living the best version of me? Absolutely not!*

Then she underwent emergency surgery, and under anesthesia her uncle who'd just passed spoke to her in a dream. With his boisterous laugh he said, "You don't have to drink!" Leia realized she had a choice to be different. She didn't have to be like everyone else.

Okay, these are enough signs. I'm going to stop drinking.
Leia stopped drinking, discovered "clarity is priceless," and her ambition multiplied by ten.

Her first public speech about her struggles with addiction went viral. Her high school volleyball coach referred her to an author interviewing people about their brave stories. This person connected her to a program where she wrote and published her book, *A Star for Stella: A Mother's Journey to Overcome*.

Now sober and strong, Leia's added motivational speaker, mindset coach, and author to her quiver. She role models having conversations without shame, teaches people it's never too late to change, and gives others hope.

> "Never in a million years
> did I imagine I'd be this person."

Because of Leia's custody crisis, she discovered why she had a problem with drinking and overcame it. She depended on her support network to get her through. Amping up her relationship with God, she received the needle-moving divine intervention. With the help of professional therapy, she connected the missing dots and pieced herself back together. Support and her determination to transform who she was led to breakthroughs that haven't ceased to open new doors of possibility.

KEY TAKEAWAYS

DOS AND DON'TS

- Don't resist help.
- Seek help while maintaining sovereignty in the process of accessing and using help. This is your ship you're sailing.

- Don't stop with the first idea.
- You can overcome and get help in many ways.

- Don't skimp on help.
- Pay for the best-quality professional help you can find and afford. It's *the* time to invest heavily in yourself.
- Don't second-guess opportunity.
- Serendipity, divine intervention, God—when the supernatural manifests, it's not by accident. The universe makes harmony in mysterious ways. If we acknowledge and welcome it, we can access joy even during hard times.
- Don't hang out with people who aren't the right fit.
- This applies equally to professionals, family, and friends. Be extra choosy when onboarding support team members. Let self-compassion be your guide.
- Don't go this alone.
- Find and cultivate connection, company, and fellowship with others in the same boat. You might consider using this book to start a support group with kindred folk.

RESILIENCE

When you feel alone and like no one can understand your predicament, know that others have survived to thrive. Trust the process. You're not the first to overcome this particular struggle. You too will find your way. You are a bold becomer.

UNANTICIPATED OUTCOMES FROM SEEMINGLY INCONSEQUENTIAL CONVERSATIONS

As beliefs shift during FIT, we let down barriers and often find new and surprising forms of support.

I was so desperate. I had this once-in-a-lifetime opportunity to actualize my dream of becoming a couturier—a maker of fine, handmade clothing. I had the teacher I needed,

Simmon, and time to do it. But fatigue kept me from allowing myself to even dream of what I could do with this opportunity. Because of my health, I was afraid to get my hopes up and then be disappointed. I couldn't count on having the energy I'd need for following through.

Dismayed with how many hours I spent in bed, I thought fatigue was because I always overworked. But a year had passed since I stopped working due to my hand disability, and I was still just as tired. Doctors had no answers.

Only half the time did I complete my homework for Simmon. The other half I did it in class. I felt so bad for "wasting time" like that. I had to keep reminding myself of my reality; I was doing the best I could.

In a conversation with a physical therapist, I learned about a metaphysical healer in Brazil. She'd gone there and said people go there when doctors can't help them. The healer was the medium John of God (more recently he's been defamed and arrested for sexual assault).

Coming from a science background, with Dad being a high school biology and natural history teacher and Mom a nurse, I was skeptical. But the more I slept and didn't make fast progress on my patternmaking course, the more I thought about what life would be like if I had the energy I needed.

My friend Jovita, who's part Brazilian, told me even though some people scoff at this kind of healing modality, that doesn't mean it doesn't work.

Listening to a book on tape during a long drive
home after dropping my son off at summer camp,
I made up my mind to go.

The author, Deepak Chopra, a Western-trained physician, read a passage about his cousin. He was cured of a virulent disease with no Western medical cure with the same kind of spiritual healing.

I'm a linear person, and I went to Brazil for one purpose—to have more energy. So that's what I asked for. I didn't ask for help with my hand injury because I didn't want to ask for too much.

One day I went to a lady's house to see how she sewed zippers into jeans. Taking a few notes, I stopped, grabbed, and massaged my wrist. Even that little bit of writing hurt.

The lady stared at me and asked, "Just from *that*?"

"Yes, just a tiny bit of writing hurts my hand."

She gave me some arnica cream to rub on it. Walking back to the hotel, she said I should ask John of God for help with my hand. That's why she'd come to John of God— because her hand was injured and swollen—and now she could work again.

I told her I didn't want to ask for too much.

She said I had to ask for everything I needed.

I told her I didn't really need my hand to be okay because now I didn't have to write. She didn't buy that and told me I needed my hand to be okay. I capitulated because it was true.

So I asked for everything I needed. The translator did a double take reading my long list of body parts needing help. During my next treatment, I got help with my wrist. I didn't know, though, because the treatment was invisible, until I wrote a birthday letter to Simmon. I had two sides of a page written before I realized how much I'd written, and it had been essentially pain-free. I'd had a healing, but it turned out only to be a partial healing.

I could write, with relatively no pain, things that could only come from within me. No matter how much I *love* to fill out forms, take notes, and document things, that's not what the healing allowed for. I was being freed only to write some kind of original content. I knew if I'd gotten a full healing I would have returned to work and that content would never get written. At the time, I didn't have a clue of what I'd write about. But I wrote another two pages to Simmon.

In Brazil I learned things happen that are beyond scientific measurement or any current methods of proof, and the spirit world makes its own decisions on what to prioritize. What I think I need and what they think can be completely different. Our job is to ask for what we desire, take what we get, and run with it.

I discovered I am connected to something greater than myself. I'm not alone. I have support I never knew existed, which can be summoned and accessed from anywhere at any time. The spirit world is real and ready to help when we ask.

ROBUST SUPPORT SYSTEM ESSENTIALS

This is adapted material from the University of Buffalo School of Social Work's website (2022).

SUSTAINING CURRENT RELATIONSHIPS

Quality and consistency matter. It shows up in the give-and-take of a relationship. Intention is a choice, and awareness and preparation are key to powerful intention. Here are some best practices:

- Show appreciation.
- Stay in touch.
- Be available when needed.
- Anticipate how you can help without being asked.
- Accept help.
- Keep the lines of communication open.
- Use courage to have those tough conversations today rather than later.
- Support success.
- Respect needs and limits.
- Acknowledge and take action when a relationship isn't supporting you.

Your support system should help reduce stress, not increase it. Ups and downs are inherent in any relationship, and patterns of belittling, undermining, or being ignored isn't support.

IDEAS FOR BUILDING YOUR SUPPORT SYSTEM

- Volunteer.
- Take up a sport or the gym.
- Start a book club.
- Attend seminars, workshops, and personal growth events.
- Meet your neighbors and coworkers.
- Join professional organizations.
- Use online social networking resources.
- Don't let the belief that in-person support counts more than online.

YOU'VE GOT THIS

I'm here, cheerleading you on as you have the conversations you've been putting off, so you live by design rather than default. You deserve everything you need. You can be the one to make change happen. You're so much stronger, wiser, and competent than you think.

APPLICATION OF THE EIGHT PRINCIPLES OF MASTERING CHANGE

The chief task in life is simply this: to identify and separate matters so that I can say clearly to myself which are externals not under my control, and which have to do with the choices I actually control. Where then do I look for good and evil? Not to uncontrollable externals, but within myself to the choices that are my own...

—EPICTETUS

Part III Introduction

This is where we pull everything together. In the following chapters, we'll analyze the stories of different individuals who applied the eight principles of mastering change in the context of FIT. These illustrate how people overcame adversity when mind, heart, and soul were tested to the max.

As review, your needle movers to keep front of mind are:

1. Courage	5. Self-care
2. Purpose	6. Mindset
3. Grief	7. Productivity
4. Clarity	8. Support

A short analysis after each story, combined with the seven steps I teach below, will prompt you to look at your own story from different angles.

As the individuals in these stories let go of *perceptual bias*—skewed interpretations of information based on assumptions from preexisting beliefs—they're able to support new decisions that might have previously been out of reach.

The gift of FIT is that we see things from new perspectives. This opens the door for new possibilities. We're able to find new places to belong where we no longer must discount our values and beliefs. We no longer settle for functioning on auto-pilot and ignoring information that contradicts our values and beliefs. We become willing and able to sniff out *confirmation bias*—the act of seeking out what we already know to reinforce our beliefs. We expand our options as new ideas become part of our equation for growth, happiness, and success.

Part III's *Bold Becoming* stories include a range of identity loss catalysts, each of which disrupt identity in major and unique ways. They fall under the umbrellas of three categories:

- Career
- Health
- Relationships

Everyone falls on a spectrum of how they handle challenge based on their general life skills, previous experiences, and coping skills. Here, we showcase how ordinary people generate extraordinary results through learning and growth from their struggle and harnessing challenge.

My work is to give readers hope that all is not lost and to help you recognize you have and can develop more personal agency. You can avoid getting stuck and, instead, grow your way out of sorrow and trouble. We're all small containers for giant experiences. Some losses are total and ultimate. In others, you lose only pieces. Both offer immense opportunity.

Forced identity transition is a gift.
It's a time for respite and reorganization,
an opportunity for rebirth and transformation.

SELF-REFLECTION

As you read these last chapters, I invite you to create space to listen to your own stories playing inside your head. This phenomenon is called *parallel storytelling*. Others' stories lead us to better understand our own, even if they barely overlap with our experience. A sort of cross-pollination occurs, sometimes prompting personal breakthroughs. Others' stories expand our perspective, helping us connect our own dots and leverage our experience in new ways.

Below I've outlined a set of steps for you to use on your own, or with others, where people can be transparent about their transition process together. Doing it together provides opportunity for social learning and can speed up and deepen the process in positive ways.

These steps might be done in a group at regularly scheduled meetings. If you go through these steps with others, you're likely to leverage change and reap its benefits more fully. Peer-to-peer interaction helps us make up our minds and take action. You probably know of someone who, like you, needs to understand what's happening around identity loss. What might it look like to get them a copy of this book and organize a support group?

HARNESSING THE POWER OF PARALLEL STORYTELLING

We're all authors creating our future. Our next chapter awaits a solid plotline in congruence with our best self. Here's how to get the most out of these stories:

1. When reading, notice your mind's own parallel storytelling. As you listen, be curious about matching similarities and

where your brain takes you. It automatically connects dots about your own story, often revealing insights.

2. Keep a notebook, and after each story, jot down your thoughts. Don't judge or analyze. Just record what surfaces. While reading and afterward, in places like the shower, capture:

   a. Insights;

   b. Takeaways; and

   c. Feelings that come up.

3. Read the story a second time. Look for any of the eight principles of change. See what comes up in relation to your own story. Record insights on how you might better apply the principles to your own situation.

4. Journal about how you might get one of these principles to consistently land in your day. Start with one, not all at once:

   a. What would the impact be if you showed up differently with this quality/habit?

   b. When have you leveraged it successfully in the past?

   c. What did you do to create that success?

   d. How might you bring that past success into the present and apply it to current circumstances?

   e. What's stopping you from stepping up with this today?

5. In your answer to that last question, which of the three fears are involved (see Courage chapter)? Release any self-judgment, and curiously explore fear.

    a. Loss pain

    b. Process pain

    c. Outcome pain

6. What does the worst-case scenario look like, and what would you do? Generate various options for taking action.

7. What if the outcome was totally different because you took a different perspective? Based on knowledge about where the fear is coming from, what new perspectives can you choose to adopt?

    a. How might you apply one or more of the eight principles to create this different outcome?

    b. From this new vantage point, what new options for tackling your challenge can you generate?

The goal is to figure out *why* you get stuck. Identifying what's in the way helps you understand how to change. Fear is often involved. Applying clarity, courage, and purpose results in better choices.

You don't have to have lived a story anything like one of these to benefit from parallel storytelling. It happens automatically when we listen to any story. I invite you to practice awareness and leverage it.

Career Catalyst

My body knew it was time for a full stop, not a pause.
I needed time to rediscover what else wasn't ticking,
because something wasn't ticking right in there.
As I was pushing to feel fully better, I had to resolve
a tension in me: Do I want to feel better as a person,
or do I want to feel better as a teacher?
That was a big choice I had to make.

—REBECCA RAE EAGLE, RETIRED PUBLIC SCHOOL
TEACHER, AUTHOR, PODCASTER, ENTREPRENEUR

...

CHAPTER 11

Losing an Identity in Waiting

This identity loss catalyst was a lost dream. For a decade, my actions and psyche had prepared for an expected outcome when poor health blocked me from continuing my chosen self-actualization trajectory. Before becoming the person I dreamed of becoming, it forced me to pivot and become someone else.

...

I remember my United Nations interview like it was yesterday—a sunny day in 1990, in a downtown San Francisco highrise. I'd worked ten years to get qualified to work in public health and planned to work in West Africa. I'd first been exposed to African culture when playing pick-up soccer at Stanford on Sundays with the Stanford African Allstars. I loved the music, textiles, food, and people, the interconnectedness and sense of community. Becoming a United Nations volunteer was my ticket to more of all that.

My desire for preventing health problems (public health's mission) began during a year abroad in Colombia, South America. Here, I witnessed untold pain and suffering. Desire turned into dedication during my public health master's program. I learned how structural and systemic problems contribute to people's suffering and, to a certain degree, were preventable. Public health was the answer to the privilege guilt I'd come home with after living in Colombia. It was how I'd do my part to lift people up.

I'd also discovered I was a natural at connecting the dots and finding practical solutions to complex problems. Reverse-engineering and strategic planning were skillsets I had in spades. Program evaluation was my sweet spot—using measurement to improve efficacy.

At that interview I felt a sense of pride I hadn't felt for years. It wasn't solid as a rock, like when I was a star athlete, because I was at the beginning of my career. But it was solid enough. I'd prepared myself to become the person I'd wanted to become. I'd jumped through hoops and opened doors of opportunity in front of me. I was positioned to carry out my promise to myself after returning from Colombia—to use my privilege to prevent unnecessary suffering.

I passed the interview and was placed on their volunteer roster. When positions opened, they'd choose three people off the roster to offer a chance at the position. Once selected, you had to travel to your assignment within two months.

The first offer was a position on some island, working with Vietnamese refugees teaching breastfeeding. Completely uninterested, I declined. I didn't know the first thing about breastfeeding other than it being the best way to feed an infant. And it wasn't Africa.

In the meantime, I got my first job out of graduate school. Ironically, it was working as a social work case manager for pregnant and parenting teens. (I'd gotten a master's in social welfare at the same time as my degree in public health.) I cut my teeth in social work at a place I'd revered for years: La Clínica de La Raza. By the end of my first year, I'd gained enough competence and confidence to feel like a real social worker. During this year I got another offer from the UN—a position in Zambia, working in the country's HIV/AIDS program.

By now, I'd had time to evaluate where my life was and where it was heading and to rethink plans set in stone years earlier. So when I got the Zambia offer, I made a heartbreaking decision. I'd already lived in a developing country, Colombia, where I was sick half the time and knew the health risks involved. Graduate school had chewed me up and spat me out in terrible health. I was only now beginning to regain my health. Functioning on autopilot, I'd powered through with my plan when applying for the UN position. But it wasn't until I had to make a decision about accepting the Zambia position that I came to terms with reality. I wasn't physically in shape to live in a developing country. My health was too delicate.

In my last year of graduate school, my chronic health problems had hit crisis level. This was when I started macrobiotics—a mainly plant-based, whole foods diet used for its holistic and natural healing power. By now, my health had already improved dramatically, but in Zambia, continuing with macrobiotics would be unfeasible. I wouldn't have access to macrobiotic staples (e.g., brown rice, miso, sea vegetables). Apart from that, I knew about living in a foreign country. You're always invited to meals, and people get really put off when you don't eat their food. Not liking the food was initially one of my biggest problems in Colombia. It was hard enough to eat macrobiotically in my own country. People were constantly misinterpreting that because of my food choices, I was insulting theirs. Those supporting my macrobiotic path were few and far between.

I agonized over the choice I knew I must make,
but I couldn't turn my back on myself.

Not now that I had a clear path forward for my healing. Citing health concerns, I sent the United Nations a letter requesting to be removed from the volunteer roster. That was the death nail to my dream of being an international public health worker, but I had to do it. I couldn't go back to eating whatever I wanted. I couldn't risk losing the ground I'd made to regain my health nor the chance to fully heal.

With that letter, I lost a dream I'd worked a decade to actualize, but I didn't let sunk costs influence my decision. Past investments were no longer relevant. I let go of things that were important because they were no longer a good fit. My health forced me to put myself first and to shift my priorities.

I pivoted my efforts to setting goals and measuring productivity around self-care instead of service.

I was getting better and chose to keep my healing project as my top priority. It was sad to part with my vision of being this person, using all my education to work on a big, important thing. It came down to saving myself first.

So I grieved my loss and replaced the void of the lost dream career with social work. I continued to heal myself physically, in the comfort of my own home. I gave up the status I'd envisioned—using strategic planning to make an impact on large groups of people. Instead, I used my therapeutic voice as a social worker, helping one person at a time. This tempered the blow from losing my ten-year dream and of facing reality head on. I simply couldn't actualize that dream.

I've never doubted I made the right choice, even while deeply saddened by having had to make it. At the time, it seemed like my dream didn't work. I now see it served its purpose. It gave me a vision and purpose that directed my life through the uncertainty of my twenties—difficult years filled with health and academic struggles stretching me to a breaking point. That dream was the inspiration that delivered me to an alternate destination I would surely have missed had I not had a specific and important mission to accomplish.

A career in international public health was not a lost dream but a transmuted dream. It activated a dormant calling—my therapeutic voice—what lights me up and is the force behind my intentions. The dream allowed me, in a roundabout way, to reconnect with my north star by opening a path I'd set aside. I celebrate this loss as a life giver.

ANALYSIS

We can lose something we don't yet have. A lost dream can be as significant as losing something you already have. Identity and dreams share the same real estate—the mind and heart. They commingle to create one's desired reality. Just because it didn't manifest does not negate the impact of losing access to that option.

Before becoming the coveted identity I dreamed of, I had to let go of it for one I could attain. By that time, I'd gotten used to pivoting and fortunately had a second career up my sleeve. Because I had an option already lined up, I avoided the exploration and discovery phase in FIT. But to get to that point, I relied on the principles of change.

- Starting macrobiotics, shortly before the UN decision, had already given me a new *mindset* and with it, *clarity*. I'd adopted the macrobiotic worldview of taking full responsibility for my choices. I had a path forward to regaining my health. This kept me from spiraling into depression, and it kept me willing and able to focus on what mattered most—regaining my health.

- Losing my dream career didn't cause as much *grief* as it could have had I not already had a plan B. Acknowledging my grief made it possible to accept reality and let go of my dream. I'd been through this before (losing competitive athletics, chapter 5) and knew how to handle being between a rock and a hard place. Allowing and not resisting change (once it's happened) is the secret because fighting reality is futile.

- *Courage* made it possible to ignore sunk costs around the career loss and people's criticism of macrobiotics. Courage and leveraging personal agency were the linchpin to self-determining my destiny. They made it possible to pivot both my career and health trajectories.

- *Self-care* became my new measurement of *productivity*. I allowed myself to shift focus from career advancement to action steps on my macrobiotic path to health.

- Initial outcomes after starting macrobiotics gave me the *clarity* I needed to be able to put my own oxygen mask on first, to pivot my life *purpose* from serving others to serving myself. And at work, an organic shift in purpose occurred, one client at a time. I replaced large-picture dreams of population-level impact with witnessing my impact on individual lives. I found purpose comes in many different sized packages.

- I drew on the tiny circle of *support* I had around practicing macrobiotics and buffered myself from those who discounted or tried to dissuade me from my healing path choice.

Had I allowed myself to get angry and depressed about losing my dream career, I would have wallowed in depression. This would have added yet another challenge to my self-healing path. As it was, as a social worker, I honored my gift of therapeutic communication with individuals. I'd been ready to put that aside for the bigger picture of public health's focus on populations, and that, I believe, would have been a mistake. Of course, not every dream identity loss has a happy ending. I lucked out.

CHAPTER 12

When Everything Points to Change

Source: personal interview.

A health crisis was Becca Rae's catalyst for unexpected identity loss. It prompted her to remember she was more than the role she served at work. After a few tense and tumultuous months on medical leave, she chose ambiguous transformation over staying in the familiar zone.

...

Two years into exhausting COVID teaching, Rebecca Rae Eagle went to the doctor in January 2022. She'd worked October through mid-December with a sinus infection and migraines. A forty-six-year-old eleventh grade English teacher in New York State, Becca Rae knew she was overworking. She spent twelve-hour days commuting, teaching, and helping with the after-school program.

"Bawling, I said to my husband, 'I need to see a doctor. I'm sick of being sick. I'm depressed beyond limit. I don't know what to do with all this.'"

She was "physically done and emotionally taxed." Her stellar dedication to self-care no longer worked. She couldn't even walk across the room to pick up papers to grade. She was forgetting names of coworkers and wondered if she had early Alzheimer's. "I felt like my body and mind were revolting."

Pouring her heart out during the hour-long medical appointment, Becca Rae's emotional pain snowballed. Her provider told her, "It's time to go on medical leave. You're going to take a month off." Becca Rae responded, "You're nuts! Teachers don't take a month off. The system doesn't work that way."

Promising to help her work it out, her provider started by scheduling appointments with an ear, nose, and throat specialist (ENT), a therapist, and a psychiatrist, "which is a bit jarring when you don't even know you have a problem." She was diagnosed with anxiety, depression, and PTSD.

Over the last two years with COVID, Becca Rae had lost her identity as a teacher "in the foreign system." On Zoom, some of her students never showed their faces or spoke up, but she still had to give the same amount of love, care, and attention to their needs.

"That caused a kind of mourning over what COVID had stolen from me. I'd been teaching for twenty-one years and was a really good teacher, nominated—I can't even tell you how many times—as 'teacher of the year.'"

Becca Rae's losses were dogpiling. In 2019, she lost both her mom and mother-in-law to brain cancer. Just as she was recovering from those, COVID deaths started, without proper ways to grieve. At one funeral for a friend, only three people attended. Then her birth father died of COVID in October 2021. An adopted child, she'd only just reunited with him three years earlier. They'd loved getting to know each other. The sadness around that loss was devastating. Her sinus infection started right after that.

When her provider told her she needed to take a month off, Becca Rae had an out-of-body experience. "It was like I wasn't really sitting there, but at the same time, the words were entering my ears. What? A month? I don't take a month off from school!"

She realized more was going on than the sinus infection. She acknowledged how much pain she was in and knew her body was telling her it was time for a full stop, not a pause. She needed to find out what wasn't ticking right. With a "broken heart and a broken body," she took that first month off to figure out how to heal both. As a person of faith, she trusted God had a plan.

At the follow-up appointment, Becca Rae was ordered to stay home another month. Driving home, "disconnected," she totaled her car going ten miles an hour. She was upset because she'd done everything the specialist said, but the sinus infection still wasn't better. It didn't clear up until almost March. To top it off, during this time she and her husband got mild cases of COVID.

She was, however, finally getting enough rest. She was no longer physically exhausted. Her memory improved, and mentally she felt a lot better because she didn't have to "put out all these millions of fires all at the same time with all the sick kids."

The ENT's orders were *not* to wear a mask. So because of the mask law in New York State, she was stuck at home. She couldn't even go to the grocery store. As her leave turned into a third month, she was desperate for the mask law to change, so when she got well she could get back to school.

At the same time, Becca Rae was at a crossroads.

She was conflicted. She loved her work, and she loved her newfound freedom. Having time to journal, listen to music, and read books for pleasure, she realized, *There's a human behind this teacher whom I'd forgotten about.*

This awareness forced her to resolve the tension. *Do I want to feel better as a person, or do I want to feel better as a teacher?* She had a big choice to make.

During her leave, because her job was to feel better, she'd joined an online support group to help keep her mind positive. One by one, she added to her days things that only brought her joy. She started evaluating what was important to her, apart from her career, son, and family. She started writing again, found a book hidden in her journals, and remembered ever since she was little she'd wanted to be an author.

As she engaged with positive people online, she wanted to lean into that more. Then when she was sick with COVID, she listened to a couple of audiobooks by Marth Beck and Joe Dispenza and realized, *You're more than a good teacher. You're headed in the right direction, remembering things you'd forgotten for twenty-one years.*

In April she was released to go back to work, but New York State still had the mask mandate, which meant she couldn't go back to work, per doctor's orders. And she didn't have her car or a ride to work, after asking everyone who might be able to help. On top of this, she felt devalued by her school administration, like just another person behind a desk.

All these factors, with the thawing memories of who she was, pushed her to declare, "This is done! This is locked, sealed, delivered, and I'm resigning.

The person she was blooming into because of the full stop was more valuable than being in a role behind a desk. She chose mental health and happiness over security and predictability.

If she had just said, "Nope, you're a teacher. That's what you're gonna do," she'd never have had any of these things.

If she hadn't fallen on her back and taken the time to get to know herself again, listened to her inner knowing, if she'd settled, the opportunity to boldly become a new version of herself would have passed her by.

Before, Becca Rae was a person who loved her students and found joy in helping them grow. Now she's made herself her own student as she ventures into entrepreneurship. She wrote her first book, *Embodying Joy: A Heart Journal.* She started *The Joyful Journaling Podcast* and her business, The Writing Well, to help others bring their words to life.

ANALYSIS

Becca Rae's health crisis catalyzed an unlikely change: leaving her job without a viable plan forward. Forced medical leave became transformative fertile ground where she reconnected with buried passions and dared to step through doors to growth and greater fulfillment.

When Becca Rae discovered her identity as a teacher would no longer suffice, she accepted reality. Using the principles of change and her faith in God, she released it to walk into an unknown future.

Becca Rae maximized the principles of change to make her decision about whether to return to her job.

- Using awareness and acknowledgment of *grief* and loss, she faced reality for what it was, in real time, and grappled with her many challenges.

- She sought out *support* and followed professional advice. This opened the door to a new kind of self-care: reconnecting with repressed passions.

- Her dedication to healing and *self-care* was key to transformation. It amplified her ability to gain clarity and harness her growth mindset to explore, experiment, learn, and pivot.

- She leveraged her growth *mindset*, maintaining confidence in her ability to figure things out, grow, and make decisions without clarity on outcomes.

- She used *clarity* of intention—the unwavering pursuit of joy—to avoid settling in the face of uncertainty. She believed her inner wisdom while lacking clarity about next steps on her future path.

- Her *courage* to listen to and act on inner knowing made it possible to make decisions without full clarity on a plan forward.

- Shifting her *purpose* to center around joy legitimized taking the risk to walk away from all she knew.

If Becca Rae hadn't hit the ground running, already armed with a growth mindset and a willingness to wrestle with grief, she may have stayed stuck in depression. This could impact her immune system, putting her at risk for additional medical problems, apart from other maladies connected with depression such as an impaired ability to take action. Instead, she opened the landscape to what's possible, filling it with new options and allowing for pivots as the iterative process of transformation unfolds.

CHAPTER 13

The Empty Space in Her Soul Revealed

Source: personal interview.

Sarah's identity loss catalyst was her move away from her creative muse—the ocean. No matter how she sliced it, living in landlocked Colorado blocked access to her muse, forcing her into identity transition. Her story is a snapshot of a person taking her first step over the threshold, out of the liminal space.

...

Since high school, Sarah Thee Campagna wanted to live next to the ocean in Florida. "I belong near the water," says the self-proclaimed mermaid. Sarah made it to Florida and stayed for almost two decades, promptly swapping out her career as a computer systems analyst for being an artist. As an analyst, Sarah created tools to improve hospital patients' health and make doctors' careers more fulfilling. As an artist, being next to the ocean gave her happiness and was the source of inspiration for her work.

From that happiness and joy, Sarah's art sort of created itself. Working with glass and metal objects, "they would begin to tell [her] what they wanted to be." Doing the work for the object was an act over which she only had so much control. Art would "come in from [her] soul, through the skill and precision of [her] hands." She loved being that person and was proud of her work because it spoke to people. She felt like she was doing something of value.

Sarah earned good money as an artist and her art made people happy. Then her husband got a new job and they moved to Denver, Colorado. Sarah knew living in Florida was important to her, but she hadn't known moving would become an obstacle to artmaking. She was supportive of the move. Her husband knew how important Sarah's art was to her. They both took great care making plans to get her new studio up and running as fast as possible.

At the time of our interview, Sarah had been in Denver for four years. She could not produce work that had any joy in it. To her surprise, she'd taken a long time setting up her studio. She finally got inspired enough, recognizing, *I have to do this because this is who I am.*

Her studio was beautiful, but the only art she produced was "forced and completely out of [her] head, not from [her] heart, not from where [her] muse is." Describing it as having no spark or soul and depressing, she didn't want to show it to anybody. She feels like her "heart is being choked."

> Three years in, Sarah started to give herself
> permission to begin thinking of herself as
> somebody else.

But her friends, who were mostly artists and knew her as Sarah the Artist, would disagree when she'd mention she might not be able to make art anymore. They'd tell her, "You're wrong, Sarah." This invalidated her experience. When she'd try doing other things they'd say, "No, that's not who you are, Sarah. You'll do art again."

But Sarah's tried everything—things that worked before when she lost her muse. She even moved her studio three times in the new home, but no art came. Completely frustrated, crying all the time, what Sarah needed more than anything was to hear something like, "Whatever you're doing, I'm with you," and, "Tell me about what you're doing now." Instead, some of her friends disappeared. With many others, she stopped telling them what she was up to. They knew her as an artist. They wanted her to be an artist again. They knew she was happy being an artist. As an artist, they could recognize and understand her, but not now.

Sarah had lost her identity before with different job changes, but it had never been this hard. She felt like her life "was a bridge with supports under it, and too many of them got knocked out at once and the bridge couldn't stay up anymore." Recognizing defeat and the need for a total pivot *and* because she's committed to living in Denver with her husband, Sarah spent the last year "working to find new supports for the bridge."

She started finding new things. She made homes for solitary bees but felt no spark. She'd just reconnected with contra dancing, joined a gym, and she and her husband were about to buy a small winter getaway in Florida when COVID hit. Because her husband is a transplant recipient, they had to be extra careful. Sarah's one foray into something new during COVID was volunteering at the Denver Museum of Art and Science, where she worked with dinosaur bones and one other masked person.

She felt like she was swimming upstream, but on July 3, 2021, "a light bulb switched on."

> She started feeling a new identity emerge
> as she reconnected with a part of her that she'd
> always been interested in, a subject she'd
> never given herself time to study—magic.

Her sister is very experienced with magic, and Sarah always wanted to learn and engage in it. But since she's a scientist, she's a bit wary of what people will think. It took this forced identity transition for her to cross that Rubicon.

"Since it's my job to spend time finding what I'm supposed to be doing, I'm actually giving myself permission to identify with this subject that for so many years I'd not." She's let go of the idea of always having other people agree with her before moving forward. She's selective with whom she shares her journey during this "tender stage."

Sarah believes magic is around us all the time, and we overlook it and miss out leveraging it. People call it different things; it's part of religion, and some call it God winks. She started developing a course to help people recognize and access it as part of their daily life and a podcast called *Salt and Fire Spellworks*.

She's totally lit up with her work. In fact, it keeps her up at night thinking how many people she can help. She wants to start a movement, helping people connect with something bigger and more important than our individual selves. She teaches people how to become aware of and observe the cues the universe gives us, telling us what the right thing for us is. Her mission is to make it easier for people to trust their inner guidance and take the risk to follow it.

Sarah believes she was guided to do this work and it "wasn't just from desperation to find a new identity." She has full support from her husband and sister. Regarding her times of struggling, she says, "It's extremely helpful that I truly believe I'm supposed to be doing this." Finding a way back to doing something that helps people motivates her: "I never really felt like my art helped people, even though it made them happy. It always felt like a selfish pursuit."

Sarah realizes without having things taken away from her, she wouldn't have noticed the empty space in her soul. She never would've had a reason to look. She might have never connected with this interest that had been inside, waiting for attention and expression.

ANALYSIS

Nothing in Colorado would coax out Sarah's muse, forcing her to give up working as an artist after her relocation from Florida. The discovery process that followed led her to find the answer to her purpose already residing within her. She pulled it out and brushed it off. We're all waiting to see it in its full glory.

- Sarah's growth *mindset* set her up for taking this loss in stride. It might not have lessened the impact, but it gave her the confidence she would figure this out.

- Sarah's support system thwarted her *grieving* process and efforts to grapple with reality. So she put up guardrails, becoming selective with what she shared with whom.

- Grief forced her to seek *clarity* around what's next. She did the necessary exploration and discovery until she discovered a repressed desire.

- Sarah's *self-care* was her conscious effort to "find out what she was supposed to be doing." This became her *productivity* barometer—seeking purpose.

- She knew her *purpose* was connected to service, and that helped her release the lost career as an artist. It helped give her the *courage* to let go of an identity she dearly loved and enjoyed.

- Sarah's willingness to adjust her expectations around and manner of engaging with her *support* system allowed her to be nurtured by those who could and to protect herself from those who couldn't.

Had Sarah not listened to and followed her own inner knowing and let go of the pressure to return to whom she'd lost, she might have missed her opportunity to start doing magic. She would likely have gone further down the rabbit hole with depression. That would have made exploring, discovering, and taking action on new ideas unlikely, leaving her stuck in liminality. Instead, trusting herself and recognizing she was being guided got her through her moments of doubt and uncertainty.

CHAPTER 14

Goals Fueled by False Beliefs

Source: personal interview.

Classifying an identity loss catalyst is not an exact science. Damiun's identity loss catalyst is a chicken-or-egg paradox, a tossup between career and relationship. Because career was where his focus was, I've put this story in the career section. But had Damiun had a better relationship with his dad, this career story might never have happened. The relationship could have been the forced identity transition catalyst. The two are inextricably linked.

...

Damiun Moore was a typical kid who needed a close and satisfying relationship with his dad. But he harbored anger and resentment toward him because his dad was raising his sister and married to his stepmother. Damiun had a strategy he thought might create the level of connection with, and dedication from, his father he so craved. He'd become a pro basketball player.

Damiun lived with his mom, who worked two to three jobs and spent a lot of time with his dad. They connected most through sports. His dad had been a great football player in high school. He was also a boxer and loved to share athleticism with his son.

When Damiun was twelve, he watched a cousin go pro right out of high school. His cousin had a great relationship with his dad. Damiun was trying to emulate that for himself by following the same path. He knew what it took to become pro because he watched his cousin do it. He "saw the difference in his attitude and approach, how he carried himself and how he believed in himself." This inspired Damiun. He liked how people lit up around his cousin. He wanted the same for himself.

At sixteen, he went to live with his dad and carry out his plan. Going all in, he followed in his cousin's footsteps. Because of his cousin, he knew being a pro ball player was attainable and put on blinders to actualize his dream. He knew the sacrifice, focus, and disciplined mindset it would take. He was setting himself up to have the support he needed. He was counting on his dad's help to get him to that next level. He needed that hands-on approach, the leadership, and the guidance his dad could give him. Damiun's drive was "insatiable." He believed, *I'm gonna make it. There's no other option.*

Unfortunately, his carefully curated plan to create the relationship with his father was "dead on arrival." The personal connection he wanted, to make up for the past, didn't happen.

What Damiun got wasn't what he'd hoped
it would be, and he started to rebel.

He stopped trying to get what he couldn't get from his father. He followed his own path, "engaging in a negative social environment."

Around this same time, one of his teammates, Trevor Martin, was diagnosed with leukemia at age fifteen. Damiun had never encountered death or the possibility of death. He was by Trevor's side for the next year as he fought and lost his battle with cancer. Damiun examined his own identity for the first time and "learned the power of faith." Trevor's last words were, "Stop trippin'. It's okay to die when you know you're goin' to heaven." Those words made Damiun question his belief in himself, God, the universe. "Trevor taught me a level of mental discipline I couldn't get from athletics or anywhere else up until that point because he didn't complain."

The journey with Trevor made Damiun "seek clarity early." He learned what freedom meant, watching his friend be okay with giving up his body to death. Damiun realized, "There's something bigger to this experience that we can't fully understand, and I have to do my best to pursue it." This is when he learned about choice. We always have the choice to choose freedom. We can either be a victim or a champion, and we have free will to make that decision.

Trevor's death shook Damiun to the core, and he didn't have the tools and support he needed to process it. "I went through a period where I was completely lost. I felt it on a deep level but couldn't articulate it mentally." So he started rebelling in anger, lashing out and getting in trouble at school: "I took an easy path and started to morph into this bad boy image to give people the idea that I was untouchable because I was really afraid, knowing how vulnerable I was."

He pretended like nothing mattered. He did whatever he wanted without regard to consequences or how it impacted people he cared about. At the same time, he'd always been an empathetic person and knew this wasn't who he really was. "I felt like I lost the sense of compassion, and my personal life became incongruent with what I know is true about myself." Even so, he wanted to hold on to the feeling of being hurt and justify it through his actions.

This phase lasted into college. He continued being a great athlete and got a scholarship to play in Division II college basketball at Felician University. But his disregard for how he was showing up in life caught up with him when he got a knee injury. He tore his MCL playing basketball, "completely doing something [he] shouldn't have been doing." He was out for the season, and he didn't get the support he needed to "bounce back and come back stronger," the way some athletes do.

> Instead of seeking support, Damiun isolated.
> "I didn't want people to see me as this wounded warrior, so I just went inward, in my shell."

"I didn't ask for the help I needed and wasn't honest with myself in the recovery process." He was still angry and had "stopped feeding the relationships" he needed to recover. On top of that, he didn't think anybody would understand because he was on a different path than most, performing at a higher level. He went back to basketball too soon, got a second injury, and ended up retiring from basketball.

It wasn't his physical injury that he needed help with; it was his mental battle he couldn't recover from on his own. It was the first time he had to face the possibility of not continuing with basketball and therefore needed to think of a career post-basketball. *I'm no longer this person who can live off of sheer will.*

At this point, Damiun discovered personal development and "the possibility that there was more to life than basketball." He found Tony Robbins and Brendon Burchard and went "on a mission to tackle personal development" like he'd been on with basketball. He read one hundred books that year, went to seminars, and started volunteering at events. He started doing some coaching, but he didn't do the work of taking action on what he was learning. He gained some clients and knowledge, but not his own transformation.

At this same time, with the help of some college roommates and teammates who did photography, he got into modeling. This was 2016, when Instagram was new. His plan was to develop a network and then leverage the network to do something with personal development. But he didn't have a clear vision of an endgame. The modeling generated a following of 130,000 people on Instagram within four months. This led to opportunities in the entertainment industry, but his success led to further isolation and hardening. He started to believe he was better than other people and nobody could understand him or do what he was doing. In the end, he never fully committed to modeling or personal development because he "was still holding on to the pain of not fulfilling [his] basketball dream."

He found a mentor who took him under his wing. He helped Damiun uncover the "pain of not feeling good enough or that [he] had a fair opportunity to give [his] full effort with basketball." With that understanding and the mentor's support, Damiun gave up modeling and personal development. He deleted his social media and took the opportunity to train with the pros. He was invited to the Drew League and played semi-professionally that summer, where he could possibly go pro.

But the closer he got to fulfilling his dream, the more he questioned whether this was what he wanted.

He ultimately recognized, "Through the guidance of [his] mentor, the drive and desire to be a professional athlete was to finally get the acceptance from [his] father that [he] was good enough." In the end, he realized that wasn't going to happen, and it wasn't what he wanted. So he stepped away from basketball.

Damiun was able to see he'd never been looking at reality. He'd been telling himself he wasn't good enough because he was misinterpreting reality. He realized the resentment he felt toward his dad, because he was taking his dad's treatment toward him personally, wasn't necessary. He saw it from a new angle: His dad wasn't "doing that to [him]."

When he realized that, Damiun was able to forgive his father for something he didn't even know he did. And Damiun could release himself from seeing himself as someone who had been hurt. "It took almost fulfilling that childhood dream to find my own path in life."

Damiun could then pick up his passion for personal development. He serves as a certified high-performance coach, helping connect people from where they are to where they want to be.

Because of our interview, here's what he wrote me, illustrating the power of sharing your tough stories:

"I want to share that our interview inspired me to speak to my father and share the realization that I was at peace now, pursuing my heart's calling. I recognized the way I was living was pushing him away. It brought generational healing because he shared with me that he wished he could have done that with his father. We both gained a greater understanding. Now, I'm raising my son in honor of what was given as opposed to rebelliously striving based on what wasn't."

ANALYSIS

When I interviewed Damiun, I thought I was getting a career loss story. As it turns out, his identity loss catalyst stems from childhood, where his true identity was nipped in the bud. He spent his energy trying to be someone who could win his father's approval instead of discovering who he really wanted to be. Because he used the principles of change, when it was time to make these career decisions, he could walk away from the ones not congruent with who he really is.

- Damiun had unprocessed and ongoing *grief* throughout childhood because of the kind of relationship he didn't get to have with his father. It's possible that with the death of his friend, he was able to feel those feelings fully, and this might have contributed to the force behind his anger. Not having the support he needed around these losses could have influenced him not to get the support he needed when he first injured himself in basketball.

- On the other hand, from an early age, Damiun recognized and harnessed the power of *support*. He tried to get it from his dad and later found it in a mentor.

- The death of his friend fast-tracked him into seeking *clarity* around life's *purpose* and magnified his well-established *mindset* he intentionally developed by following the role model his cousin set for him.

- Damiun demonstrated *courage* when he chased his dream to be that elite athlete and more so when he gave it up, once he realized the motivation wasn't from his heart. He ignored sunk costs and followed his inner wisdom.

Had Damiun not given up basketball, he would likely not have gotten back to where his true desire lies—personal development. His role modeling would have been limited to one area, sports, instead of helping people be who they wish to be. He would likely have missed out on the breadth life now offers him, demonstrating high performance in all areas of his life and helping others do the same.

Health Catalyst

My eyes have been opened to realize we're all pieces of a big,
beautiful whole, like a diamond.
Each of us shines out from that in our own unique way,
and when we do that to the best of our ability,
we can find what brings us joy and those gifts we have to offer
to everyone else. Then that shines out so brightly
and adds to the whole and brings the whole together,
yet allows everybody individually to be themselves.

—JEAN OLNEY, MOTHER,
CAREGIVER FOR A DISABLED CHILD

...

CHAPTER 15

When Mental Illness and Addiction Rob Your True Identity

Source: personal interview.

Thomas's early family life set negative patterns in place that stayed with him. Then, both severe mental illness and addiction robbed him of his sovereignty over thought and judgment. For years, his identity was controlled by forces that thwarted self-actualization and delayed him from reaching his full potential.

...

Thomas S. wanted to be close to his daughter. He lived in Trinidad and she in England. He needed a way to live in England. In 1966 he found a way to make that happen. While in the US, on his way home after representing his country in Senegal as a professional dancer (performing the flaming limbo), he enlisted in the US armed forces, which promised he'd be stationed in England.

In basic training in Georgia, as a twenty-three-year-old Black man who grew up in a country with considerably less racial segregation, he was ruled by demeaning Jim Crow laws. He quickly learned to navigate "signs telling colored people where and where not to be." Interfacing with drinking fountains and restrooms to movie theaters and waiting rooms at bus stations, every day was a lesson in white supremacy.

Later, while stationed in Germany, he and a Black friend went to a bar where the tragedy that would set the trajectory for the rest of his life occurred. Thomas witnessed a fellow US serviceman murder his friend because he was a Black man talking to a White woman, and after the murder, someone repeatedly put hangman nooses in Thomas's bunk.

That murder and the nooses left Thomas saddled with PTSD (post-traumatic stress disorder) up until today, almost sixty years later.

"It devastated me. I've never been able to take that vision [of the murder] out of my head." It set him up for a life of addiction and crime that robbed him of his true identity and ruled his decisions for years to follow.

Thomas was a rebellious child. He was fifth of nine children and the first boy. At about age eight, he stopped minding his mother. He started abusing his acolyte and altar boy positions in the church, drinking leftover wine when cleaning up after events and taking funds out of collection baskets. He became "a sneaky thief." At school he got expelled for pushing a bookcase down on a teacher.

At home, he was trying to get the same attention as he used to get—attention now directed toward his sisters, whom his mom was "trying to keep from having early babies." He got attention, but it was negative. His mom and sisters, using extreme measures, failed to force him to behave. They went as far as putting him in a gunny sack, pretending to take him to the river and lowering his bottom into the water. (In reality, they would put him in a sink.) By the time he was fifteen, they began locking him out of the house. He slept on people's garage roofs "eating mango morning, noon, and night." Around that same time, Thomas attempted suicide by cutting himself and drinking iodine. He told his sister to tell his mom "she don't have to worry about [him] anymore." Thomas stayed rebellious. His time in the service was underscored with "earning stripes, being demoted, and then earning them back again." Problems included low-level criminal activity, such as having extra ration cards for cigarettes and liquor and getting arrested for having a pistol.

His struggle with addiction started in Thailand in 1968. Two years after the murder he was finally given treatment for "interim anxiety." They didn't know about PTSD yet, but he was waking up at night screaming from nightmares feeling like he was being strangled, and he had flashbacks. They gave him Valium but abruptly discontinued treatment because it required another service member to lose work time accompanying him to appointments.

With an unchecked mental health challenge, now addicted to Valium and forced to withdraw cold turkey, Thomas discovered heroin. Without telling him, a friend gave him a cigarette laced with Red Rock heroin. It felt good. After a couple of weeks smoking these cigarettes, Thomas didn't like it when he didn't have them. Thus began his heroin addiction. Drugs served as self-medication for the PTSD symptoms. They also exacerbated his tendency for rebelliousness.

PTSD and addiction robbed Thomas
of his identity by taking control of his mind.

He initially used heroin to take the edge off of PTSD symptoms, but addiction impacted his decision-making. It intensified his loss of sovereignty over his mind and who he was choosing to be. It turned him into a person in pursuit of a fix.

While the military shirked responsibility for Thomas's mental health needs, it made accommodations for its servicemen in other ways. Everywhere Thomas served, he was surrounded by bars and women who prostituted. Coming from Trinidad and Tobago, where drinking and partying was part of the national culture (it's touted as the place with the greatest party on earth—Carnival), Thomas made the most of this and started doing dance shows in clubs. But instead of paying him, the owners let him pick three women to spend the night with, and sex became another obsessive compulsion.

Thomas spent eight years in the service being demoted and promoted. He left at the same rank he'd entered. He still didn't know addiction was a disease, but he did know he was "doing suicide on an installment plan." One time he put a gun to his head because he needed a way to shut up the voices in his head.

Once out of the service, still addicted to heroin and without civilian skills other than his dancing, he fell into serious criminal activities. He and his girlfriend had a massage parlor that was a front for prostitution. They were arrested and charged with pimping and pandering. This arrest, and a subsequent murder conspiracy arrest, became Thomas's turning point.

He became homeless, living in his car and riding with his motorcycle club. His family would lock their doors when they heard his motorcycle arriving.

He was facing deportation when the conspiracy case got dropped. On the recommendation of his attorney, who shared his drug use and Vietnam veteran status, the judge sent him to drug treatment. In a detox program, Thomas got off heroin. He's been in treatment for addiction and PTSD ever since. "I just continue to work on myself. I stay in treatment. I stay with a therapist. I still have flashbacks."

His lifestyle didn't change overnight after getting clean, but now he hangs his "mask of deceit" on his wall instead of his face.

Everything Thomas went through prompted him to continue to search for a different, honest, ethical way to live. He's on "a spiritual path, still becoming a better person." He believes part of his problem stems from arrogance and insecurity. He works on being humble and surrendering. He focuses on staying clean, one day at a time, and helps others do the same. He surrounds himself with people who know how hard it is and who help him do that. He calls upon God to guide him. He meditates and prays.

Thomas is amazed, delighted, and emotional about his accomplishments, despite his pain. More people than can be counted have benefited from him becoming his true self, free from addiction. In 1984, he returned to Trinidad and Tobago and started a recovery program.

As one of the founding members who started San Francisco Carnival, he brought the best of his culture to the San Francisco Bay Area. Carnival attracts over four hundred thousand individuals each year and involves hundreds of local Bay Area artists and arts organizations, making it the largest multiethnic festival in California.

He's received various awards from local politicians and the Caribbean community. The City Council of Oakland, California, gave him a proclamation: May 17 is Thomas S. Day.

Thomas remains active in the recovery community. Addictive cravings still pull at him. PTSD still invades his peace, and he continues to find and define his best self despite it all.

His daughter in England called him on her twenty-first birthday and they've had a wonderful relationship ever since.

ANALYSIS

Thomas's identity loss began in childhood when he turned "rebellious." His story is an example of nipping one's identity in the bud. His identity is undermined by repercussions of adapting to adverse childhood events (ACEs) (in his case, extreme disciplinary measures, absent parent). ACEs have a tremendous impact on future violence victimization and perpetration as well as lifelong health and opportunity (CDC 2022).

Coping with his situation and the consequences of his actions, Thomas seems to have developed an identity of being "untouchable": "I'll do as I please. You can't hurt me because I'm already broken and rejected." Racism was the catalyst for PTSD and addiction. These outcomes added overwhelming new challenges to his self-perception. This combination of factors blocked his inherent potential from emerging until after he got clean.

Thomas used key principles of change to transform:

- Leaning on *support*: detox program and recovery community, God, therapists, only associating with people who contributed to his recovery; he accessed resources needed to transform.

- Learning about addiction and how to manage it made it possible to build a new *mindset*. One based on the possibility of being a different, better person.

- Gaining access to *clarity*, made possible in recovery, improved his judgment so he made better decisions.

- Clarity, mindset, and positive support made it possible to *courageously* cut ties with those not contributing to his recovery and to disengage from his criminal lifestyle even while not yet knowing how he would support himself.

- Choosing more effective *self-care* options—therapy, meditation, prayer, recovery group—gave him better outcomes than drugs and denial.

- Helping others recover from addiction gave him *purpose.* This contributed to the motivation and resilience he needed to stay on track with his own recovery.

Harnessing these principles of change to achieve and stay in recovery, Thomas regained his sovereignty. He was able to choose who he was boldly becoming instead of addiction and early coping mechanisms—arrogance and rebelliousness—controlling who he was.

Had Thomas not become a master of change, addiction and criminality would likely continue to plague him, and others whose lives he touched, with anguish and distress. Now he lives up to his responsibilities and is a shining example of resilience, redemption, and the depth of human capacity.

CHAPTER 16

Between a Rock and a Hard Place

Source: personal interview.

The birth of a child with severe disabilities turned Jean's identity inside out. It moved motherhood into a different universe, one that demanded she maintain high performance motherhood while annihilating her own future dreams.

...

Jean Olney is the mother of Gabe, a 100 percent physically dependent child who cannot walk, feed, dress himself, transfer from chair to toilet or bed, and whose communication only close family members can understand. He's cognitively bright and highly engaged in life. His main challenges are both stiff and loose muscles. "It's been hard to find ways to help him," says Jean.

She prefers not to name her son's diagnosis but rather to talk about symptoms and capabilities, struggles and hopes. When she says the diagnosis, people put the conversation into a box that leaves out both hope and all the strength and wonder that have been part of their journey.

Gabe sustained a traumatic brain injury during birth and was not expected to survive. Now in his early twenties, he is Jean's eighth child. She was about to wind down motherhood and plan her empty-nest phase of life.

Jean loved being a mother, and when Gabe was born, her life changed forever. Apart from grieving the loss of her dream of having a child who would develop normally, she couldn't comfort Gabe. Nothing she knew to do worked, and he cried for the first three years.

> Jean lost the dream of raising another child to enjoy, and who would get the most out of life.

Becoming a "forever caretaker" became her new reality. With this, she lost her future dream of doing what *she* wanted, after all the kids grew up and left.

She buckled down with her new task of raising a disabled child. She thought she'd "just do it differently." But nothing she knew from parenting her other kids worked. On top of that, medical treatments didn't work either. Some made things worse. In Gabe's case, she learned "less is more when it comes to medication."

Because things didn't work, this actually kept hope alive because she kept searching for solutions and trying new things. To this day, Jean keeps hope alive that the doctors are wrong and someday her son may walk. Many therapies sound promising—therapies that *allow* the body to move instead of trying to force it—but are out of reach financially, and insurance won't pay.

Another thing that keeps hope alive is a vision Jean had of Gabe ten years before he was born. She saw his face clearly and thought he was going to be fine. Because of this, she's been patient with him "moving along at his own pace" and believed eventually "something was going to click and he'd put things together" because he's really smart. However, "every year that didn't happen."

One of the things Jean struggles with as a caregiver is lone-liness. Even though her family is supportive and helpful, she's the one primarily caring for Gabe.

Mixed in with the loneliness is grief about the change in her life plans and "not feeling like there's a place for [her] anymore."

Jean's plans to go back to school and engage in hobbies are off the table for now. She's "in limbo, supposed to be an empty nester but still a full-time caregiver." Every step forward she makes toward her own goals she realizes "it's not gonna work because the focus has to be on Gabe."

She's in constant struggle with her identity. *Am I this? or am I that? And really, how can I be both?* The more she thinks about what she wants to do for herself the more she has to balance it with the reality of the moment. Yet when she stops dreaming for herself, she "moves into depression, hopelessness, victim mentality, grief, guilt, and failure."

Jean sees her role as caregiver as a choice, pointing to group homes where he could live. But because of the quality of care, that's not an option. He would end up "medicated and in a diaper in a corner in front of a TV, drooling off the side of his chair." She cannot put her son in a place where "they don't honor his life."

Compounding Jean's challenges are fears about Gabe's welfare once she's gone. "I have panic attacks. It breaks my heart thinking about that." Her other kids assure her they'll take care of Gabe, but she worries how he'll manage a change in caregiver. She can't win for losing.

Jean uses her faith in God to keep her going. While she believes God will never give her more than she can handle, she often thinks she's got more than she can handle. Her faith is being "very tested," and she still questions everything but doesn't get specific answers.

Over time, she's developed more trust in her intuition, especially when it comes to advocating for her son with the medical establishment. She knows her voice counts, and regardless of their training, she knows more about her son than they do.

Jean's life is a duality. She grapples with anger, depression, hopelessness, and fear, but so much beauty is in learning from Gabe who is "very real." Gabe "doesn't have those conditioning and patterns we normally acquire. He's just himself, and *all* of who he is."

Jean's learned to look beyond the physical and appreciate the innocence about him—something so different from how others show up in life.

Her perspective about life has expanded from a narrow view of the world to seeing beyond the physical aspects of life. She now sees more exists than "what the world says and all these expectations or ideas about how things should be." She's not trying to find a silver lining. Accepting reality for what it is, she lives in the moment and responds with grace, gratitude, and acceptance to what needs attention.

> Jean uses mindset to keep herself positive,
> choosing to be a hero over being a victim.

She takes care of herself because of him. "How I feel rubs off on Gabe; he mirrors my feelings." She's learned to love herself "through difficult feelings" so she can help him do the same. Jean and her family have "grown so much in ways that would have never happened without Gabe," and she describes her experience as "the best worst thing that ever happened."

Jean has become the master of "stepping outside of the box" and "allowing openness" to hold the possibility of "maybe

[she] can be all these things," without having to decide. She's listening to "those little whispers" and when she's uncomfortable and her heart is saying pivot, she does. She's willing to shift directions in her thought patterns and belief system and simply look at things differently. "I don't have all the answers," she says. "I'm open to seeing what new pathways open up."

ANALYSIS

Having a disabled child was Jean's identity loss catalyst, forcing her to transform her parenting methods and expectations, to release dreams for her future, to accept a tight paradigm to live in the moment. She wears the mantle of a perpetual, interdependent role with grace and has gratitude for every small win.

Jean's story has no clear resolution. She's made peace with that while keeping hope alive. When her universe collapsed, she learned to see and appreciate life in single moments rather than whole events or chapters. Tenuous fulfillment comes in micro-installments, prompted by nuanced gifts Gabe shares by simply being himself.

Jean runs the gamut of harnessing the principles of change:

- Accepting her *purpose* is to serve as a lifelong caregiver to her son gives Jean the freedom to see her form of *productivity* as valid and enough.

- Mastering her *mindset* allowed Jean to embrace the challenge God's given her and grow into rather than resist her lot in life.

- She leveled up her *courage* skills to match the need by trusting her intuition. She sets others straight and is the fierce and competent advocate her son needs.

- One of her main *self-care* activities is actively managing *grief.* With complicated grief, painful emotions don't improve with time and are so severe you have trouble recovering and resuming your own life (Mayo Clinic 2022). Acknowledging and addressing rather than burying grief, Jean's kept depression at bay, which makes her able to fulfill her caregiving role.

- Continually seeking *clarity* about how to manage her life and dreams and allowing for pivots helps Jean maintain hope as she navigates life trapped in this liminal space.

- While many parents in her shoes have inadequate *support* systems because of the immense and ongoing needs involved, Jean's family and faith in God's plan give her enough support to make it through each day.

Jean's is a complex case of forced identity transition where discovery of who she's boldly becoming is highly limited. The exploration and experimentation needed for identity transition she does is mainly through introspection and spirituality.

Had Jean not come to peace with her constraints, depression could overtake her and impede the high-functioning parenting needed to ensure Gabe's well-being. Or, she might have settled by putting him in a home and have to live with that decision.

CHAPTER 17

Blocked Access to Sherry's True Identity

Source: personal interview.

Like Thomas S., Sherry's is not a classic forced identity transition story. There's no before/after inflection point causing identity loss. Depression, since childhood, nipped identity formation in the bud. It cut Sherry off from her whole self. Because she mastered change, her identity evolved into a duality—accessing and radiating love and joy while battling suicidal ideations.

...

Sherry Richert Belul never remembers being happy as a child. Three things troubled her:

1. Feeling out of place because she was different.

2. Her father's abandonment.

3. The tremendous amount of heartbreak in the world.

Sherry's father abandoned the family when she was very young. She grew up in a rural, conservative town in California with her mom and brothers. The religion she was brought up in didn't resonate with her. Her mom was on the other side of the fence politically, in a cookie-cutter town where individuality wasn't expected or appreciated.

Early on, Sherry identified with being a person "always lost in depression." She was an expert at showing one part of herself while feeling something else. For decades, depression nipped a more comprehensive identity in the bud. Mental illness impairs the mind, changing the way people think and process the world. It kept Sherry from discovering another part of her identity—a person filled with tremendous love and joy.

A highly sensitive, empathetic person, Sherry cried a lot because so much heartbreak was in the world and she felt things so deeply. She also grieved the abandonment of her father although she didn't realize this until her twenties. She managed her emotional pain by being a high achiever, staying busy, and never making any waves. She was a straight-A student. She was in every club, a cheerleader, the president of things, yet nobody knew what was going on deep inside, how she desperately wanted to be loved. All the accolades never gave her what she needed.

Sherry hated herself and thought something was wrong with her. As a child and young adult, she believed, *I'm the wrong person. I was just born wrong. A screw got turned the wrong way.* She thought she was "a mistake" and about "how to exit the world."

In college things went from bad to worse. Her sense of not belonging deepened. A fish out of water, she was in a very conservative college filled with wealthy classmates heading for corporate jobs. She didn't relate to them at all.

As her self-questioning and lack of belonging escalated, so did suicidal ideations. Constant thoughts were:

- *How do I get off?*
- *I could jump right now in front of this train.*
- *Which bridge could I jump off?*
- *What could I take?*

This was the beginning of her deep dive into depression. She felt no matter what she did, she'd *never* belong. Filled with constant anxiety, depression, and OCD, she says, "I saw myself as a dark cloud." *I'm just trouble. I'm not adding anything.* She felt separated by a thick, solid iron wall that kept closing in on her. All she saw was absolute darkness.

In this solitude, she felt, *I can't express anything, and there's no way for anything to come in.* In this state she felt like she was suffocating. It still happens. She even felt the sensation talking about it during our interview.

Sherry knew she wasn't living up to who the person inside of her was and believed she never would. This better version of herself was inaccessible. So she'd try to disappear by not eating because she "wanted to be gone." She believed the voices inside her were true. She didn't belong.

When things were unraveling in college some seeds of hope were planted. While working for the school counselor, she had some sessions with her. This was the first time she'd had counseling. Around the same time, a professor in her creative writing major told her, "You're going to die here. You need to go to the New York Arts Program." He saw in Sherry what she didn't yet see. She was a creative person who was trapped.

The semester in New York, on the one hand, saved her because she discovered things about life she hadn't known. But it also deepened her sense that she could never be who she wanted to be. She saw people with spiky blue hair and wildly colorful clothes and loved them, but she felt disconnected from this person she desperately wanted to be because it "felt impossibly far away." While inspired, her sense of being the wrong person deepened.

Sherry graduated college. She didn't get a corporate job. She worked in a New York museum. She still couldn't figure out how to be who she really was, and things remained too hard. She just "wanted off this planet," but she gave herself more time.

Her darkest period came when she relocated to San Francisco and broke up with her boyfriend. Then, a friend, gifting her a book about meditation, provided her breakthrough catalyst.

She started practicing Zen meditation and learned to see life in tiny moments. One day, in *one* in-breath, she heard herself say, *I don't want to kill myself right now.*

> Meditation gave her a path, tools, and practices that allowed her to be sad yet connect with joy.

That in-breath was the first time she could remember *not* feeling like killing herself. It was the first "pinprick of light" she saw in the iron wall. That's when Sherry realized the wall wasn't solid, and that changed everything. If it happened once, it could happen again.

Sherry started looking for light, one small pinprick at a time, and realized she didn't need to wait for these moments but that she could create them. She now had a path to something other than depression.

> She also learned she had a right to think differently, and this was a choice. We all have this personal freedom.

Finding pinpricks of light and using freedom of thought opened the floodgates. It connected her with previously inaccessible parts of her identity. She was no longer trapped behind that iron wall. Sherry gained sovereignty over her mind.

Over time Sherry began to live with both things happening—still depressed and having suicidal thoughts *and* moving forward with her "guiding philosophy of pinpricks of light."

She started practicing joy by appreciating little things, like a casual conversation with a stranger, a cup of coffee with a friend, or a beautiful painting.

She made a practice of finding singular moments
where she didn't feel like killing herself.
She would notice something she enjoyed
and tell herself, I don't want to die right now.

This ability to focus on singular moments became part of her mental health practice. She said, "A million times a day, my way of being in the world is a moment. It's just a moment because I can pause, I can make a choice, and this is the opposite of the iron wall."

Sherry's breakthroughs continued. Now she knew joy and beauty were there for the taking, she set up expectations that she'd find and express them. One day, instead of saying, *I don't want to die right now,* she changed her language to: *I'm love and light.* Her new identity was emerging and becoming more complete.

She stopped believing she was a mistake. She started helping others—people in the dark, grieving and sick, disappointed and lost. Sherry's healing process developed into a practice of using moments to create *gifts of love.* The first one she did was called *a love list*—all the reasons why she loves someone. It was a way for her to feel love and joy. "I didn't want to kill myself when I was making those lists." She started sharing her tools with others. Her purpose shifted from distracting herself from feeling anxiety and depression to something bigger. She now had something more to do than just survive.

In her book *Say It Now,* she helps others develop a practice of sharing joy, celebrating life, and expressing love. As a certified high-performance coach, Sherry supports people in living their best lives, full of joy, success, engagement, and meaningful relationships.

Through her work she also found, "The deeper I let myself feel the pain and sorrow and sadness, the more room there is for joy." Although Sherry still thinks of suicide at least once a week, she says "Depression is not who I am today." She's able to separate singular moments and not let any one moment "mutiny other moments."

She transmuted that identity—*I'm trouble and not adding anything*—into *I'm love and light and spreading it everywhere I go.*

This is the Sherry I met a few years ago. Her over-the-top positivity was genuine from a mile away and so contagious I *had* to find out what was up with her happiness quotient.

ANALYSIS

Sherry's story is one of excavating a force from within strong enough to survive and manage severe mental illness with flying colors. It illustrates the profound power of applying the masters of change principles. Her need to become her true self forced an identity transition—even when her mind, exactly what she needed to survive, was going toe-to-toe against her.

Sherry believed she didn't belong in this world. This was her identity loss catalyst. It blocked her connection with her inherent, true nature—a deeply loving, engaged, and empathetic person. Her essence was always to share love and light, but the wall of darkness derailed its manifestation.

Sherry's successful application of the principles of change, persistence, and determination kept her alive until she found a way to manifest her core identity.

- *Courage* was the air she breathed, luring her into each moment of each day, helping her decide to give life another try.

- Sherry knew her *productivity* priority was keeping herself alive. Laser-focused on that, she took the bull by the horns to defeat suicide, one minute at a time.

- Using *support* as her lifeline, Sherry followed the breadcrumbs put in her path. Each action—from getting counseling and going to New York to learning to meditate—got her one step closer to accessing that person she knew she was.

- With *clarity* about freedom of choice of thoughts, she harnessed the ability to change. Her guiding philosophy (pinpricks of light) allowed her to consciously restructure her thinking into a *growth mindset*.

- Inventing her own *self-care* tool, she leveraged intentionality to find moments of joy and then choose new thoughts. She replaced feelings of dying with these moments of joy.

- Shifting her *purpose* from survival to contribution—helping others experience joy and suffer less—transformed her identity from being a depressed person to a person of service. Her mission augments the courage and mindset needed to keep suicidal ideations at bay.

Had Sherry not chosen to boldly become, every single day, we might have lost her. If she'd let a fixed mindset win, her symptoms, beliefs and behaviors robbing her of a more complete identity could have resulted in suicide. Because she tackled her mindset, love, light, and joy are amplified, spreading like wildfire as we speak, one person at a time.

CHAPTER 18

With Schizophrenia, Will My Son's Life Be Empty?

Source: personal interview.

Liz's identity loss stems from losing the dream of being the parent of a child who will grow up to be independent. Because severe mental illness changed this trajectory, Liz added on to her identity by taking on a different role as a parent and changing expectations for her and her son.

...

"Eric wants to kill himself" were the words school psychologist Liz Rebensdorf heard her son say that day in the kitchen. Liz was sitting at the table with Eric behind her, and those words sent shock waves to her bones. He'd never talked in the third person or about killing himself.

Eric was sixteen or seventeen and had "regular adolescence challenges," but this was in a different league. Liz's response was, "Oh shit!" She got up and threw away a knife. Then called a social work friend and, talking in psychobabble code so Eric couldn't understand, asked what to do. The police took Eric to a psychiatric ward and the psychiatrist determined it was a drug reaction from LSD. He said it wasn't schizophrenia because Eric was still interested in social connection.

Liz and her husband were relieved. "It was just a glitch." They brought Eric home, realizing things were going to be okay… until the middle of the night when he started screaming, "I'm back!" and threw something through the window. This was the beginning of a completely new and unexpected life for Liz and her family. She began her never-ending quest to find ways to help Eric, and those around him, live more comfortably and with at least with a modicum of sanity and joy.

> During the beginning stages of severe mental illness, it's hard to take care of the person because they don't want care.

Eric had countless meltdowns, emergency room visits, and locked psychiatric hospital stays for erratic psychotic behavior. "He would explode, be really agitated, and pace when he was normally a compliant kid." Liz and her husband put Eric in every program they thought might help. It was traumatic for everyone. Eric didn't know what was happening, and Mom and Dad and Eric's little sister had to learn what was happening and how to handle it.

Eric did, in fact, have schizophrenia. He initially lost his sense of humor, as do many with schizophrenia. If Liz could get him to smile at a joke, "that was progress." He began living inside his head and lost interest in social connections.

Schizophrenia is a thought disorder—versus depression and bipolar, which are mood disorders—that compromises one's ability for logical reasoning. "His thinking was out the window." He did things like go to his sister's room and think she was Mary and he was Jesus. He'd try to be on playdates with her girlfriends, not realizing it was inappropriate. The lowest point was coming home to find he'd taken all the things off their desk where the bills were, put them in the garbage can, and used a hose to fill it with water.

In the beginning he had a lot of anger toward his parents because he could no longer behave as they wanted him to. The old parenting techniques didn't work any longer. Nothing worked well. They had a dog Eric cared for. He acted like a therapy dog for Eric, but whenever the dog didn't want to be in his room, Liz knew he was even too much for the dog to handle.

Liz's relationship with Eric changed.
She had to learn to protect him from reality
while making sure he understood reality.

She still has to do this. It's not how she expected her life would be. Liz and her husband had to recalibrate what to expect from Eric while sustaining one loss after another as the avalanche of things he couldn't do never stopped.

He would never be the park ranger he might have become. Every life and daily goal had to be narrowed down and many let go of forever. He would never get a license and drive because, rather than being totally aware of the environment, he's in his head and not looking at anything around him. At the same time Liz's son lost his life's trajectory, another couple, friends of Liz and her husband, also had their child come down with schizophrenia. Their concern was he'd never get a college degree. Another friend's concern was her child with schizophrenia wouldn't have friends. Liz's concern: *Will his life be empty?*

Eric never recovered. Now in his fifties, he's still unable to live independently. Liz and her husband remain in their caretaking roles. The sister moved out of the picture to the other side of the United States, although she's prepared to take on necessary administrative roles once Mom and Dad are no longer able. Conversations are still like pulling teeth.

Not following logic, they contain bizarre cause-and-effect reasoning, so Liz often doesn't know what to say. But since Liz is fascinated with how the brain works, this curiosity helps her enjoy their conversations in a different way. Out in public, he misreads situations and yells at people. Some days he stands outside the Safeway grocery store and recounts his recovery story to middle school kids who laugh at him.

Fortunately, Eric's not aware of what he's missing. Some people in his situation are, and they feel their life is over. They don't like what they're going through and become depressed. Eric on the other hand, jokes about being "goofy and loonier than a hoot owl." One time he told his mom he was proud of having schizophrenia.

Fortunately, he's a kind and gentle person, and now with maturity and proper meds, things have mellowed out. He has fewer explosions, and his parents know how he needs to be coddled. They modify things to fit his needs because he's incapable of being different than he is. Liz has adjusted to him being a different kind of person and found joy in knowing him as he is.

Regarding identity loss, Liz doesn't see her experience as one of having to take on a new identity after losing her dream of being the parent of a healthy child who will grow up and become independent. Instead, she's "added things on" to fit with her new reality. She's still the same person, with added qualities. A playbook doesn't exist for how to handle when your child or family member comes down with severe mental illness. Each person changes in their own way depending on what they bring into it, how they make sense of it, how the illness manifests, and a multitude of variables inherent in the person who is ill.

Liz's life became a juggling act. She met the crisis by educating herself and sharing what was going on. She had friends in the social service field and lots of support. Showing up to work after meltdowns forced her to rise to the occasion as a professional. Work kept her busy and from wallowing in tragedy. Compartmentalizing her life helped keep her functioning. Liz uses the Serenity Prayer as her mantra, and beyond that, her various interests have also kept her going. Being the mother of a person with schizophrenia is only one part of who she is. Besides being very social, she loves gardening, crafts, art classes, art history and many other things. At eighty-one she still teaches the Family-to-Family class for NAMI (National Alliance on Mental Illness) and runs support groups for people with family members with severe mental illness. She helps them avoid revolving their whole life around their ill loved one by building other things into their lives, things to look forward to.

Liz's perspective is she's one of the lucky ones.

Her son has food, clean clothing, and a roof over his head with heat and electricity. Eric escaped the ranting and raving stage. He's not a foreigner who doesn't speak English, so he can understand what people say. He lives well-situated next to public transit, the bank, and a grocery store. He's not left to fend for himself and eat out of garbage cans or roadkill, like the poor soul in San Francisco Liz saw on the news. This man was taken for a psych evaluation after eating a dead raccoon but deemed not in grave danger because he "knew how to find food."

I asked Liz to give me a before and after picture of who she was and became. She said she has a much richer, multifaceted, and full life. She used to have a narrower view of the world and her son's illness "opened up her eyes."

Her biggest concern, one she worries about constantly, is *What's going to happen when I'm gone?* She and her husband have made plans, but because services are always changing, there's no certainty. In a recent conversation Liz had with Eric about the future, he asked, "Well, when are you going to die?" Liz said she didn't know, but it could happen any time, to which Eric said, "Well, rest in peace."

ANALYSIS

Having a child with schizophrenia forced Liz to become a person she never imagined—a mother in perpetual teaching mode, protecting her son as best she can. She let go of dreams of her son living independently, having a fulfilling career, getting married, having grandchildren, or having him to support her in old age. The tables turned on Liz. She's supporting him and worrying about who will take her place once she's gone.

Mastering the principles of change helped Liz make the most of her situation rather than wallow in despair.

- She leaned on *support*. She didn't keep things bottled up and used her support system to release the pressure from the immensity of change and emotional pain from her son's loss of his mental faculties. She reached out and connected him with programs and professionals to guide and assist. She educated herself about what was going on and what to do.

- She dealt with *grief* by accepting reality. She used her support system to share her pain and dismay. She's had to endure ongoing grief because her and her son's challenges continue. Working on plans for his future once she and her husband are gone is a way of managing grief rather than avoiding it.

- Liz used *courage* to keep herself in the equation, not allowing her life to be overtaken by this high-risk, high-demand health condition. She paid attention to and acted on the need to keep her emotional pain and stress levels under control by pursuing things that bring her joy. She keeps *self-care* as a top priority.

- *Mindset* has been her savior. As a psychologist who believed in the ability to transform, she used it on herself. This helped her face reality for what it was rather than spending critical time in denial, making excuses that didn't line up with what was happening. This mindset helped her face the grief at hand and make sense of it. It also helped her hit the ground running with the *clarity* she needed to know what was important and find ways to shift her focus and pursue these things.

- By accepting reality and shifting expectations for her son's life, she was able to change what *productivity* looked like for both of them. She allowed him to live his reality without demanding he do things he could do before but no longer. Her role as protector changed drastically as the definition of independence changed. She started to count little things in life we take for granted, such as getting him to smile. She also put more attention toward her *self-care* than she might have done otherwise. She let go of long-term plans and dreams for her son and replaced this with accommodations so he could get through each day without a meltdown.

- As Eric stabilized and Liz had time to catch her breath, she began giving back. She turned her tragedy into *purpose* and started helping others navigate life with a family member with severe mental illness.

If Liz had wallowed in grief over her lost dream as a parent or not had the courage to face reality straight on, a cascade of worse things could have happened. Schizophrenia has a high rate of accidental death, and early diagnosis and constant accommodations help prevent this. Divorce often takes place when there's an ongoing family medical crisis. Eric might have suffered longer than needed before getting whatever help was available. As it happened, Liz rose to the occasion and has given her son the best life possible, found joy within their lives, and helped others do the same.

Relationship Catalyst

I can literally feel my heart and soul and mind growing and changing and evolving. It's a really beautiful thing, a beautiful outcome out of a traumatic experience. I'm unrecognizable today from where I was a few years ago.

—LIVIA RISMONDO, *Emotional Wellness Coach*

...

CHAPTER 19

When the "Worst of the Worst" Become Indispensable

Source: personal interview.

John has many catalysts of identity loss or blocked opportunities for positive identity formation. They are all relationship-based: not knowing who his father was, his mother's murder when he was a boy, taking the fall for his guardian's criminal offense, joining a gang in prison. Despite a tragic story that went from bad to worse, support transmuted John into a leader of hope and healing. Now he's solving one of the most intractable social ills cops and government never will—gang violence.

...

John Jackson lost his mother when he was eleven years old. "My last memory of my mother was when she kissed me goodnight and tucked me into bed before leaving to work the graveyard shift as a waitress at Denny's." The next morning, walking to school, he saw her car parked by the side of the road. Looking in, he saw her blood. This was his mother's murder scene, where she'd been beaten to death.

After his mother died,
John never felt like he belonged to anyone.

He didn't know who his father was, so he went to live with his mom's sister, who sold drugs. Although she took him in and he knew she cared for him, he also knew he wasn't her top priority. She had kids of her own.

Then one night, he gained her love and acceptance. He was seventeen, and he was with his aunt when she was pulled over with drugs in their car. He remembers the lights flashing and his aunt saying, "John, if the cops find the drugs, say they're yours. I'm already on probation. If I get caught with drugs again, I'll go to prison."

In jail, John felt proud. "I'd done what I felt I needed to do—protect my family from going to jail." When he got released a few weeks later, his aunt celebrated and praised him.

He craved more praise: "I committed my first aggravated robbery a couple of weeks after my release, gave her some money, and got more praise." Little did he know at the time, taking that drug charge for his aunt set the trajectory for spending the next eighteen consecutive years in prison. Before the end of that year, he was convicted of four aggravated robberies and seven felonies and headed to a maximum-security prison as a "skinny teenager."

In prison, John found the family he so desperately needed—one that loved and protected him and put him first. He earned his way into a gang by proving he was more violent than others. "The gang provided, in spades, the community, love, and caring you needed and didn't have." Joining a gang gave him the family he'd been missing. It was a way to gain power and respect and to be accepted. But it was a lifetime commitment "'til the casket drops."

At seventeen, instead of being in school, John was schooled in criminality by men twenty, thirty, and forty years his senior.

"I found purpose in using my skills to create
harm and destruction. I believed that was
what I was born to do."

He went on to develop and misuse his leadership qualities
instead of healing from his traumas. In prison, John says, you
learn "emotional suicide"—to kill your feelings, to stuff them
down and act as if they don't exist in order to survive the atroc-
ities witnessed and sustained. He had no room for empathy
and compassion in that environment.

This repressive environment eventually took its toll. Twelve
years later, crying one day alone, he thought, *I was meant for
more than dying in a prison cell.* He wanted anything but to die
in a box. This was the first time he realized he wanted to go
home. He was supposed to be released the next day. Instead, he
was starting another four-year sentence for crimes committed
in prison.

He was now thirty years old. His "choices to engage in gang
violence and criminal behavior" resulted in him doing four
terms in solitary confinement, where he was locked in a cage
the size of an elevator, never seeing the sun or feeling wind on
his face. Because of his choices, six more years were added to
his prison sentence. He knew if he continued to engage with
gang and criminal activities, he'd die in prison.

In 2017, a lady named Cat came to Pelican Bay where John
was. This supermax prison houses those the California Department of Corrections and Rehabilitation labels "the worst of
the worst." She called a meeting with the top gang leaders of
some of the gangs—the Crips, the Bloods, and the Mexican
Mafia. Cat asked them, "Do you only want to be known for
the worst things you've ever done?"

Catherine Hoke, an entrepreneur, had worked with incarcerated and formerly incarcerated people in various places nationally and internationally. Her programs maximize the potential of people affected by incarceration. Cat told the Pelican Bay gang leaders, "You can do better. You can use your voice and your leadership to tell the next generation that there's something better for them than to follow in your footsteps."

In that first meeting, John Jackson saw a tender side of his family he'd never seen. One of them said he plays teatime with his granddaughter when she visits. He yearns for her to grow up seeing him so much more than the worst of who he is. That day, Cat planted the seed in John that would grow into a completely different life.

Cat expressed her care for them as fellow human beings. She offered to help them become known for more than their rap sheets. She validated their worth and in exchange, they gave her their trust. This is where Hustle 2.0 was born, a program reducing crime, violence, and recidivism, and eventually the first ever gang retirement plan was introduced by these gang members.

Until Cat and the 2.0 writing team members started working together, gang members had no retirement option. The only exit options were death and snitching. And if you snitch you die.

With the help of Cat, John slowly started to change, with baby steps. "They weren't huge, gigantic steps. It was, 'Today, I'm not going to pass drugs. I'm not going to involve myself in a criminal conversation today.'" He was threatened and ridiculed but stuck with it. He gave up his privileges as a high-ranking gang member—selling drugs and cell phones, engaging in the micro economy of the prison.

"Eventually I told my homeboys, my fellow gang members, I'm not doing this anymore."

They asked, "Is this what you really want?" He said, "Yes, that's what I want. I want to go home." They said, "Alright, if that's what you want, you can go home. You're not one of us anymore." They told him he was "a square." He wasn't really a gangster. He was only pretending to be one and he could go home. They didn't want to see him die in there. They realized he didn't belong there, that he could do more. They told him, "Go home. Mind your own business, and everybody will leave you alone." They left him alone, and after two years, John paroled and was released from prison in 2019.

Since being out of prison, he's nonstop "turning pain into purpose" (when he's not on the ski slopes). He's a Seth Godin altMBA leadership program graduate. He's the director of curriculum development at Hustle 2.0, a TEDx speaker, and an author. He offers what was previously never available—a gang retirement plan to incarcerated people *and* proof it works.

When I met John in 2021, they had Hustle 2.0 in over seventy jails and prisons. As of December 31, 2022, Hustle 2.0 is now in over six hundred jails and prisons, and in all fifty states! No one can stop John and Cat's mission. They're putting "an army of some of the most resourceful, intelligent, and dedicated people out in the communities to prevent gangs, crime, and people going to prison." They're transmuting this massive, untapped talent pool into a force for good.

John gave up his family and took on new values. He's on the other side now because of them. "My family saw value in me and told me to go home." He found a fulfilling and service-oriented mission and is working to bring his family with him. He's one of the five percent who hasn't returned to prison as a prisoner.

Boldly becoming the best version of himself, John's putting his vision and leadership to use making a positive impact. He's transforming gang culture and creating safer communities. He's helping others go legit with their own entrepreneurial strengths, born out of struggle and pain.

ANALYSIS

John's identity formation was negatively impacted from essential relational needs not being met growing up. In prison, he replaced his patchwork identity when he became a gang member. Later, he rebuilt his identity from scratch. Exiting gang life alive and more whole than he could ever know was possible, he defied reality.

- *Grief* about not going home gave John the *clarity* that he didn't want to stay in prison and needed to change. He stopped settling. He shifted focus to leverage what he learned from prison versus grieving all he lost.

- Once John was clear he wanted to leave prison, he changed his *mindset.* He chose to think and act differently. He always believed things would work out. This fueled his courage and resolve to pivot away from comfort, safety, and belonging. By believing and acting on the knowledge that he was the expert of his life, he made better choices.

- Once John made the decision to change, his *productivity* shifted from gang and criminal activities to ones that could get him out of prison. He did the classic identity transition activities—explore, discover, experiment, iterate, pivot, and build more effective *support* systems. He chose different options based on new beliefs and values of hope, healing, and giving second chances.

- John demonstrated *courage* by withstanding threats and humiliation as he opted out of criminal gang involvement. He gave up the only sense of belonging he'd known since losing his mother. He made choices that might have cost him his life.

- He used *support* from incarcerated peers who convinced him he didn't belong in prison and Cat to keep him moving in the right direction. He leveraged his belief in God as another support pillar he could count on and his updated belief that he was meant to do good, not harm.

- His *self-care* was his productivity activities, which included upgrading his support network.

- His change in mindset eventually gave John a new *purpose*—helping others transform, heal, and reject crime and violence. He gained a life-affirming, service-based purpose larger than himself.

Had John not become a master of change, he would have stayed a statistic of a boy who didn't have the dad he needed. A statistic of a kid who society let fall through the cracks after the thread of stability he had disintegrated. A statistic of a kid who society locked up and threw away the key. Instead, he saved himself, a perfect example of the phoenix who created his rebirth from the ashes. He became a role model and facilitator for others to follow him on this previously unattainable path.

CHAPTER 20

Grieving a Breakup

Source: Personal interview.

Livia's identity loss happened invisibly, over time. The catalyst was a relationship. It wasn't until Livia was outside of the relationship, after it ended, that she realized part of her was missing. This put her on a journey to discover who she was at her core and rebuild from there.

...

In 2015, Livia Rismondo was a twenty-two-year-old, adventure-seeking Canadian in Australia. She went backpacking and traveled around until she'd "burned through a bunch of money and needed a job." She got a job, met an Ozzie gentleman, and began a five-and-a-half-year relationship. Then everything changed, leading to a two-year period of massive growth as she rebuilt herself.

The breakup was traumatic. "It left me in a really dark, lonely, scared place." Now twenty-seven, she'd spent the majority of her adult life with her "identity intertwined with, kind of rooted in that person, and then all of a sudden, they're not there and you lose that piece of you." She said, "It was almost like a physical piece of me was gone."

A large part of the trauma was she didn't even know how it had happened. She'd poured so much love into that person, and then he caused so much pain. With "a heavy cloud of sadness," she felt lost in the woods, completely discombob-ulated, not sure which direction she was going or how many steps to take this way or that. Everyday menial tasks no longer had any meaning because they'd always been done with that other person in mind. Rather than cooking dinner, she'd have a piece of toast.

> Livia questioned everything, especially
> her own choices, trying to understand how
> she'd gotten to where she was.

"It wasn't always so dark and terrible, and then suddenly it was." Failing to understand what had led up to that change, she fell into a depression, and "just waking up, getting out of bed and brushing [her] teeth became major accomplishments."

She had to call in sick for work because she used dangerous equipment—chainsaws and chippers—on her tree job, and not being able to mentally focus, she would put everyone at risk. She got the doctor's note to take off work and was diagnosed with depression and anxiety.

This mental health condition was completely foreign to a person who'd always been "outgoing, bubbly, and happy." Livia had to learn what it was and how to come out of it. She chose therapy over medication. She went about researching in books and online how to combat depression and anxiety. While she was scared, she knew "since this had developed because of circumstances," she could get over it.

During her recovery, she had to rediscover what gave her life purpose. She loved to help others but realized the habit of doing more for others than herself needed adjusting. She didn't understand self-care, so she Googled it. She started paying more attention to her own needs and learned to "just say no" without guilt.

Her breakthrough came when a friend told her,
"Ask yourself, 'What would my best friend say?'
And then take that advice."

Turning this into a powerful self-care practice, she began to
consciously coach herself using this tactic. She became adept
at recognizing when she was doing too much and making
sure she took care of herself first. As she gave herself more
time for her own needs, she found that when she had projects
scheduled on her calendar, it was easier to say no. Making sure
she had projects to work on helped her find new interests and
opportunities, which continued to add more fulfillment and
joy to her life.

Livia also used a strategy she'd used in the past when she
wasn't happy. She relocated. But since this was during COVID
and she couldn't just pack up and go anywhere, she adapted
how she changed her environment. She went to work in some
mines in Western Australia, which involved FIFO—flying in,
flying out. She'd be away at work for two weeks and home for
one week. This ability to "just pack up and move" was a critical
tactic she used during her darkest moments.

Livia started some spirituality practices, focusing most
on tarot cards. These validated things as she tapped into her
intuition to interpret their meanings. She had a daily practice
doing this with a friend.

What helped most were the people she associated with.
As she rebuilt herself, she had to build a whole new social
network and ended up with incredibly supportive friends.

Livia recalibrated her "bullshit meter and was a bit ruth-
less," now having zero tolerance for unacceptable behavior
and circumstances. Her friends support her "in ways [she]
could never even ask," and she now values "human connection
on a level that's otherworldly."

This shift caused Livia to understand
"home wasn't a place anymore; it's a feeling,"
taking expat living to a new level.

She came out of this knowing life's about:

- Making the best decision for yourself in the moment and trusting you can figure things out.

- Knowing no decision is wrong, so it doesn't matter what decision you make, but you must make decisions.

- Avoiding disappointment by not planning too much and releasing outcome expectations while striving for your goals.

- Choosing where you give more power—to your fear or to the courage it takes to make new choices.

- Getting comfortable with being uncomfortable so you don't get stuck in inertia.

In the end, allowing herself to feel, knowing the terribleness would be temporary, was how Livia became "unrecognizable" from the person she was a year ago.

ANALYSIS

Livia's identity loss catalyst was the end of a relationship. The suddenness of this ending, with no inkling of what was in the works, made it traumatic. Livia not only had to grieve the loss of the relationship but also had to recover from trauma. Her growth mindset helped her mobilize internal and external resources to heal and transform in record speed.

- Livia used *courage* to face her *grief* head on—"feeling the terribleness of it"—thereby processing grief instead of burying it.

- She harnessed her growth *mindset* to recognize she had the power to change and grow and trusted she could figure things out.

- Livia put *self-care* as her main priority. She explored and learned about her condition and then took action steps to counteract it—therapy, self-coaching, calendaring time to set boundaries, etc.

- *Clarity* emerged as she learned more about her condition and experimented with options and solutions. She made new definitions for what was and was not acceptable in relationships. She discovered more of what she wanted and didn't want in life and how to hold to those new standards.

- She got the help needed by leaning heavily on her *support* network, both personal and professional. They helped her connect the dots as she made her way through the darkness.

- Livia went through the classic FIT steps of exploration, discovery, and experimentation. She found new friends, interests, and opportunities. Along with self-care, these *productivity* activities were key to transformation.

- She demonstrated *courage* by establishing boundaries with her bullshit meter and acting on its readings and by learning to be comfortable being uncomfortable.

- While making self-care a priority and gaining clarity, Livia spent time on things only for her. She shifted her *purpose* inward as she explored what was important and considered where to put her energy and focus. She could now readjust her give and take ratio to an equation that filled her up instead of depleting her.

Had Livia not sought help from professionals and friends, she could have stayed isolated, and depression could have taken a turn for the worse—especially since this was during COVID, when people were already isolated. Had she not leveraged her growth mindset, she might have spent her time looking backward and blaming, instead of actively exploring and creating what would come next and reaching next-level fulfillment.

CHAPTER 21

Adoption and Identity

Source: personal interview.

Damon's identity loss was from not knowing his family roots because of adoption. He had a wonderful experience as an adoptee, which tempered but did not negate the grief and questioning about identity that all adoptees experience. Reunions with his birth parents filled in the missing pieces so he could finally get clear on who he really was.

...

What's it like to live thirty-six years knowing you're disconnected from your biological identity? Damon Davis, born Michael Anthony Sullivan, knew he was adopted and was perfectly comfortable with it. He grew up in a racially mixed neighborhood in Columbus, Maryland. Damon is Black American, as were his adoptive parents Veronica and Willie.

Because Damon's family looked like a biological family, there was no cause for uninvited public discussion about his status. He and his family went about their business with adoption under the radar unless they chose to bring it up. Because his parents let him know from the get-go he was adopted, they were all playing on the same team. His identity as an adoptee was not subverted.

Damon had been in foster care for three months before his adoption and, to this day, knows nothing about that period of his life. In his adopted family he was an only child. "Thankfully, I got a lot of hugs, kisses, and love, and all the support and encouragement I needed to be the best person I could possibly be. I was nurtured in fabulous ways, and it made me into the man I am today."

At the same time, children who know they're adopted live with chronic, unanswerable questions—*What if I had retained my biological family life?*—trying to discover the core of who they are or could have been.

Damon had this question, but he was happy with his adoptive family, so he didn't do anything to get those answers.

Adoptees who know they're adopted have full awareness that a life rooted in ties to their biological family, one that would have resulted in them becoming a different person, was nipped in the bud. It will never blossom, for better or for worse. This causes a grieving process for the person they wish they could have been had things "worked out." Grief begins with the fact your mother relinquished you.

With their alternate (or original) potential identity inaccessible, thoughts and emotions of loss and grief are constant companions.

This happens to different degrees based on many variables and impacts everyone differently. This grief was part of Damon's experience, and again, he was happy, so his grief was on the low end of the spectrum.

Nevertheless, the curiosity—and sometimes longing—for a life that might have been possible if things had just been different is ever present. No matter how well-adjusted or treated an adopted child may be, grief is a part of their journey through life.

On top of this baseline grief comes more grief, if and when children reunite with their biological parents. There can be acceptance and inclusion, and there can be rejection. If they develop a relationship with a biological parent, they have more people to mourn when they die. Instead of losing two parents (your adoptive parents), you may have four people you will lose, not counting siblings and other biological relatives.

Being adopted keeps grief and loss on your plate at every turn, even if you don't seek reunion with your biological family. Fortunately for Damon, his positive experience as an adopted child balanced out that grief. He could focus more on what he had than what he didn't have—until the tables turned.

Damon's first major identity shift, apart from being relinquished as an infant, happened when he was thirty-six and his adoptive mother fell ill with paranoid schizophrenia. In a tragic blow, he lost the parent-son relationship. "I went from being the son whose mother was always in a position of nurturing, to basically becoming the parent."

This involved making many decisions, including having his mother removed from her home after she stopped paying the mortgage and lost it on the auction block. As he grieved the loss—"the person who was there before is gone"—he adapted to the startling change in her identity. He took on the incredible challenge of being the one making care decisions while she still wanted her autonomy.

During this abrupt, terrifying, and unwelcome transition, a friend suggested he seek out his biological mother, and he started the process. During this same time, his wife gave birth to his son.

"We created the first biological relative I ever knew.
It was a massively impactful moment."

A social worker in Baltimore City, where Damon was born, found his birth mother, and he had an amazing reunion. On their first phone conversation, he said, "We had instant rapport, a phenomenal discussion." Since she worked two blocks away from him, he surprised her on her birthday the next day. They sat at lunch together, staring at each other and crying. He doesn't remember a word they said; only the experience of seeing his face in hers.

From there, the next step to piecing together his whole identity was a bit rockier. She told Damon his father's name. Damon sensed the pain in her voice and didn't pursue finding his father, based on the story she told him... until the passing of his birth mom six years later, when "curiosity got the better of me."

Damon tracked down the person his mother named as his father and called him. They had no rapport, and talking to him "was like nails on the chalkboard." Damon still wanted to check the box of having been face to face with his biological father. Before he got the chance, he received a note saying, "I'm sorry. I'm not the guy," and that was the end of that. Turns out, his biological mom was wrong about who his father was.

After a family relative used Ancestry.com to trace her family roots, Damon decided to use it to find out more about himself and his son. He found a man who shared more DNA with him than his own son. With this, Damon tracked down his biological father, and they had a wonderful reunion. In Las Vegas, "for the second time, I saw my face in another person. It was really astonishing."

Damon was one of the lucky ones. He got the warm and fuzzy reunions all adoptees wish for when they seek their biological parents.

> "It was a grounding experience to come face
> to face with your biological relatives
> and have them accept you."

Many people aren't willing to risk opening that Pandora's box, but for Damon, it helped answer the question, *Who am I really?* He now supports others in answering that question as they piece together their history, with his podcast *Who Am I Really?* and his book *Who Am I Really? An Adoptee Memoir.*

ANALYSIS

Damon's identity loss catalyst was being relinquished by his birth mother as an infant. Loss of this relationship made it impossible to fully know who he was, but his loving and safe adoptive home environment made for a smooth and positive identity formation. Reuniting with his birth parents gave him answers he didn't seek until the right time came, unifying his sense of who he was.

- Being honest and disclosing his adoptee status, Damon's parents made it possible for him to *grieve* what he lost and would never have. Since their *support* also gave him a life of happiness, this diminished his grief, allowing him to minimize energy and focus on his adoptee status and thrive.

- Capitalizing on the catalysts brought about by loss of his adopted mother's deteriorated condition and the birth of his son, Damion sought *clarity* around his biological roots.

- He demonstrated *courage* by following through on the supportive friend's suggestion and sought out his birth parents.

- Damon's identity transformations resulting from reuniting with his birth parents morphed into a service-based *purpose*, helping other adoptees reconnect with their roots.

Had Damon's adopted parents failed to help him thrive, he could have ended up a bitter, sad, and confused man. Had Damon not sought out his birth parents, he would never have known his roots. As happy and well-adjusted as he was, he might still be like a tree living as an air plant, flourishing while dangling in the air. With his roots not exposed to nutrients from the soil, he might never have gotten that feeling of being grounded that now fuels his mission to help other adoptees find wholeness and feel settled.

Conclusion

Nietzsche was the one who did the job for me. At a certain moment in his life, the idea came to him of what he called "the love of your fate."

Whatever your fate is, whatever the hell happens, you say, "This is what I need."

It may look like a wreck, but go at it as though it were an opportunity, a challenge. If you bring love to that moment—not discouragement—you will find the strength is there.

Any disaster you can survive is an improvement in your character, your stature, and your life. What a privilege! This is when the spontaneity of your own nature will have a chance to flow.

—JOSEPH CAMPBELL

IDENTITY RETOOLING:
ROCKET FUEL FOR TRANSFORMATION

When destiny steps in, will you allow or resist it? FIT is a journey in which we discover the roots of who we are—the essence that remains no matter what identifiers we've lost, what's still there even when we are sick or feel broken. Within that chasm of lost status roles—lost job titles, relationships, health statuses—who are we left with? What is our inherent magic?

Many people's lives are uprooted by unexpected identity loss events, and/or their identity is negatively impacted from adverse childhood events, including societal offenses such as racism, sexism, ableism, etc. These nip their identity in the bud by creating detours and moving people away from who they could have become. The flip side of FIT is that often through challenge and adversity we discover our superpowers and purpose. Bold becomers cannot live on autopilot, and we move from living in the context of pain, into fully engaged living. Where some see barriers, bold becomers see breakthroughs, each breakthrough leading to the next.

If we're alive and possess our mental capacity, choice is where our superpower resides. No one can take that away, even if the only choice we have is over our perspective.

The liminal space of identity loss is filled with uncertainty and lack of clarity. Unless we make choices based on incomplete information, we're at risk of staying stuck. Once you take action and trust the process, magic happens. Next steps reveal themselves but only a few at a time. Knowing this has given me comfort. I've seen it come true for myself and others. It's something we can count on. It's happening to me right now as I finish writing this book and prepare for where it's leading me.

In 2016, I did Seth Godin's altMBA leadership program, feeling like a complete fraud. At the time, I was still trying to do my custom clothing business, the furthest thing from leadership. But I honored my inner voice and took the opportunity in front of me. It led me to next steps, a few at a time. It's been hard work learning new skills and I've definitely had cold feet often, but not doubt. When we act on our inner wisdom, we have questions that are different from doubt.

Are you ready to face your fears and transform your pain, suffering, grief, and loss into purpose and fulfillment? Some things cannot be fixed inside of grief. Acting on what can be changed is where our power lies. Masters of change choose to harness opportunities because they want what's on the other side more than staying where they are or the hard work involved in transformation, even without yet knowing what transformation will look like. They see the tip of the iceberg and trust the whole exists.

Are you:

- Ready to get comfortable being uncomfortable?

- Able to let go of the familiar for the unknown?

- Equipped to deal with rejection and build new support networks?

- Willing to ensure you have the energy necessary to bring your vision of change for yourself to fruition?

- Willing to commit to not settling, not letting fear, grief, overwhelm, exhaustion, and self-betrayal dampen your vision?

- Ready to do whatever it takes during this reckoning process, as you regain balance and retool your identity?

If your answer is a resounding "yes," you already have in your hands the concepts and tools needed to master change.

I hope you keep this book handy to review while on your journey. If your answer isn't yet a resounding "yes," these eight principles of mastering change are what you need to get out of liminality and into the next version of yourself.

The gift of FIT is finding what's possible. It's maximizing our circumstances and reaching our potential. It's harnessing challenge and recognizing it as our transformation vehicle. FIT is a brilliant opportunity to untangle ourselves from our historical self, our past self. It's our chance to reevaluate our experiences, interpretations, values, and beliefs and to boldly become the person who's always been there, waiting to step into center stage.

The way to win in FIT is to take more action and to plan less. We cannot plan our way into going where we don't know we're going. New actions—exploration, discovery, and experimentation—are what's called for. Just as important is to develop the ability to say "no" and "thank you but not now." FIT challenges you to change beliefs, values, behaviors, and aspirations. This requires letting go of activities where our energy isn't vital and, while in liminality, putting much more focus on our own needs and interests.

> I invite you to awaken your dormant agency.
> Then live within the fulfillment and dignity
> of your sovereignty. You can and deserve to live
> a fully engaged life on your terms.

You are still whole, regardless of how many broken pieces you're putting back together. It's your choice to put self-compassion first and not settle. This isn't being selfish. It's redefining who you are on your own terms. It's making a conscious claim to your identity, putting a stake in the ground, and boldly becoming a new version of you by design rather than default. It's *your* time to take inspired, courageous action to connect with your full potential. It's *your* time to claim your future and live at full capacity. It's *your* time to embody your full power and cherish your truth. In the silence of your mind, your heart will deliver the answers you seek.

Acknowledgments

My deepest acknowledgment goes to Dr. Herminia Ibarra for her work on identity transition. She provided a container and words for what I've been through, and her theories are the foundation of this book.

This book wouldn't be possible without stories from my *Bold Becoming* podcast guests. Their stories broadened my perspective, and through them I found common themes in forced identity transition. This validated that my experience was not unique and that the needle movers presented in this book represent the crux of overcoming and thriving after unexpected identity loss. Their generosity in sharing how they processed their lives, and what it all meant, are priceless. I am honored to have earned their trust and am indebted to them all, including those whose stories are not in this book.

Thank you, Bold Becomers, for finding ways to own and see the power of your stories: Arletha Orr, Bandz Mabuse, Damiun Moore, Damon Davis, Diana Giraldo, Jane Doe, Jean Olney, Jill Johnson-Young, John Jackson, Josh Perry, Leia Baez, Lena Cebula, Livia Rismondo, Lori Linford, Liz Bonny, Liz Rebensdorf, Rebecca Rae Eagle, Sarah Thee Campagna, Sherry Richert Belul, Thomas Edwards, Jr., and Thomas S.

This book would also have never seen the light of day without Eric Koester and everyone at Manuscripts Modern Author Accelerator. Thank you first to Leia Baez, who introduced me to Eric's program, and Eric, for creating and delivering one of the most comprehensive and quality programs I've ever been in, for your contagious optimism, and for always having a viable answer to our problems and doubts. David Grandouiller, my developmental and revisions editor, was one-third therapist, one-third coach, and seven-eighths editor. He was my lifeline for almost a year. No words can express my gratitude, David. Thanks also to Shanna Heath, John Saunders, Sherman Morrison, Brian Bies, George Thorne, Venus Bradley, and Amy Dong for their administrative wrangling, teaching, and coaching. Thank you, Hanne Brøter, for your awesome cover design and sales video production. And thanks to the other authors who ensured I wasn't writing alone.

Thank you to my teachers who helped me learn about business development and thought leadership and, through their programs, helped me discover my identity loss topic and what to do with it: Seth Godin, Fabienne Fredrickson, Brendon Burchard, all Akimbo junkies who gave me feedback in our workshops together, and my friends from other classes who gave me input and cheered me on. Thank you to Stuart Diamond, who held a larger vision of me before I did. Thank you, Juan Fortín, for giving me the keys to freedom— macrobiotics. And thank you to my doctors who believed and supported me during my darkest hours: Drs. Mary Patton, Anne Searcy, and Bowen Wong.

Thank you to the original Bold Becomers who raised their hands to join my Facebook group. You gave me my first platform to speak about my topic and showed me my work is valuable. Special thanks to Niki Thomson, Cecilie Holter, Lynne Thomson, Judie Nelson, Jennifer Dixey, Rebecca Rae Eagle, and Andy Prestage.

Thank you, friends and family, for doing your very best to keep track of what I've been doing as I've wallowed in liminality and for always supporting me on this long and winding journey into the next chapter of my life: my dad Andy Browne, late mom Susan Browne, son Dwayne Sackey, cousins Andy and David Prestage, my very good friends Alexandra MacFarland, Amy Lee Pinneo, Cecilie Holter, Diane Hendrix Boyd, Iñigo López, my late jacket-making teacher and dearest friend Jaime Rojas, and his children Javier Alonzo and Carmen Cecilia, my Colombian exchange sister and brother Dora and Gonzalo Gil, Jessica Bernstein, Kathleen Harned, my late and dearest Simmon Sethna, and Sonja Jürgensen.

Thank you to my fabulous and generous beta readers who helped immeasurably. My editor and I could only take this so far. You put the icing on the cake. Not only that, but receiving real-time feedback was the fuel that kept me going. Especially through the arduous and usually painful first draft. You made it clear I must finish this book, so I did.

Thank you beta readers Abayomi Opaneye, Abbey Donnelly, Alexandra MacFarland, Allison Hirp, Amy Lee Pinneo, Anaya Twum, Andy Prestage, Angela McCullough, Andrea Wagner Morris, Annabelle Baumann, Carrie Klewin Lawrence, Cecilie Holter, Christina McKenna, Christine Zharova, Christy Byrne Yates, Connie Jo Miller, David Prestage, Deanna Leonard, Dwight Moore, Eline Wessels, Frances Miyamoto, Gail Boenning, Gary Kahn, Hannah Austin, Heidi Henyon, Iñigo López, Jacquewyn Chambers-Martin, Janet Benson, Janice Moreno, Jea Arzberger, Jean Olney, Jen Kline Clark, Jennifer Dixey, Jennie Byrne, Jeri Zimmerman Rubino, Jill

Brocklehurst-Booth, Kristin Oppedisano, Kristy Merson, Laura Thomas, La Verne Morris, Linda Westenberg, Livia Rismondo, Liz Zhang, Lorna McLaren, Mari Sanders, Michele Reiner, Miriam Zylberglait, Mimi Westbrook, Molamma Panicker, Muhhamed Uwaise, Nancy Brune, Niki Thomson, Ornela Maric, Pamela Bye, Paul Meyer, Paula Tavrow, Pawnee Simons, Perrine Rambeau, Rob Boyle, Robert Pardi, Rebecca Austin, Rebecca Rae Eagle, Russell Smith, Rachael Blair, Rosa Tomrop-Hofmann, Sabrina Fritts, Sana Fayyaz, Stewart Uyeda, Suma Ibrahimi, Susan Brown, Susan Deitrick, Tammy Afriat, Terumi Okano, Tricia Morrissey, Wayne Pernell, Wilson Silva, Ying Wu.

Thank you to the following people who gave the book early praise and reminded me why I did what it took to write this book: Adam Teitelbaum, Amanda Bush, Amy Lee Pinneo, Anaya Twum, Andrew Prestage, Annette Reid, Annick Seys, Arminda Guerrero, Audra Caldwell, Beatriz Sandoval, Becca Rae Eagle, Becky Colwell, Bob Boyle, Cara Lynn, Carmen Cervantes, Carolyn Holmes, Cassandra Smalley, Cheryl-Anne Snow-Murdoch, Christine Zharova, Colette Holcombe, Connie Christian, Connie Jo Miller, Dana Richardson, David Prestage, Dawn Ranae, Dawn Shaw, Dayna Del Val, Debbie Bodine, Deborah Kevin, Debra L. James, Diana L. Restrepo-Osorio, Emilia Barbosa, Michelle Greenwell, Molamma Panicker, Dwight Moore, Echo Pawnee Simons, Elisabeth Caron, Frances Miyamoto, Frank Hayes, Gail Dixon, Hanne Brøter, Iñigo López Callejo, Jacquewyn Chambers-Martin, Janece O. Hoopes, Jean Olney, Jennifer Roberts, Jeri Zimmerman Rubino, Joan Advent, Josh Routh, Judith Hahn, Karla Kelly, Kathy Scatena, KR Miller, Kristin Oppedisano, Kristy Merson, La Verne Morris, Laura Thomas, Leah Eggers, Leonaura Rhodes, Lesley McShane, Lisa Smith Williams,

Liseth Kingery, Lynne Thompson, Maria McKeon, Mark Matthews, Maryjane Gertz, Michele Jones, Michelle "Shell Lightning Spirit" Mualem, Mindi Rosser, Nadhira Razack, Niki Thomson, Nurzhan Sterbenz, Pamela Bye, Patty Hayes, Rachael Blair, Roslyn Downing, Russell Smith, Sabrina Fritts, Sana Fayyaz, Sandra Grace, Sandra Sage, Seth Godin, Sherry Richert Belul, Smita Shankar, Stephanie Rose, Susan Brown, Susan Suriyapa, Tanya Levy, Vicki Cole, and Yolanda Canny.

Lastly, to everyone who backed my fundraising campaign you're the best! Thank you, a million times over: Abby Donnelly, Aesha Tahir, Amy Lee Pinneo, Amy Lindner-Lesser, Anaik Alcasas, Andrew Browne, Andrew Prestage, Angela McCullough, Annick Seys, Annie Stevens, Bob Boyle, Brian Paulsen, Cara Lynn, Carl Sorenson, Carlo Mahfouz, Cassandra Smalley, Cecilie Holter, Charity Youngblood, Christine Voorhees, Christine Mountford, Christy Yates, Cindie White, Claire Brindis, Connie Christian, Colette Holcombe, Connie Jo Miller, Constance Kilmartin, Courtney Foat, Cynthia Vann, Daniel Gates, Danielle Luhrs, David Prestage, Dawn Hanlon, Debra Lee James, Dwayne Sackey, Dwight Moore, Elaine Gerbert, Eric Koester, Eugina Jordan, Ev Bryant, Gail Dixon, Gale Berkowitz, George Papadoyannis, Heidi Henyon, Iñigo López Callejo, Jean Olney, Jeri Zimmerman Rubino, Jill Brocklehurst, Jill Celeste, Jonathan Stark, Joy Foster, Judie Nelson, Judy Sims, Krysta Barraford, Laura Wade, LaVerne Morris, Livia Rismondo, Liz Zhang, Lynne Thompson, M.J. Brune, Margaret Hollander, Marge DeStaebler, Marie Hannaman, Mark Matthews, Mary Haran, Michele Elmore, Michele Reiner, Michelle "Shell Lightning Spirit" Mualem, Nancy Brune, Niki Thomson, Pamela Bye, Paula Ewington, Penny Harris, Robin Toews, Roslyn Downing, Russell Smith, Ryan Alford, Sabina Feinberg, Sarah Thee Campagna, Sharon

Briscoe, Shawn Whittemore, Smita Shankar, Sonja Jürgensen, Stephan "Chip" Bianchi, Stephanie Brentin Rose, Stephanie Phillips, Stewart Uyeda, Sudeep Roy, Susan Suriyapa, Suzi Wright Blaue, Swati Doshi, Tammy Afriat, Tanya Levy, Todd Foos, Tracy Eng, Trish Barber, William Cane, and Willow Coberly.

Appendix A: Story Index

CATALYTIC EVENT TYPES

CAREER

HEALTH

Appendix B: Podcast Interviews

If you'd like to listen to the *Bold Becoming* podcast episodes where I interview people mentioned in the book, they're here:

Chapter 3: Courage and Grit
  Scarier than a Brain Tumor
  Josh Perry
  https://spotifyanchor-web.app.link/e/UDUdkOAKVxb

Chapter 4: Purpose
  When Money and Meaning Elude Each Other
  Bandz Mabuse
  https://spotifyanchor-web.app.link/e/v3yyUOAKVxb

Chapter 5: Grief and Loss
  Widowhood Rules Aren't for Anyone
  Jill Johnson-Young
  https://spotifyanchor-web.app.link/e/Z72JKNAKVxb

  From Unimaginable Loss to Happiness
  Arletha Orr
  https://spotifyanchor-web.app.link/e/PnL59RAKVxb

Chapter 7: Self-Care
  Extreme Self-Care: It Can Either Kill You or Keep You Alive
  Lena Cebula
  https://spotifyanchor-web.app.link/e/1O6A2Z0KVxb

Chapter 9: Productivity
When What You Do Doesn't Support Who You Are
Liz Bonny
https://spotifyanchor-web.app.link/e/UCh3b40KVxb

Sorting Out Her Garbage Led to a Rebirth
Lori Linford
https://spotifyanchor-web.app.link/e/jSHNLQAKVxb

Chapter 10: Support
Thomas's Healing Trifecta—Feedback, Fellowship, and
Professionals
Thomas Edwards, Jr.
https://spotifyanchor-web.app.link/e/o4cdaRAKVxb

When Tragedy Turns You into Someone Unimaginable
Leia Baez
https://spotifyanchor-web.app.link/e/JC44p30KVxb

Chapter 12: When Everything Points to Change
Becca Rae Eagle
https://spotifyanchor-web.app.link/e/BvQh2SwKVxb

Chapter 13: The Empty Space in Her Soul Revealed
Sarah Thee Campagna
https://spotifyanchor-web.app.link/e/6tokz40KVxb

Chapter 14: Goals Fueled by False Beliefs
Damiun Moore
https://spotifyanchor-web.app.link/e/rKcH2K0KVxb

Chapter 16: Between a Rock and a Hard Place
Jean Olney
https://spotifyanchor-web.app.link/e/8awxaTAKVxb

Chapter 17: Challenges Blocking Access to Sherry's True
Identity
Sherry Richert Belul
https://spotifyanchor-web.app.link/e/WGxjSz8tUzb

Chapter 18: With Schizophrenia, Will My Son's Life be Empty?
Liz Rebensdoft
https://spotifyanchor-web.app.link/e/3iKeurpKVxb

Chapter 20: Grieving a Breakup
Livia Rismondo
https://spotifyanchor-web.app.link/e/ocHaX40KVxb

Chapter 21: Adoption and Identity
Damon Davis
https://spotifyanchor-web.app.link/e/NlW9DSwKVxb

Appendix C: Chapter Tools Index

These are the end of chapter tools:

Appendix D: References

INTRODUCTION

Burchard, Brendon. 2017. "My Car Accident." Brendon. com. December 6, 2017. 22:30. https://www.youtube.com/watch?v=zfOlmihVXX8.

Edwards, Roxanna, and Sean M. Smith. 2020. "Job Market Remains Tight in 2019, As the Unemployment Rate Falls to Its Lowest Level Since 1969." *Monthly Labor Review*, US Bureau of Labor Statistics. April 2020. https://www.bls.gov/opub/mlr/2020/article/job-market-remains-tight-in-2019-as-the-unemployment-rate-falls-to-its-lowest-level-since-1969.htm.

Horowitz, Juliana Menasce. 2022. "More Than Half of Americans in Their 40s Are 'Sandwiched' Between an Aging Parent and Their Own Children." Pew Research Center. April 8, 2022. https://www.pewresearch.org/fact-tank/2022/04/08/more-than-half-of-americans-in-their-40s-are-sandwiched-between-an-aging-parent-and-their-own-children.

Ibarra, Herminia. 2017. "Identity and Transition in Professional Careers." Filmed October 2017 in Saïd Business School, University of Oxford. Video,1:15:15. https://www.sbs.ox.ac.uk/events/what-got-you-here-wont-get-you-there.

Kacha-Ochana, Akadia, Christopher M. Jones, Jody L. Green, Christopher Dunphy, Taryn Dailey Govoni, Rebekkah S. Robbins, Gery P. Guy Jr. 2022. "Characteristics of Adults Aged ≥18 Years Evaluated for Substance Use and Treatment Planning—United States, 2019." *CDC Morbidity and Mortality Weekly Report* 71, no. 23:749–756. June 10, 2022. https://www.cdc.gov/mmwr/volumes/71/wr/mm7123a1.htm.

Kochanek, Kenneth D., Jiaquan Xu, Elizabeth Arias. 2020. "Mortality in the United States, 2019." *CDC NCHS Data Brief No. 395*. December 2020. https://www.cdc.gov/nchs/products/databriefs/db395.htm.

Lazic, Marija. 2022. "Retirement Statistics for 2022: 15 Important Facts You Should Know." *Get Your Daily Fix of Legal Insights*, Legal Jobs. November 18, 2022. https://legaljobs.io/blog/retirement-statistics/.

National Coalition Against Domestic Violence. "National Statistics Domestic Violence Fact Sheet." *Statistics.* Accessed March 13, 2022. https://ncadv.org/STATISTICS.

National Institute of Mental Health. 2020. "Mental Illness." *Mental Health Information, Statistics.* Accessed March 13, 2022. https://www.nimh.nih.gov/health/statistics/mental-illness.

Okoro, Catherine A., Hollis NaTasha D., Alissa C. Cyrus, Shannon Griffin-Blake. 2018. "Prevalence of Disabilities and Health Care Access by Disability Status and Type Among Adults—United States." *CDC Morbidity and Mortality Weekly Report* 67: 882–887. August 17, 2018. https://www.cdc.gov/mmwr/volumes/67/wr/mm6732a3.htm?s_cid=mm6732a3_w.

RAINN (Rape, Abuse & Incest National Network. "Child Sexual Abuse is a Widespread Problem." Children and Teens: Statistics. Accessed March 13, 2022. https://www.rainn.org/statistics/children-and-teens.

Vuleta, Branka. 2022. "14 Divorce Statistics You Need to Know in 2022." *Get Your Daily Fix of Legal Insights*, Legal Jobs. January 18, 2022. https://legaljobs.io/blog/divorce-statistics/#:~:text=9.,single%20day%20in%20the%20country.

CHAPTER 1

Ibarra, Herminia. 2003. *Working Identity: Unconventional Strategies for Reinventing Your Career*. Boston, Massachusetts: Harvard Business School Press.

Ibarra, Herminia. 2017. "Identity and Transition in Professional Careers." *Clarendon Lectures*. Filmed October 2017 in Saïd Business School, University of Oxford. Video, 1:15:15. https://www.sbs.ox.ac.uk/events/what-got-you-here-wont-get-you-there.

Pasricha, Neil. "'You Learn' by Jorge Luis Borges." Accessed June 29, 2022. https://www.neil.blog/full-speech-transcript/you-learn-by-jorge-luis-borges.

CHAPTER 2

Clear, James. 2018. *Atomic Habits: An Easy & Proven Way to Build Good Habits & Break Bad Ones*. New York, New York: Avery.

Cozolino, Lou, Chloe Drulis, and Carly Samuelson. 2021. "The Science of Intuition: How the Body Translates Unconscious Information into Gut Instinct." *Psychology Today*, October 20, 2021. https://www.psychologytoday.com/us/blog/executive-functioning/202110/the-science-intuition.

CHAPTER 3

ADL (Anti-Defamation League). 2018. "Nike's Ad and Believing in Something." *Anti-Defamation League—Table Talk: Family Conversations about Current Events—Tools and Strategies*. October 11, 2018. https://www.adl.org/resources/tools-and-strategies/nikes-ad-and-believing-something.

Boren, Cindy. 2020. "A Timeline of Colin Kaepernick's Protests against Police Brutality, Four Years After They Began." *The Washington Post—NFL*. August 26, 2020. Accessed May 5, 2022. https://www.washingtonpost.com/sports/2020/06/01/colin-kaepernick-kneeling-history/.

Burchard, Brendon. 2015. "Fear vs. Happiness." *High Performance Masters Program, Growthday.com, Week #2, Session #3*. Video length 37 mins. https://www.growthday.com/hpa-masters.

Burchard, Brendon. 2016. *"High Performance Academy."* The Burchard Group. San Diego, California, September 23, 2016.

Burchard, Brendon. 2017. *High Performance Habits: How Extraordinary People Become That Way*. Carlsbad, California: Hay House, Inc.

Duckworth, Angela. 2016. *Grit: The Power of Passion and Perseverance*. New York, New York: Scribner.

DuVernay, Ava, Sheldon Candis, Robert Townsend, Angel Kristi Williams and Kenny Leon. 2021. *"Colin in Black & White."* ESPN Films and 40 Acres and a Mule Filmworks. Film length 3 hours. https://www.netflix.com/watch/81229665?trackId=14170286.

Graham, Bryan Armen. 2017. "Donald Trump Blasts NFL Anthem Protesters: 'Get that son of a bitch off the field.'" *The Guardian—NFL News*. September 22, 2017. Accessed May 5, 2022. https://www.theguardian.com/sport/2017/sep/22/donald-trump-nfl-national-anthem-protests.

Martin, Michel, and Nate Boyer. 2018. "The Veteran and NFL Player Who Advised Kaepernick to Take a Knee." *NPR All Things Considered*. September 9, 2018. Accessed May 5, 2022.

https://www.npr.org/2018/09/09/646115651/the-veteran-and-nfl-player-who-advised-kaepernick-to-take-a-knee.

Wyche, Steve. 2016. "Colin Kaepernick Explains Why He Sat During National Anthem." *NFL News*. August 27, 2016. Accessed May 5, 2022. https://www.nfl.com/news/colin-kaepernick-explains-why-he-sat-during-national-anthem-0ap3000000691077.

Mangan, Dan.2019. "Colin Kaepernick Reaches Settlement in National Anthem Kneeling Collusion Case Against NFL." *CNBC—Politics*. February 15, 2019. Accessed May 5, 2022. https://www.cnbc.com/2019/02/15/colin-kaepernick-reaches-settlement-in-collusion-case-against-nfl-lawyer-says.html.

CHAPTER 4

Burchard, Brendon. 2016. *"High Performance Academy."* The Burchard Group. San Diego, California, September 23, 2016.

C-SPAN. 2003. "Military Deployments in Iraq." *C-SPAN Video Library*. September 9, 2003. Video length 1:35:34. https://www.c-span.org/video/?178098-1/military-deployments-iraq.

Gafni, Marc.2012. *Your Unique Self: The Radical Path to Personal Enlightenment*. Tucson, Arizona: Integral Publishers, LLC.

Hillman, James. 1996. *The Soul's Code: In Search of Character and Calling*. New York, New York: Warner Books, Inc.

Moore, Michael. 2004. *Fahrenheit 9/11*. Dog Eat Dog Films. Length 2h 3m. https://www.peacocktv.com/watch-online/movies/fahrenheit-911/9336dd35-b173-33df-9296-46f3a0e2a7be.

Moore, Michael. 2021. "Michael Moore & Former Marine Corporal Abdul Henderson." *Michael Moore*. September 16, 2021. 25:50. https://www.youtube.com/watch?v=kP5AAKJ-kNI.

CHAPTER 5

Leech, Peter, and Zeva Singer. 1988. *Acknowledgment: Opening to the Grief of Unacceptable Loss*. Laytonville, California: Wintercreek.

CHAPTER 6

Eyal, Nir, and Julie Li. 2019. *Indistractable: How to Control Your Attention and Choose Your Life*. Dallas, Texas: BenBella Books, Inc.

Kahneman, Daniel. 2011. *Thinking Fast and Slow*. New York, New York: Farrar, Straus and Giroux.

Klemp, Nate. 2019. "Harvard Psychologists Reveal the Real Reason We're All So Distracted." *Inc.com Productivity—This Morning*. June 24, 2019. https://www.inc.com/nate-klemp/harvard-psychologists-reveal-real-reason-were-all-so-distracted.html.

Murray-Serter, Dan. 2021. "How to: Focus and Become Indistractable with Nir Eyal." *Heights Briancare*. March 3, 2021. Video length 59:05. https://www.youtube.com/watch?v=7XKx8Wt_eFg.

Pardi, Robert, and Phyllis Melhado. 2022. "*Chasing Life: The Remarkable True Story of Love, Joy and Achievement Against All Odds*. Prominence Publishing. https://www.robertpardi.com/my-books.

CHAPTER 7

Aihara, Herman. 1991. *"Basic Macrobiotic Cooking."* Vega Study Center. Oroville, CA. February 3–8, 1991.

Briscoe, David. 2020. *"Acid/Alkaline Made Easy."* Macrobiotic America-Macrobiotic Global—Macrobiotic Counselor Year-Long Training Course.

Burchard, Brendon. 2016. *"High Performance Academy."* The Burchard Group. San Diego, California, September 23, 2016.

Danaei, Goodarz et.al. 2009. "The Preventable Causes of Death in the United States: Comparative Risk Assessment of Dietary, Lifestyle, and Metabolic Risk Factors." *PLOS—Public Library of Science—Medicine.* April 28, 2009. https://journals.plos.org/plosmedicine/article?id=10.1371/journal.pmed.1000058.

Kahneman, Daniel. 2011. *Thinking Fast and Slow.* New York, New York: Farrar, Straus and Giroux.

Kaiser Permanente. 2022. "Forest bathing: What It Is and Why You Should Try It." April 8, 2022. https://thrive.kaiserpermanente.org/thrive-together/live-well/forest-bathing-try.

Leech, Peter, and Zeva Singer. 1988. *Acknowledgment: Opening to the Grief of Unacceptable Loss.* Laytonville, California: Wintercreek.

Mills, Jason, and Michael Chapman. 2016. "Compassion and Self-Compassion in Medicine: Self-Care for the Caregiver." *The Australasian Medical Journal* 5, no. 9 (June): 87–91. https://eprints.qut.edu.au/107931/1/2583-13266-1-PB-1.pdf.

Nelson, Jill et.al. 2018. "Self–Compassion as Self-Care: A Simple and Effective Tool for Counselor Educators and Counseling

Students." *Journal of Creativity in Mental Health* 13, nl. 1 (June): 121–133. https://doi.org/10.1080/15401383.2017.1328292.

Planned Parenthood. "6 Kinds of Self-Care." Accessed April 6,2022. https://secure.everyaction.com/p/Pg5bqblugE6-NGIdo9RIcQ2.

Pruitt-Young Sharon. 2022. "A New Program in Canada Gives Doctors the Option of Prescribing National Park Visits." *NPR—National Public Radio—Health.* February 9, 2022. https://www.npr.org/2022/02/09/1079356799/a-new-program-in-canada-gives-doctors-the-option-of-prescribing-national-park-vi.

Romano, Ryan. 2020. "Repairing the Identity Crisis." March 23, 2020 in Dallas, Texas. TEDx Mountain View College, 5:59. https://youtu.be/wdvR6VFg-K.

Smith, Anita, and Kelly J. Cone. 2010. "Triage Decision-Making Skills: A Necessity for all Nurses." *Journal for Nurses in Staff Development* 26, no. 1 (January/February): E14–E19. https://www.nursingcenter.com/static?pageid=1071278.

Ugelo, Linda. 2018. "Becoming Your Own Best Friend." *Women Inspired—Bedford TV, Massachusetts.* Aug 30, 2018. Video length 29:25. https://www.youtube.com/watch?v=4IoZ9ooi3iQ.

WHO—World Health Organization. 2022. "Self-Care Interventions for Health." *WHO Newsroom Fact Sheets.* June 30, 2022. https://www.who.int/news-room/fact-sheets/detail/self-care-health-interventions.

Winters, Susannah. 2019. "Self Care: What It Really Is." Filmed January 4, 2019 in Hilton Head Island, South Carolina. TEDxHiltonHeadWomen. Video length 9:59. https://www.youtube.com/watch?v=dBnoETS6XDk.

CHAPTER 8

Dweck, Carol. 2006. *Mindset: The New Psychology of Success.* (Audio book.) New York, New York: Ballantine Books.

Morgan, Adam, and Mark Barden. 2015. *A Beautiful Constraint: How to Transform Your Limitations into Advantages and Why It's Everyone's Business.* Hoboken, New Jersey: John Wiley & Sons, Inc.

Reinhold, Niebuhr. 1943. *"The Serenity Prayer."* Used in a sermon at Heath Evangelical Union Church, Heath, Massachusetts.

Purdy, Amy. 2011. "Living Beyond Limits." Filmed June 8, 2011 in Costa Mesa, California. TEDxOrangeCoast. Video length 9:36. https://www.youtube.com/watch?v=N2QZM7azGoA.

Sun, Las Vegas.1999. "Las Vegas Teen Amy Purdy Battles Devastating Illness." October 3, 1999. https://lasvegassun.com/news/1999/oct/03/las-vegas-teen-amy-purdy-battles-devastating-illne/.

Stanfield, Morgan. 2022. "Amy Purdy: The Star Behind the Scenes." *Amplitude—Newsletter.* March 23, 2022. https://livingwithamplitude.com/article/amy-purdy-the-star-behind-the-scenes/.

CHAPTER 9

Browne, Julie. 2022. "Widowhood Rules Aren't for Anyone." *Bold Becoming Podcast.* Episode 26, June 22, 2022. Length 1:18:31. https://spotifyanchor-web.app.link/e/ixsCosSY9wb.

CHAPTER 10

Burchard, Brendon. 2012. *The Charge: Activating the 10 Human Drives that Make You Feel Alive*. New York, New York: Free Press.

University at Buffalo School of Social Work. 2022. "Developing Your Support System." Accessed November 3, 2022. https://socialwork.buffalo.edu/resources/self-care-starter-kit/additional-self-care-resources/developing-your-support-system.html.

CHAPTER 15

Centers for Disease Control. "Adverse Childhood Experiences (ACEs)." *CDC website—Injury Center—Violence Prevention*. Accessed June 14, 2022. https://www.cdc.gov/violenceprevention/aces/index.html.

CHAPTER 16

Mayo Clinic. "Complicated Grief." *Mayo Clinic Website—Health Information*. Accessed July 17, 2022. https://www.mayoclinic.org/diseases-conditions/complicated-grief/symptoms-causes/syc-20360374.

Made in United States
Troutdale, OR
05/15/2024

19899019R00226